National Differences, Global Similarities

National Differences, Global Similarities

World Culture and the Future of Schooling

DAVID P. BAKER AND GERALD K. LETENDRE

Stanford Social Sciences
An imprint of Stanford University Press
Stanford, California

Stanford University Press
Stanford, California

Printed in the United States of America
on acid-free, archival-quality paper

Library of Congress Cataloging-in-Publication Data

Baker, David, date–
  National differences, global similarities : world culture and the future of
schooling / David P. Baker and Gerald K. LeTendre.
      p. cm.
  Includes bibliographical references and index.
  ISBN 0-8047-5020-3 (cloth : alk. paper)—ISBN 0-8047-5021-1 (pbk. : alk. paper)
  1. Comparative education. 2. Education and globalization—Cross-cultural
studies. I. LeTendre, Gerald K. II. Title.
  LB43.B25 2005
  370'.9—dc22   2004027281

Original Printing 2005
Last figure below indicates year of this printing:

14   13   12   11   10   09

Designed by Rob Ehle
Typeset by Classic Typography in 10.5/12 Bembo

To Mimi, Tirzah, and Harry. DPB

To Gerard and Anna. GKL

Contents

Tables and Figures

SCHOOLING IS ubiquitous in our modern world. On a given workday, more people in the world participate in schooling than in any other formal institution, including health care, the military, and even the entire labor market. In most places in the world, just about every child from the age of five or six until well into the teens daily attends a school, and an increasing proportion of older youths and adults take part in some type of postsecondary education. The teachers and administrators operating the world's schools make up a significant portion of the labor force in each nation, and the parents of all those children are frequently drawn into helping with and monitoring their child's schooling as a daily routine.

Although on a political level schooling is a national enterprise, the essential educational activities of curricula, teaching, and administration are shaped not just by local and national influences but increasingly by transnational forces. This is becoming more obvious in all categories of nations. Examples abound. U.S. educators now routinely talk of "benchmarking" their schools' performance against international standards; some school districts routinely compare their students' achievement against students in Singapore (a top mathematics and science performer). Singapore educators suggest that their high-performing educational system has room to improve. South Korean administrators worry that gender differences in learning mathematics among their students are large by international comparison. Kuwaiti educational administrators wonder why their schools are so violent compared to schooling in other nations. A number of Asian nations are concerned about a runaway trend in the use of private tutoring and how it influences fairness in schooling. There is a heated debate in Germany over the relative differences in international competitiveness of schooling among its individual provinces. Icelanders ask why their science scores are not higher internationally. Politicians in Chile see relatively low scores and ponder what that means for the international competitiveness of the country's future workers. And so on, through all nations. Everyone is concerned about how their schools perform internationally and what to do about it in the future.

This book tells nine tales of how schooling functions in some fifty nations around the world. The stories are about specific trends, but they blend together to paint the bigger picture of schooling as an institution with currently unprecedented involvement in the daily lives of students, teachers, and families. All the stories point to the global nature of education; they are written for the scholar of education, the educational policy maker, the educator, and the consumer of schooling in modern society.

Schooling is shaped and changed by a world culture of values about education that sometimes mixes with (and other times flattens) national and local cultures on a massive scale, producing remarkable similarities in what is taught and learned in school all around the world. Yet there are striking differences from nation to nation, and from place to place within nations, that help us understand how the institution of schooling is evolving.

On the basis of a four-year project of analyses of unique international information on schooling and its consequences over a selection of the world's nations, we examine important trends in mass education and speculate on where these trends might take this institution in the future. Looking inside the workings of the institution, we try to see how it actually functions in many places today and how it might work tomorrow. Our tales are told without complicated statistical jargon, but each is based on a published technical statistical journal article. In each chapter, a summary of the analyses is the point of departure for an essay on the implications of a particular trend for mass schooling in the world now and in the future. There are, of course, many other trends that we do not comment on here, but the ones chosen are particularly informative about the institutional workings of schooling.

The stories are about how children are schooled, how parents participate in schooling, and how national governments shape education in their societies. All suggest some ways in which schooling might morph itself in the near future to something that would have been difficult to predict just a few decades ago. The information we use focuses on teaching and learning mathematics and science in the fourth, eighth, and twelfth grades, but the trends we identify apply to elementary and secondary schooling in general.

Although the tales are comparative and discuss trends cross-nationally, in each we draw some attention to the U.S. case for several reasons. First, one can argue that the United States, for better or for worse, is often the leader in the institutional development of schooling. Second, a large share of the readers of this book are familiar with the U.S. school system, and it can serve them as a reference point regarding the cross-national trends. Lastly, like a number of other nations, the United States has just gone through a particularly active period of education debate and reform that in large part originated with the publicizing of several key international studies of school achievement; the data from two of these studies are used here.

The global environment is particularly important for American educational reform movements, because in the past impressions from international studies were the impetus to make sweeping decisions about what should be done to improve U.S. schooling. To cite three salient examples, the Sputnik crisis in the 1950s led to development of federally funded science and mathematics training; the *Nation at Risk* report in 1983 defined an image of an internationally mediocre American school system; and recent large-scale international comparisons and ideas about reforming the American mathematics and science curricula along international standards. In each case, international comparison of schooling in the United States with other nations motivated major change in the American school system. Also in each case, there were a number of misuses of international data and exaggerations of images about American schooling from overly simplified comparisons to schooling in selected nations. Nevertheless, international comparisons and their influence are not going away and may very well intensify their influence on the policy landscape in the near future.

People in charge of running and improving schools need to know that there is much to learn about schools in general by comparing what goes on in them across nations, well beyond the usual sound bite. We hope our stories provide an alternative to what has become an annoying and common public reference by educational policy makers to "international findings." These sound bites about what is happening in other nations are frequently simplistic and often ill informed, yet they can have major consequences for how a nation thinks about the health of its school system.

One important consequence of all this internationalization of education and its successes and failures is that there is now more sophisticated information on schools, teachers, students, and their learning than ever before. Here we use the Third International Mathematics and Science Study (TIMSS), which in 1994 collected a massive amount of data in schools in forty-one nations across three grades (fourth, eighth, and twelfth), and for some analyses we also use data from the TIMSS-99, an identical study done in 1999; together these studies furnish data on some fifty nations.

This type of information has been available for the past thirty years, but there have never been international data sets as extensive as the two TIMSS studies. Probably without knowing TIMSS was the source, just about everyone who reads a newspaper or watches TV news has at least heard some of its basic findings about American mathematics and science performance relative to other nations. But TIMSS has much more to tell.

Since this book is not about basic facts and figures of various national school systems, a statistical profile of education worldwide would serve as a useful reading companion to this book. The best is the series *Education at a Glance* (OECD, 2003). Also, UNESCO, the branch of the United Nations dealing with education, has recently instituted a database on educational data for all the nations of the world.

Acknowledgments

We want to thank our former students and collaborating colleagues, Motoko Akiba, Fernanda Astiz, Brian Goesling, and Alex Wiseman, for their effort on the analyses and certain essays in this book. These colleagues are now working independently on significant research issues in education; we hope the long hours put in on the "TIMSS project" helped their development as scholars. We benefited from collaboration with colleagues who participated with us in the TIMSS analyses project: Erling Boe, Robert Boruch, and Susan Furhman. We also thank Scott Davies, Gero Lenhardt, John Meyer, Francisco Ramirez, Catherine Riegle-Crumb, and Maryellen Schaub for their valuable comments on earlier drafts. We are grateful to the U.S. Department of Education's Fund to Improve Education and the National Science Foundation for funding the project on TIMSS analyses, and to the German-American Fulbright Commission and the Max Planck Institute for Human Development's Center for Education Research for support during the writing of this book. Lastly, we would also like to thank our colleagues at the Pennsylvania State University for numerous discussions and insights over the years, and the staff members who gave us logistical support.

March 2004

DPB
Berlin

GKL
Bremen, Germany

National Differences, Global Similarities

CHAPTER 1

The Global Environment of National School Systems

WHATEVER SUCCESS human society has mustered over the past hundred years is in large measure a result of widespread educational investment by nations in the skills, attitudes, and behaviors of all children. Schools are part of the essential fabric of life in a modern society. Although schools are so commonplace we often overlook them, they play a crucial role in the making of our social world. In the global community, a high-quality public system of education is the *sine qua non* of a modern democratic society. Many economists and others who study how nations develop stress that high-quality schools are essential for the human capital development and economic growth of nations (OECD, 2001). Beyond economic development, a nation would be hard-pressed to consider itself a functioning country without a national system of education.

With all the importance attached to schools, it is no wonder that politicians and policy makers around the world place much emphasis on providing quality public education to their constituents. Operating and regulating a nation's schools—public or private—is of extreme importance to national leaders, and governments everywhere guide and direct the kind of education that children receive. In a very short time, public schooling has become the major means by which governments try to promote positive economic change, strengthen national identity, and inculcate citizenship values and behavior in entire populations of people. Consequently there is incessant public discussion about schooling, and political campaigns in all sorts of nations make educational policy and the performance of schools a central point.

By and large, most people most of the time think about education as solely a national undertaking. The trends we examine here, however, lead to quite a different vision, one where there is a considerable global process at work. To make sense of this contrasting globalized world of education, it is helpful first to describe the common image of schooling as a national enterprise. It is a vision with several components.

The everyday vision of schooling as a national enterprise sees it as chiefly a unique product of a nation's culture and governmental effort to foster prosperity for its citizens. This is thought to be true regardless of the particular level of governance of schools within the nation. It is common, then, to refer to French, Chilean, Japanese, American, and South African (or any nation's) schools as separate national entities. After all, what could be more deeply embedded in a nation's society than its schools preparing children for future adult lives in that country? The reigning image of education today is that schools are designed and managed within a national context for the specific needs and goals of a particular nation.

This vision also assumes that schooling is organized to educate and socialize children in a specific way that is directly linked to the future welfare of a particular nation. For example, German schools are thought to produce German adults with the technical skills, linguistic capabilities, and cultural awareness necessary to carry forth the entity of Germany into the future. A national product of educated citizens issuing forth from the school system is the main image of what schooling does in every nation. Educators may be aware of the larger global world, but their predominant image of a nation's schools is as a means to pass on a sense of national uniqueness and heritage, as well as meet the technical needs of its particular labor market. This image implies that schooling is limited to the specific needs of a nation, therefore schooling would not expand except as is needed for national reasons. Nor would schools engage in education that is separable from traditional values of the nation. Additionally, this image of schooling holds that because labor markets are hierarchical, so should schooling be hierarchical. For efficiency, the argument continues, the best and the brightest of a nation deserve the best educational opportunities for the best national outcomes, and those with lesser endowments should receive less. All of this is wrapped up in the picture of a national system of education operating uniquely to produce efficiently adults with the kind of skill necessary for a range of tasks in the labor market and adult life within a national context.

This common image of schooling bound up in a national context is further reinforced by the rhetoric of official comparisons of education across nations (Schümer, 2004). Observing schooling across nations is thought to reveal significant differences in specific and unique national features causing relative differences in academic outcomes, such as national achievement among nations. A common extension of this idea is that the specific characteristics of a nation's schools are partly responsible for its relative position in the world's economy, and that nations are different enough from one another in their implementation of education to make it possible to learn unique lessons from one another on how to develop and manage schools better. Listen to how the founder of modern empirical comparison of academic outcomes of nations' schools in the late 1960s, Torsten Husén, describes the logic behind cross-national studies:

The more we have recognized education as an investment in human resources and as an instrument for bringing about economic growth and social change, the stronger has been the *need to investigate the roots of the educational systems* of which the world around us shows such a striking diversity. In the *search for causative factors behind the development and "productivity" of educational systems* there is a need for empirical data and for cross-nationally valid variables pertaining to these systems as they actually function [Husén, 1967, p. 19, emphasis added].

Now listen to how he perceives schooling as inseparable from national context: "Any educational system can only be fully understood in the context of the culture, traditions, history and general social structure of the *nation it is designed to serve*" (p. 220, emphasis added).

This image of national schooling is how many think the educational world works, but ultimately it is mostly inaccurate, and becoming more so every moment. In spite of the fact that nations (and their subunits, provinces, and states) have immediate political and fiduciary control over schooling, education as an institution has become a global enterprise. We show here that there are all kinds of trends suggesting that ideas and demands and expectations for what school can, and should, do for a society have developed well beyond any particular national context. The same global ideas, demands, and expectations filter into nations, greatly shaping their schools in union with school all over the world. Over the last century, there have been both steady expansion of schooling into our daily lives and deepening of education's meaning for things people hold dear. The current situation in schooling across nations is wholly unpredictable from the image of unique national models of schooling.

All the while that schooling has been considered a national technical project, from nation to nation considerable global forces are at work shaping and changing schooling in fundamental ways that many people are unaware of as they view education mostly from a national perspective. But just like the shrinking of the world's marketplace, media, and politics, education too is undergoing intensive globalization. Whether you find them in Mexico City, a small town in Pennsylvania, or in rural Kenya, schools all over the world appear to run in much the same way everywhere. Whether we were educated in a public school in New York City or a Catholic school in Tokyo, we experienced the same basic patterns of education. Today we can walk into almost any public school around the world and be able to understand

why global? (handwritten marginal note)

what is going on, even though the specifics of the lesson might be totally incomprehensible. Even if we do not know the language, social mores, or dominant religious dogma of a country, we can still identify central features and make sense of the general patterns when we step into a school there. We all recognize schooling just about everywhere because it entails a similar set of ideas about education held consistently throughout the world. This commonality—and the amazing story of what produces it—often goes unobserved, and its substantial consequences on the everyday world of students, parents, teachers, and administrators remain mostly unappreciated.

This book is about the global state of education, and about how worldwide forces interact with local ones to create educational change among students, their families, teachers, and administrators in your neighborhood school. Although we focus on mathematics and science in the fourth, eighth, and twelfth grades, we generalize to all academic subjects in elementary and secondary schooling. We tell this story of globalized education through nine separate tales of educational trends, using some of an ever-growing stream of complex information intended to compare schooling across many nations.

Over the past three decades, there has been an explosion of information comparing schools and their outcomes, particularly the academic achievement of their students across nations. In most nations, this kind of information has become part of the dialogue about education improvement. But this information is often misinterpreted or misused, deliberately picked through for certain results and highlighting a particular political position within a national debate. Two good examples are the massive debates resulting from the Reagan administration's *Nation at Risk* report, with its overly gratuitous negative misinterpretation of American student performance relative to other nations (Bradburn, Haertel, Schwille, and Torney-Purta, 1991), and last year's debate in Germany over the causes of achievement differences among its provinces on the international assessment called PISA, in which politicians attributed educational outcomes to all sorts of unrelated policies.

With this recent flood of international information about schooling in various nations, it is not clear that national policy makers, educators, and even some policy analysts really understand how to interpret such data in conjunction with the global forces driving their school systems. We recognize that educational policy for running and improving schools is mostly aimed at national or subnational issues, and always will be. As the saying goes, all politics is local. Policy makers all over the globe have been organizing and reorganizing national school systems nationally or seminationally since at least the end of World War II, and in some nations well before that. But there is another major part of the story (increasingly becoming the main part of the story), namely, the effects of the globalization of schooling. As national and local educators alike are bombarded with comparative information that shows the results of this international process, the need to understand education on a more global level is inescapable in today's world.

Further, how global trends affect the operation of local schools is little understood by legislators and administrators who regulate and oversee them. These effects, we strongly suspect, will only increase in the future, with yet more globalization accompanied and reinforced by a growing array of international tests, studies, and politically motivated comparisons as well as the workings of numerous multinational and regional agencies such as the World Bank, OECD, and development foundations (see, for example, Dale and Robertson, 2002).

Using analyses of the data from the Third International Mathematics and Science Study (TIMSS), we give the reader a look at how schools work around the world, and how complex forces are affecting all nations, shaping both their understanding of educational problems and solutions to them. We highlight the dramatic changes that have occurred in the recent past and speculate on where current trends will take the institution of mass education in the future.

TIMSS collected a massive amount of data in 1994, in schools in forty-one nations across three grades (fourth, eighth, and twelfth). In addition, for some analyses we use data from TIMSS-99, an identical study (done in 1999) that also included other nations, making a total of fifty-three nations participating in one or both TIMSS studies.[1] TIMSS sampled thousands of students in hundreds of schools and classrooms in nations as diverse as the United States, South Korea, Kuwait, Colombia, Germany, and Latvia. In addition to a mathematics and science test, students were asked a number of questions about themselves, their schooling, and their parents. Their mathematics teachers and the headmaster of the school were also asked a number of questions about the mathematics and science curricula, teaching, and the school. This huge data set was then compiled by the International Association for Educational Achievement and Evaluation (IEA) and made available to nations and researchers. We augmented the original cross-national data with more than one hundred indicators of other qualities of nations drawn from a range of international sources. Complete technical details about the TIMSS data and study can be found in Martin, Gregory, and Stemler, 1999.

If we combine the nations represented in the TIMSS of 1994 and the TIMSS-99, there are now extensive data on how schools run and what kind

study design

1. Australia, Austria, Belgium (Flemish), Belgium (French), Bulgaria, Canada, Chile, Chinese Taipei, Colombia, Cyprus, Czech Republic, Denmark, England, Finland, France, Germany, Greece, Hong Kong, Hungary, Iceland, Indonesia, Ireland, Islamic Republic of Iran, Israel, Italy, Japan, Jordan, Republic of Korea, Kuwait, Latvia, Lithuania, Macedonia, Republic of Malaysia, Moldova, Morocco, Netherlands, New Zealand, Norway, Philippines, Portugal, Romania, Russian Federation, Scotland, Singapore, Slovak Republic, Slovenia, South Africa, Spain, Sweden, Switzerland, Thailand, Tunisia, Turkey, United States.

of achievement level they produce in more than fifty nations. This represents only 15 percent of all of the world's nations, but given that a significant number of the total of three hundred or so nations in the world today are micro states with a population less than one million, these nations represent a reasonable number, and in terms of cross-national comparisons this is a large sample. Further, the TIMSS sample of nations comprises a range of national qualities such as size of school system, cultural background, history of school growth, participation of females in higher education, average wealth of citizens, political regime, economic productivity, level of violence, and many others.[2] Most of the OECD nations are here, along with nations from North America, the former Soviet East Bloc, and the Pacific Rim. There are, however, no sub-Saharan African nations, not many in South America, and not many extremely poor ones. So we take some liberty when we say that the trends described here are worldwide, but we are confident that they are in fact trends found in developed nations and many developing nations alike. In the case of extremely poor nations, or those with severe health or political crises, it is less clear what is happening in their educational systems; we consider what the case might be for nations of this kind only in passing. A full picture of education in the most impoverished and politically dysfunctional nations is much needed, but it is beyond the scope of this work.

Each of the nine tales is interesting in itself; together they plot the global state of education now and what it might look like in the near future. Like all good stories there are subplots, and ours has three.

Subplot One: The Worldwide Success of Mass Schooling

In developing these tales about cross-national trends in education, we are struck by how successful schooling is in the world. But we don't mean just any kind of schooling; rather, we refer to a particularly successful type of schooling that has spread around the world and has become the *singular model* of educating children, regardless of a nation's political regime, level of economic wealth, cultural heritage, and social problems. This is often referred to as *state-sponsored mass schooling*, or "mass schooling" for short. It is mostly public schooling for large masses of children, hence the name.

2. The TIMSS sample of nations is technically not a random one; all nations are invited to participate and those that wish to are included. In each participating country, a two-stage sampling design was used in TIMSS, where first a probability proportional to the size of the sample of schools was selected from a sampling frame of all schools in a participating country that had most of their students in the target ages. The second stage sampled all students in up to two mathematics classrooms per school with an equal probability of selection. Sampling weights are used to take into account any disproportional sampling of subgroups and adjustment for nonresponse (U.S. Department of Education, 1999). Some variation applies to the study at the twelfth grade, which is noted in some of our technical papers.

The history of the spread of public mass schooling and its accompanying mass enrollments around the world is the biggest success story ever known about the implementation of education (Fuller and Rubinson, 1992). Funding for schooling now rivals military and other social welfare expenditures in most national budgets, and educational spending continues to grow worldwide.

Comparing mass schooling with that of the education in premodern societies that has gone on throughout most of the history of human civilization shows how revolutionary an idea mass schooling really is. For most of recorded history, education was practical, situational, and highly limited—as with an apprenticeship to gain a set of skills—and it often did not require literacy. Most of the time, children learned all they needed to know within their family, clan, or tribe. Much of the content of premodern formal schooling was "religious" in nature: learning the legends, beliefs, and sacred traditions of a people or culture, and some limited literacy for reading religious texts. It was in this situation that premodern schooling became most elaborated; a small, elite group of students were taught how to read, write, and memorize the texts important to that culture. Practical apprenticeships were education for some nonelites, but this was not available for all and was aimed at a specific craft.

This all started to change some 150 to 200 years ago with the rise of mass schooling in many Western nations. There were still elite forms of education, but over time schooling was developed in principle for all children to learn academic skills through a more or less common curricula. Since then mass schooling has become one of the most impressive cases of successful transmission of a cultural model in the history of human society, developing and spreading in a relatively short time without limitations. Using mass schooling, most nations have achieved mass literacy within just the last hundred years, and currently there are no real alternatives to mass schooling anywhere. Full enrollment in elementary education was achieved before the middle of the twentieth century in wealthier nations and over the next forty years in poorer nations. Mass secondary education expanded to the same full enrollment a decade or two after elementary reached full enrollment, and the growth of higher education continues unabated in many nations today. Mass schooling has developed and intensified over time as an institution, deepening its meaning for everyday life. A big part of our story is what effects this resilient institution has on students, families, teachers, and school administrators.

Subplot Two: Schooling Is an Institution

At the core of the spread of mass schooling is a set of fundamental ideas that were unique just a short time ago but now have become widely accepted and even cherished. For instance, the ideas that all children should be educated;

that the nation has an interest in this and should furnish funds; that education is for the collective good; that children should start early and receive continuous instruction for a relatively large number of years; that tradition of statuses such as race, gender, religion, or language should not be barriers to mass schooling; and that academic cognitive skills are useful to all children are institutional foundations that underpin and give modern schooling widespread meaning in society. Adding to these powerful ideas is the rise of the exclusive currency of the educational credential, required to hold almost any position in labor markets all over the world. Now in human society, formal schooling has an unprecedented monopoly on the issuing and control of these credentials that lead to so many aspects of adult life.

Our stories lead us to appreciate how these ideas about mass schooling have formed a broad globalizing process making schooling a pervasive and powerful institution. As we have just described, the schooling-as-a-national-enterprise perspective tends not to appreciate the complex institutional nature of education, or its ability to reach across national borders as easily as the ideas behind modern capitalism and democratic government have spread worldwide. A big part of this underlying subplot is what is happening to the institution of mass education, more than what is happening educationally in any one nation, or even type of nation.

Education is an institution, like modern health care or the family, that may take on differing forms from nation to nation and even from region to region within a nation, but that at a deeper level is strongly affixed to global norms and rules about what education is and how schools should operate. If one turns a blind eye toward the image of schooling as a world institution, one is easily led astray in interpreting trends in schools, particularly cross-national trends that appear to differ so much from our individual experience (chiefly with a particular nation's schooling).

The trends we describe in this book are essentially meaningless without the aid of this institutional perspective. For example, why is it that in all the TIMSS nations the educational background of parents has a large impact on school achievement even though school quality has been on the increase over the past three decades? Why have gender differences in eighth grade mathematics almost vanished across so many national school systems? Why do teachers from diverse nations have similar core beliefs about the role of teaching and the role of the student? Why have so many national administrations of schooling produced a paradoxical mix of centralized and decentralized operating procedures for managing schools? The answers to these questions, and similar ones asked in each chapter, are found in understanding the consequences of the deepening of institutional ideas about mass schooling and how nations respond to this institutional force.

Certainly not all nations are alike; nor do they experience global institutional forces in exactly the same way. Patterns of cross-national differences within overall trends help us detect the larger institutional picture, but without the notion of a world institution these trends are little more than cross-national curiosities, like so many unexplained relics from a nineteenth-century travel adventure.

We admit that it is easier to say "institutional perspective" than it is to communicate exactly what that means. In part this is because institutions themselves are simultaneously so fundamental to our behavior and so powerful in constructing how we make sense of our daily world that they are hard to observe. All of us are part *of* institutions, within them more than we are outside observing them. Historians have long known that time offers a useful perspective on institutions, and to a degree we use that perspective here. Also, cross-national difference, or a perspective from multiple places, is a useful technique to observe institutions. If we hold the social world like a prism at just at the right angle to the light, we can see something of its institutional structure underneath; cross-national analyses help make that happen.

Institutions are the building blocks of human society at any time or place. By _institution_ we do not mean a specific place with bricks and mortar, as in the vernacular sense that a particular mental hospital is an institution. Instead we mean a set of rules for behavior and social roles to be played in a particular sector of life. Institution is more process than entity, more cognitive than physical, powerful in its control of human behavior through the production of shared meaning in all realms of human existence. The social world is a world of social institutions providing meanings and values about how to think and act in the everyday world. Individuals and collectives—formal organizations, informal groups, and the individual human—obtain realities through social institutions. From an institutional perspective, the very essence of social change is institutional change (see Berger, Berger, and Kellner, 1974). In terms of schooling as an institution, we borrow an analogy from educational historians Larry Cuban and David Tyack: the institutionalness of education constitutes the "grammar" of how things work in schools.

Our point here is that to a large extent the grammar of schooling is global. This means that much of the grammar of schools and the ideas behind it are reproduced and reinforced at a global level. Every individual school is still influenced by local, regional, and national factors, but the basic image of a school—what it is and what it should do—is commonly defined in the same way globally. Consequently, the organization of national school systems (French, German, American, and so on) is now influenced by transnational forces that are beyond the control of national policy makers, politicians, and educators themselves yet appear to be part of their everyday world. We do not mean to say that the United Nations or other powerful multinational agencies overtly force nations to do and think in the same way about schooling. Rather, widespread understanding repeatedly communicated across nations, resulting in common acceptance of ideas, leads to standardization and similar meanings, all happening in a soft, almost imperceptible, taken-for-granted way.

As a global institution, schooling has developed powerful world values and beliefs about children, learning, teaching, and the administration of schools. Over a thirty-year research program with colleagues, institutional theorist and comparative sociologist John Meyer has convincingly established a strong case for thinking about schooling as a product of a world culture that renders education as a resilient and powerful institution in modern society (see, as examples, Baker, 1999; Meyer, 1977; Ramirez and Boli, 1987; Meyer, Ramirez, and Soysal, 1992; Fuller and Rubinson, 1992). They have shown that mass schooling takes similar forms throughout the world, and that there are common beliefs in what schooling can and should do for society. This process, they argue, has to a large degree been driven by a dynamic world culture.

By *world culture*, we do not mean a culture that is void, ersatz, or not historical. Institutionalists see a dynamic world culture that (for better or worse) evolved out of Western ideals of rationality and purposeful action (Berger, Berger, and Kellner, 1974). Rationality as a pervasive cultural product (some would say even a hegemonic product) of the historical rise of the West serves to bureaucratize, marketize, individuate, and homogenize the institutions of the world (Finnemore, 1996; Scott and Meyer, 1994; Thomas, Ramirez, Boli, and Meyer, 1987). Homogenization produces consistent norms of behavior across a set of modern institutions, thus tying institutions such as the modern nation state and formal education together in a tight political sphere. Rationality, along with its offshoots of marketization, individualization, bureaucratization, and homogenization, plays the tune that all modern global institutions march to, but it is itself a cultural product and acts as such throughout the social system.

All this is not to suggest that local and national cultures do not have influence in schooling; they do. Perhaps a better way to think of culture is in terms of a *dynamic mix of cultures*, as discussed in comparative anthropological studies. Global institutions can traverse and shape local, regional, or national versions of particular areas of human life such as education. Thinking from the perspective of wide-open dynamics of culture, national cultures—if they exist at all—have only vague boundaries. Culture is far too dynamic to stay purely national, yet subglobal cultures do mix with global ones (see

G. Spindler, 1974; Spindler and Spindler, 1990; Tobin, Wu, and Davidson, 1989; LeTendre, 2000).

Culture is a continuous transforming process, often shaped by economic, political, or social change (see Spindler and Spindler, 1990). From this perspective, schools do not simply transmit culture; they are themselves cultural products not contained within national borders. In Louise Spindler's important book on culture and society, *Culture, Change, and Modernization,* she writes:

Culture . . . refers to shared designs for living. It is not the people or things or behaviors themselves. Culture can be equated with the *shared models* people carry in their minds for perceiving, relating to, and interpreting the world around them... . . . Sociocultural systems therefore include customary, agreed upon, *institutionalized solutions* which influence most individuals to behave in a predictable manner most of the time, but never all of the time [1977, pp. 4–5; emphasis added].

One of the major consequences of a dynamic cultural model is that world cultures are easily imagined, as are global or transnational institutional solutions applied to common human problems across nations (Boli and Thomas 1999).

An institution heavily shaped by a world culture of schooling more accurately depicts the cross-national trends we observe here than a vision of many national cultures of schooling operating independently. Further, such a perspective offers a rich description of how organizations such as schools and institutional ideas interact to produce consequences for the people participating in them. This also offers us a way to think about what will change in schooling in the future, and this leads us to the last of our subplots, educational change.

Subplot Three: Educational Change Is Institutional Change

Institutions by their very nature impart deep meaning to our everyday world; hence they are resistant to change. When we go to a hospital, we expect things to run in pretty much the same way the last time we were there. If we were to experience a completely different organization each time we had to rely on a hospital for our health care, most of us would be extremely upset. The same is true for schools. Change does occur, but most of us expect that basic patterns of interaction have not changed all that much from when we were in school. But the schooling and the political discussions surrounding it, in most nations, are full of rhetoric about change.

In fact, institutions do change, and institutional theorists have recognized this for some time. They tend to see two main types of force that make for institutional change: those outside the institution itself and those working from within. Outside forces tend to be large and progress over a long historical period. They also interact between institutions over time. Forces from within an institution also make change, often in much shorter time. The stories here about cross-national trends lead us to think about change in both ways. In terms of the former, a number of our tales are about how school and family as institutions interact and create a situation for substantial change in both. Internal institutional change of mass schooling is also evident in other tales, and in fact we end up seeing far more of it than change from the outside.

There are primarily two types of internal force at work that have brought change and will likely continue to do so in the near future. First is the force of standardization and universalism, meaning that organizations and individuals within a particular institution tend to become more similar over time and place. The pioneering works of sociologists of neoinstitutionalism show that there are strong global tendencies toward homogeneity within the education sector. We examine this force of *isomorphism* in schooling in a number of the chapters.

The second type of endogenous change in institutions occurs through the process of institutionalization itself. In other words, as a particular institutional pattern deepens and spreads, it creates wider consequences that in turn have an impact on the original pattern. We sense this kind of process is at play in a number of our stories. For example, the deepening link between school credentials from mass schooling and the labor market has created in recent times increased pressure on families to seek help outside school for children, which in turn has an impact on the way schools themselves are doing things. Many of our tales show the consequence of greater institutionalization for educational change.

Mass schooling is the predominant model of education in the world today. It pervades every part of people's lives in modern society and creates a cultural of education unparalleled in human existence. Although nations have made, and will continue to make, their own modifications to the model, mass education chiefly develops as a world institution. But it is far from static or monolithic; global forces dynamically interact with national ones and schooling often changes unpredictably. This is the image of institutional change that we take to our stories of cross-national trends in schooling.

Stories from Cross-National Analyses of Schooling

In Chapter 2, "The Declining Significance of Gender and the Rise of Egalitarian Mathematics Education," the first of our tales of cross-national trends tells the story of how and why gender differences in mathematics and science achievement are vanishing worldwide, and it illustrates the power of formal schooling to flatten traditional distinctions between categories of people (as with male and female). Building off an analysis of gender differences in mathematics and science across nations over time, this chapter considers the role that schooling has played over the past thirty years in this decline and debates interpretations of this role.

Chapter 3, "Symbiotic Institutions: Changing Global Dynamics Between Family and Schooling," is about the changing relationship between resources of students' families and school quality and that relationship's influence on national achievement level. Contrasting family and school effects on achievement in the early 1970s with those in the mid-1990s, we find, with some irony, that the considerable institutional strength and public support of mass schooling have created a situation where smaller and smaller differences in family resources take on greater saliency in creating differences in achievement in most nations in the world.

Pressure to teach and learn mathematics and science has increased dramatically over the past few decades. This has led to growth in the supply of outside school tutoring services; rising demand by families with children in public schools to buy them is an unexpected and potentially transforming addition to mass schooling. Chapter 4, "Demand for Achievement: The Worldwide Growth of Shadow Education Systems," examines the cross-national dimensions of this rapidly growing private sector of educational services oriented toward a student's performance in public school that has been termed, as the chapter title suggests, "shadow education."

Chapter 5, "Rich Land, Poor Schools: Inequality of National Educational Resources and Disadvantaged Students," develops a related theme. Perhaps the most sacred of principles of modern mass schooling is the notion of equality. Access to schooling for all children and the fundamental social justice and benefits to society are assumed to stem from this goal and drive the organizational development of school systems everywhere in the world. The jumping-off point for the chapter is an empirical study of disadvantaged students and their mathematics and science achievement cross-nationally. The analysis shows American schools placing socially disadvantaged students at considerable risk of school failure compared to similar students in other national systems. We then examine some of the causes of this problem and compare educational resource inequalities cross-nationally, with some revealing findings about their patterns and levels across nations. The chapter then discusses the institutional basis for beliefs in universal education and the practical problem presented by inequality of resources, and it speculates where issues of equal quality are likely to take national systems of education in the future.

School violence is the subject of intense study and national prevention efforts in the United States and elsewhere; it is the topic examined in Chapter 6, "Safe Schools, Dangerous Nations: The Paradox of School Violence." Over the past decade many Americans have come to wonder if public schools can be made safe. In fact, compared to many nations U.S. schools appear quite safe. Why this paradox exists and other trends in school safety are discussed. We present an overview of how much school violence there is in the world and show which social factors are likely to predict school violence; we find some surprising results about which kinds of nations have the highest rate of violence in schools.

Chapter 7, "The Universal Math Teacher? International Beliefs, National Work Roles, and Local Practice," considers how the role of the teacher is determined by cultural values, school organization, and national and international factors. Worldwide, teaching is a tapestry with many commonalities, but a few striking differences. Teachers' work in schools is increasingly similar around the world, which in fact has created an independent "global culture of teaching." At the same time, the cultural role of "teacher" was highly developed in many nations before the modern age. The chapter ends with a discussion of what a teacher's job in the future will look like as teaching is pushed toward homogeneity by increased global discourse, but also pushed toward diversity as wealthy nations continue to reform their schools in order to increase the national level of academic achievement.

Chapter 8, "Schoolwork at Home? Low-Quality Schooling and Homework," explores the fact that homework is ubiquitous in school systems around the world but has not garnered the international attention that other teaching practices have, even though some scholars argue it can be a major factor in student academic success. Cross-national patterns in the use of homework and its relationship to the national level of achievement are more complicated than most people think. For example, in the most effective systems little homework is given. Around the world, teachers give out virtually the same type of homework (textbook assignments and worksheets), but nations vary considerably in how teachers use homework (whether it is included in grading or not, used for class discussion, and so on) as well as in how much homework they give. Homework in poor-quality national systems appears to be underused and serves as a way to try to support weak parts of national curricula.

Chapter 9, "Slouching Toward a Global Ideology: The Devolution Revolution in Education Governance," explores the dramatic change in ideology and practice of managing public school systems occurring during the past three decades. Many nations are adopting a mixture of decentralized and centralized procedures without a clear rationale for doing so. Using curricular quality control as an example, the chapter explores what this blended devolution means for school-level decision making across nations and predicts where this trend will lead nation-state governance of public schooling in the future.

Chapter 10, "Nation versus Nation: The Race to Be the First in the World," our last story about cross-national trends in schooling, is about the political and policy struggles that can result from international comparisons. The chapter starts with the observation that reform and political motivations for improving education are epidemic in modern societies; the American case of political reaction to TIMSS is used to illustrate this. The chapter describes the complicated empirical relationship between quality of curricula in nations and level of achievement of students, leading to a discussion of why the institution of schooling motivates so many to engage in educational reform and reorganization across all nations.

We conclude the book by looking to the future. If the trends we have identified continue (and there is every indication they will), then we can make some general predictions about what schools will be like, and what problems educators or reformers will have to address. These predictions also serve a scientific purpose—they suggest a future way to assess whether the institutional perspective we have used is indeed accurate. We hope that our tales and the perspective we bring to them provide some new ways to think about global trends in education in the future.

CHAPTER 2

The Declining Significance of Gender and the Rise of Egalitarian Mathematics Education

with Alexander Wiseman

MASS EDUCATION, and the beliefs it instills in all those involved in it, has flattened gender differences in technical and quantitative subjects in many nations. Gender differences in mathematics and science continue to recede worldwide, and institutional values in education as a global process have increasingly removed the use of traditional qualities of students such as gender from the process of schooling. Further, school as an institution has become the major medium by which a growing ideology of gender equality and more equal future opportunities influences individual behavior of females and males. The story about gender and mathematics and science is a compelling example of how large-scale institutional ideas in education across nations reach down and influence the behaviors and attitudes of individuals, which in turn reinforce these ideas in the world around them.

In 1990, two historians of American education, Elizabeth Hansot and David Tyack, began writing a book on how girls and boys were treated differently in the United States (Tyack and Hansot, 1990). They examined a period of roughly one hundred years that they saw as the formative period of mass schooling in the United States. They were particularly interested in assessing to what degree girls suffered from an inferior school experience or lack of educational opportunity. After an exhaustive analysis of archival material that dealt with how boys and girls went through school and were taught, grouped, and classified, their book ended up not being about gender differences in schooling but exactly the opposite—the surprising finding was how relatively little a child's gender mattered in their school experiences in the United States over the past century.

Hansot and Tyack argue that this came about because of a major institutional shift in schools as mass education expanded over the nineteenth century in the United States (Hansot and Tyack, 1988). The commonly held assumption of large gender differences in schools underestimates the institutional power of schooling to define equality of access and implement this idea organizationally, particularly in the United States. This is not to say that American culture over the past one hundred years was an egalitarian utopia for young females; it was not. But the overwhelming evidence in Hansot and Tyack's book documents how schools, at least in terms of equal treatment of females and males, did something quite different from most other institutions in the American society of the last century. From an institutional perspective, the United States, often a forerunner in global institutional trends, was just ahead of a general world trend in the production of mass schooling and growing gender equality in education.

This chapter is about the implications of the widespread rise in gender equality around the world and its extensive impact on academic outcomes of schooling. It is about how institutional change can influence change in traditional patterns of behavior among individuals over time and place. We illustrate this with the case of mathematics achievement, an area often assumed to differ substantially by gender and to have more negative consequences for females than males.

In the United States, as elsewhere, the general scientific community and the government (in the United States, under the auspices of the National Science Foundation) have taken a keen interest in the question of whether there is an insurmountable gender gap in mathematics and science hindering growth in the number of female scientists and engineers. What was once an informal (but widely held) assumption that boys on average were better in mathematics and hence more of them pursued a scientific or engineering career has in recent decades become the target of a sort of national campaign to increase economic productivity through developing a larger labor force in these fields by incorporating more women into the ranks. At the heart of this campaign is an emphasis on mathematics and science education for girls.

Global Political Ideology and the Emphasis on Women's Education

To appreciate the case of gender and mathematics achievement cross-nationally, one needs to understand the larger institutional context of mass schooling and gender. The past thirty years could be called a golden era of the female in education worldwide. During this period, many national education systems steadily increased access for females at all levels of schooling.

Wealthier Western nations long ago reached gender parity (in enrollment) in kindergarten through secondary schooling. Indeed, the massive world-wide growth in higher education has been fueled in part by incorporation of women into colleges and universities. General representation of women in higher education has grown over the past fifty years even though the distribution of women in fields of study within higher education remains uneven (for example, low participation in fields such as mathematics; see Charles and Bradley, 2002).

"Schooling for girls" has become almost a mantra among multilateral agencies that assist developing nations. As part of a much larger campaign that focuses on the importance of the quality of life for females as a development strategy among poor nations, increased access to schooling for girls has become a key objective in social and economic development from the ground up in most development programs. With the rise of vast public expenditures on education for *all* children and the recent economic notion of production of human capital as a national strategy (replacing older ideas about extraction and manipulation of natural resources), the female portion of national populations is commonly viewed in economic terms as an important underdeveloped national resource. Education is seen as the central mechanism with which to realize the value of women in national development.

Of course this more pragmatic trend toward girls and schooling has also been enhanced (some would argue actually caused) by a growing ideology throughout the world that makes it difficult to consider a person's gender as a socially acceptable limit to education and labor market opportunities. Francisco Ramirez, a comparative sociologist, describes the "demise of the culture of gender" in recent times as a product of an ideology combining the individual, the citizen, and the educated common person as a defining ideal, and replacing more traditional categories of the clan, family, and gender (1987). Embedded in a wider modern ideology of the nation-state's responsibility toward social justice and equality, gender has taken its place in a constellation of traditional qualities of individuals that are no longer legitimate in public distribution of social opportunity; along with gender, an individual's age, ethnicity, race, religion, and physical impairments are increasingly seen as *illegitimate* factors for nations to use in granting access to opportunities across a range of sectors, from legal justice to military service and the labor market. An expanded and *universalistic* notion of the individual is sweeping through social institutions everywhere. In practice, of course, gender and other traditional categories continue to be ways in which people organize themselves, and some nation-states continue to use various of these traditional categories to oppress groups with negative, even deadly, consequences. Yet even though this is true, one should not dismiss the growing world ideology embracing universalism as trivial or inconsequential; such ideas represent a clear social counterforce in the world, and this has had a profound impact on how nations organize politically (Fiala and Gordon-Lanford, 1987).

An illustration of how a universalistic ideology spreads is the case of the worldwide campaign for basic education for all children in the developing world. The World Bank, which from its inception just after World War II to the early 1980s lent money primarily to developing nations for physical infra-structure improvements, has over the last two decades developed a number of projects aimed at improving education and human capital in these nations. The bank's education-sector lending increased from an annual average of some $78 million (during 1984–85) to about $424 million in 1995. These funds, as well as the bank's considerable symbolic power to focus on avenues for national development, have played a direct role in the diffusion and accep-tance of the ideas behind gender equality in education. Along with UNDP (United Nations Development Programme), UNICEF (United Nations Chil-dren's Fund), and UNESCO (United Nations Educational, Scientific, and Cultural Organization), the World Bank cosponsored the important Jomtien Conference of 1990, where representatives from a large number of nations met to discuss plans for education within the developing world. Foremost among all the issues was education for females. The declaration stemming from the conference, *Education for All* (EFA, or the Jomtien Declaration, 1990), stated that "the most urgent policy is to ensure access to, and improve the quality of, education for girls and women."

Following this declaration, UNESCO was charged with coordinating commitments to this policy with all participating nations and other interna-tional bodies of EFA. The Dakar Framework for Action document *Education for All*, in 2000, as well as the Millennium Summit in September 2000 again emphasized the importance of providing education of girls and women for issues of national economic development and universal ideas about educa-tion as a right of all people. Given that in many traditional societies only girls from upper-class society had any chance of getting an education, these efforts on the part of multilateral agencies constitute a massive effort to reform basic cultural values in nations around the globe (Chabbott, 2003).

Over the past century we have come to think about gender and its proper role in society in a profoundly new way. The worldwide movement for gen-der rights is substantial in both its span across social spheres of life and the relative speed of diffusion. Incorporation of women as voting citizens in nearly all nations, the rise of women's issues in national and international agendas, the decline in gender differentiation in official primary and sec-ondary school curricula worldwide, enlistment of women in the military in many nations, official prohibition of gender as a job qualification in most na-tions' legal codes, and related international labor movements are all examples of outcomes of a long struggle followed by embrace of the premises of gender equality on the part of nations (Berkovitch, 1998; Meyer, Boli, Thomas, and Ramirez, 1997; Huber and Stephens, 2000; Ramirez, 2001).

Yet these are official declarations and legal abstractions occurring among national governments and global agencies. What does ideological change regarding gender and the nation-state mean for actual behavior among males and females? There is no better sector than education from which to examine this question. A fair amount of prior speculation suggests that schooling is not equal when it comes to gender and enhances subtle but persistent gender differences, particularly in the learning of technical knowledge such as mathematics and science. Everything from the image of a "hidden curriculum" in the classroom (through which girls receive messages that mathematics is a male endeavor) to educational policies working against academic opportunities and full access for girls are thought of as means by which schools reinforce traditional gender roles. Yet most of this speculation has not included a cross-national perspective in which nations vary in terms of their acceptance and implementation of more gender equality in educational and labor market opportunities. Also, much past scholarship has never really considered the possible influence of the spreading ideology of gender equality worldwide as a formidable global institutional force. Our story takes us in these uncharted directions.

With our colleagues Alexander Wiseman, Catherine Riegle-Crumb, and Francisco Ramirez, we undertook a study of cross-national patterns in gender differences in mathematics achievement in eighth and twelfth grades in relationship to the status of women in each nation's higher education system, labor market, government, and social policy regime (Baker and others, under review). This study is similar to an earlier one Baker and Jones did on cross-national patterns in the early 1980s using the Second International Mathematics Study (SIMS) data (a precursor to TIMSS, 1992). The earlier study found some interesting facts about gender differences in mathematics among eighth graders. Most notable is that contrary to the then widely held assumption that on average males outperformed females, this was not a uniform pattern across all nations in the 1980s. During that time, some researchers went so far as to argue that certain genetic-cognitive processes favored males more than females in learning mathematics, but these cross-national findings made that less plausible (Benbow and Stanley, 1980). In the early 1980s, nations fell into three groups: those with males outperforming females, those with no gender differences (the United States was here then and remains so today), and those with females outperforming males. Given the widespread idea in the United States that males tend to outperform females, it is also interesting to note that over the past twenty-five years many national studies of gender differences in mathematics have found little or no difference among American students at least until the latter part of high school (see Leahey and Guo, 2001).

If global trends in political ideology influence the overall functioning of schooling in the world, we expected that by the mid-1990s in the TIMSS data there would be a reduction in nations reporting a male advantage in mathematics from the mid-1960s and early 1980s (during which occurred respectively the First International Mathematics Study, or FIMS, and SIMS). The spread of beliefs in the national interest in human capital production among females, as well as the overall ideology of gender equality, could influence a host of factors that would increase female interest and participation in mathematics. Since this process has appeared to gain strength over time, it is reasonable to argue that one should see a decrease in gender differences in mathematics across nations.

Among the nations participating in FIMS, SIMS, and TIMSS, we found exactly this trend. Figure 1 displays the percentage of nations with male-advantage gender differences in eighth grade mathematics achievement that participated in the mathematics assessments in the 1960s, 1980s, and 1990s. Among nations participating in just the 1960s and 1990s assessments, and those in just the 1980s and 1990s assessments, the proportion of nations with statistically significant, male-dominated gender differences in mathematics scores declined from 33 percent to 9 percent from 1967 to 1994 and from about 35 percent to 18 percent from 1981 to 1994.

FIGURE 2.1 Percentage of Countries with Male-Advantage Gender Differences in Eighth Grade Math by Year of IEA Study

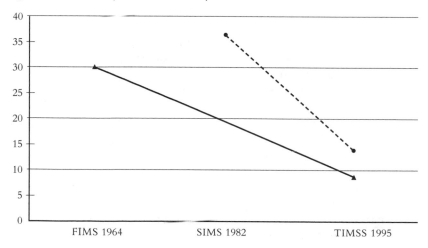

There is also corroborating evidence of this trend from national assessments of mathematics achievement over time in the United States. They report for eighth grade mathematics no gender differences in 1990, 1992, and 1996; there is also evidence that a male-dominated difference among American students in twelfth grade since the early 1990s significantly declined by 1996 (Campbell, Hombo, and Mazzeo, 2000). But these are highly aggregated national findings; they don't tell us much about the processes that we think might be at work behind them.

Equality of Opportunity and National Gender Differences

Could the shift in how nations have begun to open up educational and labor opportunities to females play some role in this decline in male mathematics advantage in so many nations? Does an emerging global ideology of gender equality in public institutions spread down to the motivations and actions of individuals? As we have already described, scholars of our changing world culture have pointed out how nations approach more equity in the education of females, as well as make policy to enhance the young female population's contribution to the economy—both of which are reinforced by an overarching global ideology toward universalism. Yet it is not clear the degree to which this actually has an influence (if any) over something so fundamental as how girls and boys approach mathematics in school. Simply achieving parity in enrollment does not mean equal access to education in the fullest sense. Even amid declining gender effects in many nations, there is still enough cross-national variation in gender differences to consider which national factors might account for the lessening of gender effects on mathematics achievement (in the eighth and twelfth grades, at least).

We found that among the countries participating in TIMSS fewer nations showed a mean difference between male and female test scores in the fourth grade than in the eighth or twelfth grade. At the elementary (fourth grade) level, mean gender differences in achievement are small, and only 27 percent of nations show a male advantage. The effect increases for the middle grades, with 46 percent of nations showing a male advantage; among twelfth graders both the difference between male and female scores and the percentage of countries reporting a difference are greatest.

So even though there has been a steady trend toward gender equality in education (at least in terms of math enrollment and achievement), differences still persist. To explain why, we collected a number of national indicators that reflect the extent to which older females are involved in higher education and the labor market in these countries: female share of enrollment in higher education, in science and engineering training in higher education, and in the labor market. To this we added indicators of the overall status of females in the national society: the number of females in upper echelons of the government and the legality of abortion. Although it is difficult to capture anything as broad and complicated as the status of a gender with a handful of indicators (we don't claim to have come close to summarizing all the facets of gender), the national measures we use reflect components of being female in different nations that come close to the forces of human capital production in the first three indicators, and a reflection of more general ideological issues in the last two indicators (Riegle-Crumb, 2000).

In a series of statistical models of the effect of a student's gender on mastery of eighth grade mathematics, we find that living and being schooled in nations with more opportunity for females in education and the labor market lessens the impact of gender effects on achievement (Baker and others, under review). Where more young women are going on to higher education, specializing in science and engineering in higher education, and going into the labor market, gender differences in mathematics are reduced on the whole. Further, in nations where there are more women with public political power and where reproductive rights are legally proclaimed, gender differences in mathematics are also reduced.

Specific analyses of twelfth grade students shed more light on this process. In 1995, when the basic national test score averages from TIMSS were reported in the capitals of participating nations, there was surprise over the margin by which boys outperformed girls in secondary school. This finding seems to negate the evidence for a declining trend in gender differences among younger students. It might, but there are several additional factors that need to be considered. First, in most systems (maybe all systems) by twelfth grade there has been some degree of choice or assignment to curricular options. In various ways by the end of secondary school, systems produce sets of students with differing access to mathematics in terms of substantive level and intensity of instruction. This can be particularly extreme in a case where students effectively end their mathematics learning before leaving secondary school in some nations. It should be pointed out that this is not necessarily because of the curricular policy of the educational system in question to create curricular differentiation by gender, but because of the increasing openness of secondary curricular decisions (such as students and parents being able to choose courses) to outside influence.

For example, in such nations as Iran, Israel, and South Korea there are pronounced male advantages at the eighth grade level in mathematics. These nations also tend to have a lower percentage of women in the labor force, in advanced science and engineering education, and employed as high civil servants. At the same time nations such as Sweden and Iceland have no gender difference in mathematics and a high percentage of women in higher education, in science and engineering education, and employed as high civil servants. The United States has no gender difference in the eighth grade and a male advantage in the twelfth grade. It tends to fall among nations that are above the world average in incorporating females into advanced education and the labor market.

Unfortunately, the TIMSS study did not capture the mathematics course history of the twelfth grade students; therefore we do not have a way to control for what might be substantial variation among students in how much mathematics they were taught since eighth grade. For example, we cannot tell if we are comparing twelfth graders with exactly the same course history in mathematics, or a sample where more boys than girls took more mathematics when given a choice. This is probably less of a concern for analyses of eighth grade students in that they are more likely to have generally received similar mathematics through most of elementary schooling. The TIMSS study did do one thing with the twelfth grade that helps in this regard. Mathematics assessments were collected from two distinct populations of twelfth graders: those in general mathematics courses, and those in advanced mathematics courses.

We did the same statistical modeling of the twelfth grade sample in basic mathematics as we did for the eighth grade and found some interesting patterns of cross-national effects. First, as with the eighth graders, in nations that have more general higher education and labor market opportunities for women, the effect of gender on mathematics achievement is lower among twelfth graders in general mathematics courses. The same is true about female reproductive rights. But contrary to these findings, among twelfth graders in general mathematics in nations where women have access to specialized higher education training in science and engineering as well as access to high civic services jobs, the male advantage in mathematics was larger! Why?

The analysis of twelfth graders in advanced mathematics courses suggests a plausible answer. In this analysis we find that gender differences among these more mathematically talented twelfth graders are lowered in nations with more specific opportunity for women with academic ability to enter advanced science and engineering training and high ranks of the civil service. Further analysis of this idea also found that nations with elite opportunities for women proportionally had more twelfth grade females enrolled in advanced mathematics courses. This process might leave more mathematically challenged (that is, low-ability) females in general mathematics in those nations, and hence increase the negative effect of gender differences in twelfth grade general mathematics. Overall, the twelfth grade findings suggest that female performance in general mathematics is enhanced in nations with opportunity for women in basic higher education and general occupations, and female performance in advanced mathematics is enhanced in nations with more elite opportunities geared for talented female students.

Taken together, the analyses of the eighth and both twelfth grade populations reveal a relationship between the level of national development of female human capital and an underlying ideology about universalism and gender equality. But what is actually the cause of these findings? On the one hand, we have mathematics achievement scores of individual students; on the other hand we have indicators of national human capital development and gender egalitarianism. Yet learning mathematics is an everyday thing. It takes motivation, effort, persistence, practice, and development of thinking skills. How then can we make sense of these findings? What is a plausible reason for higher educational and future labor opportunities influencing fourteen- and eighteen-year-olds' math ability? How can something as relatively abstract as gender status in the public sphere of a national society and the world influence students' everyday actions?

Gendered Opportunities

For several decades now, scholars have been considering how large processes in the social world shape and define the actions of individuals. Indeed, a major assumption behind an institutional perspective on the social world is that social life is *socially constructed*. In particular, this construction is rooted in, and shaped by, institutional processes. But how does this actually work? An institutional perceptive points to several ways.

One process that might cause this—one that is currently popular among social scientists—is rather simple and imagines individuals as rational seekers of the opportunities that institutions afford them for their talents and characteristics. In other words, if students and their parents perceive important future educational and occupational opportunities as being linked to current performance, their attempts to improve their performance will generally intensify. If, however, the structure of future opportunity is stratified in such a way as to not present clear opportunity for a category of students, these students and their families may not invest as much in current performance.

For example, if males are afforded the possibility of future educational and occupational opportunity as a function of their mathematics performance in school, they may try harder, teachers may encourage them more, and their parents and friends may help them see that mathematics is an area of school performance that they should take very seriously. Conversely, to the degree that future educational and occupational changes are stratified by gender (in this case, in favor of males), female students faced with the prospect of lesser opportunity tied to mathematics skills may tend to perceive these subjects as less important for their future; their teachers, parents,

and friends would reinforce this. This "future opportunity-current performance" argument is at the root of a growing literature on how stratification
of educational outcomes occurs in general. The argument has received substantial empirical support in terms of stratification by race and socioeconomic status (see, for instance, Bourdieu, 1973; Hopper, 1971; Kerckhoff,
1977; McClelland, 1990; Mickleson, 1990; Ogbu, 1978; and Stinchcombe,
1964). Furthermore, the evidence that the gender-related experiences of adult
women in their family, job, and society influence the experiences of younger
generations lends support to this process (see Eccles and Jacobs, 1986;
Janssens, 1998; Marini and Brinton, 1984; and Seymour and Hewitt, 1997).

Girls' achievement in mathematics may be particularly vulnerable to future
role expectations for several reasons. First of all, societal messages concerning
appropriate roles for women are likely to reinforce academic stereotypes of
mathematics as a masculine domain and subsequently discourage female students, leading them to direct their abilities away from mastering mathematics.
Additionally, performance in academic mathematics serves as a prerequisite to
many future educational paths toward a career in modern labor sectors that
are increasingly based on science and technology (Stage and Maple, 1996). If
girls find their future opportunities more limited in advanced education and
the labor force, they will likely lower their investment in this "gatekeeper"
academic subject (Stevenson, Schiller, and Schneider, 1994).

The future-opportunity, current-performance argument is popular, and it
does constitute a credible sociological alternative to biological or social psychological perspectives on gender differences in mathematics. We have used
it in our past work as an easily described context for our findings (Baker and
Jones, 1992). But it is less than theoretically satisfying. Not only is it a bit too
simplistic; it doesn't really consider institutions beyond their being the providers of opportunity. The image of opportunity structures eviscerates the
image of an active institution, leaving little more than a crude functional notion of institution as vessel of social roles to be played. Applying this to education as an institution results in an image of schooling passively holding out
opportunities, while an all-encompassing rationality among families, students,
and teachers is at work. Such an image does not seem too plausible.

Do youths really think, "Well let's see: what's happening in higher education and the labor market for my gender, and what should I do to take advantage of it?" Youths certainly do take as active a role as they can in deciding their educational future, but their range of choices is highly bounded by
the schools they attend and the families they have (Gambetta, 1987; Benjamin, 1997). Even if each adolescent were logically calculating his or her
odds of success in the educational or labor market, would the young person
turn this answer into more effort in math class, or less?

If adolescents make perfectly logical decisions, then why do indicators of national female political power and gender equality in reproductive rights lessen gender differences as much as indicators of "payoff" opportunities in higher education and the labor market? Further, in a worldview of passive institutions, where does this rationality itself come from? Lastly, why do things change in terms of gender? A simple, rational exchange argument is not enough to understand the larger process at work.

The Constructing Institution and Gender Equity

As we have described in Chapter 1, institutions are active creators of cognitive realities; these realities actively influence individual and organizational behavior. People operating within institutions make sense of (construct) a cognitive reality through the rules, roles, and meanings that the institution organizes. These meanings have powerful consequences for how we think, and often there are clearly collateral effects on meanings from one institution to another. Mass schooling, by defining the role of boys and girls as "students" who all share the same "job" of academic achievement, profoundly disrupts patterns of gender socialization commonly found in more traditional values. Though perhaps initially not intending to, in constructing children as students and not as boys or girls schooling undercuts, or at least limits, the extension of gender roles. Over recent history a deepening of this idea into full-blown universalism in education advances a contradictory message about gender and its traditional roles in life.

Gender is itself an institution, and the contours of the relationship among gender, school, and society do not remain stationary; they are institutionally dynamic. In the long development of human society, a person's physiological gender has always been a major defining characteristic as to what to do, how to live, and the meaning to assign to actions. Even beyond a role in sexual reproduction, gender prescribed separate worlds for females and males (Ariès and Béjin, 1985). This intensified during the beginning of the modern period. All through the eighteenth and nineteenth centuries in the West, the public sphere of life was increasingly gender segregated, and the male portion dominated with considerably more power. But this began to change during the early twentieth century. Slowly, despite considerable resistance at first and then with increasing speed in the last thirty years, this trend has been reversed.

More gender equity in the public sphere of life is part of a much larger process and the confluence of a number of social and political developments in complex modern society. The first development is the creation and spread of the modern nation as a new geopolitical form organizing human life (see Tilly, 1990). Over time, the nation and its increasing emphasis on citizen production and the importance of all citizens as potential national resources established a framework for political and social movements that agitated for rights of women in many Western democracies in the early twentieth century. An accompanying development was increased national investment and political incorporation of schools for all children (Fuller and Rubinson, 1992). Again slowly, and not without social conflict, girls were admitted to schools in many nations along with boys, and from the mid-twentieth century on females have entered all types of education, with some nations embracing this fully and others more slowly.

Gender as an institution has been transformed and weakened through the strengthening institutions of the nation and education. Both have developed and enacted the meaning of *universalism of individuals* as an idea within modern reality. Just as everyday ideas of natural racial difference have become delegitimated and considered false, so have everyday ideas of gender differences in academic domains and beyond become highly questioned, delegitimated, and considered false. One need only look at the ideas of race and gender commonly held a century ago to see how much things have changed. By the very act of educating students as students regardless of their gender in public schools, a powerful meaning about the irrelevance of gender in academic matters arises. We return full circle to the findings of Tyack and Hansot: schools may not have intentionally set out to change ideas about gender and performance, but by their very actions as an institution they have.

As the observant nineteenth-century American educator Horace Mann stated, "American schools are smuggling in the girls"—meaning that this major change happened in the early nineteenth century even though society at large was rather gendered (Hansot and Tyack, 1988). Social historian of gender Julia Wrigley sums up the history of gender in U.S. schools as "conspicuous for the widespread gender equality found in its public schools . . . boys and girls usually attended the same schools, worked from the same books, and had the same teachers" (1992, p. 4). This "institutional grammar" of public schools in the United States, and many other nations too, has a pervasive effect in weakening the notion of gender as a legitimate way to distribute opportunity.

This is not to say that schools are some extreme, androgynous place. Any visit to school at any grade sees all manner of expression of a gendered world. Girls and boys in school continue to define themselves by gender categories. The dance of gender is everywhere, its exact rhythm depending only on the age of the children. But in the midst of all of this is the message officially carried by the organization of the school that both genders receive the same status of student. Curricula are not differentiated by gender; there is no valid way to assert that boys should learn this and girls should learn that. What differentiation there was historically is increasingly wiped out until the very idea of students doing different things by gender is considered backward and just plain unfair and wrong. This has reached into every aspect of modern schooling, from the athletic field to the chemistry lab; schools manifestly organize modern forms of universalism, and gender as a valid educational category wanes as a result. This creates a clear and powerful social reality for children and adults who participate daily in the institution of schooling worldwide.

Gender may be a rich source of identity in other spheres of life, such as informal and intimate relationships, but it is not expressed that way in the grammar of schooling today throughout the world. There is a message here with real consequences for students and how they construct their world.

But although schooling has weakened aspects of gender as an institution, we do not mean to imply that it has eradicated it. Although the overall impact of other institutions such as family and religion has been considerably weakened, these institutions still play a role in shaping notions about appropriate gender behavior. In nations like the United States, the institutional logic of schooling offers a gender-neutral message of achievement through academic advancement, but adolescents face the reality of harsh choices in part defined by traditional gender roles, particularly as they near the end of secondary schooling. For example, Japanese adolescents typically make educational decisions in order to preserve what is most important to them, or what they value most, and of course gender is part of this (LeTendre, 1996a). For young Japanese women with clear academic talent in math, the path toward a college-educated life may seem clear. But what of girls whose academic talents are modest and whose families and peers place great emphasis on family over professional relations? For these girls, the motivation to continue to exert effort in academic studies may well flag.

Thinking about the interactions among institutions is a richer way to consider the links between the organization of opportunities and the behavior of individuals. Obviously, opportunity structures in society mean something, and "female-friendly" ones generate motivation for females to take advantage of them through channels such as school achievement. But this minidrama of individual rationality is encapsulated in a larger and powerful institutional transition from a weakened gender institution to strengthened educational and political institutions, which do not include (or which at least downplay) traditional social categories within their main institutional ideologies.

Some feminist theories have a darker interpretation of the trends we examine here. The removal of traditional inequalities and deep forms of institutionalized oppression of females by males is the ultimate feminist project.

why does professional aspiration trump family?

Instead of opportunity structures, feminist research focuses on the welfare state (the cluster of policies aimed at family welfare, childcare, family leave, and so forth) and to what degree it is detrimental to women's interests (see Orloff, 1996). The key idea is "women's interests," the politicized idea of gender equality achieved through active removal of gender hierarchies. Similar to our findings here, a recent line of research has examined cross-national differences in welfare policy and their effect on female versus male wages, finding that more progressive welfare regimes providing state support for the traditional roles of mothering and childcare tend to ameliorate female disadvantage in salaries in the labor market (for example, Gornick, Meyers, and Ross, 1998).

The feminist image is one of all institutions dominated by male interests and female oppression in a world that at best can only ameliorate but never eradicate this arrangement. Why some nation-states produce a more female-friendly regime is not made explicit in this work; the focus is on implications for women. Schools seen this way are also oppressive to female interests. The idea of hidden curricula that favor boys over girls in the many subtle ways that classrooms work is an attractive image from a feminist perspective. From this perspective, no matter how egalitarian schools officially become, they nevertheless reproduce gender inequality.

Although the feminist argument takes an institutional perspective, as we do, it does not have an explanation for the rapid decline of a gendered world. From a feminist position, the apparent decline in gender differences is either fundamentally false, as in trivial changes, or is only a new mask hiding even deeper male exploitation. The problem with this argument, at least in the education sector, is in the proof of the pudding. In education, instead of sustained gender-inequality reproduction in favor of males, there is growing evidence that females are actually doing better than males in many aspects of attainment of educational credentials. There is still inequality in science, technology, and engineering advanced training, but the same human capital production and ideological forces that decreased gender difference in earlier stages of schooling seem to now be at work at more advanced levels (Charles and Bradley, 2002).

But all of this is not to simply say that schooling triumphs over gender inequality; it is a far more complex process with many other factors. For example, in-depth field studies comparing extremely poor versus wealthy U.S. schools suggest a dramatic difference in the degree to which differentiated gender paths are transmitted in schools (contrast MacLeod, 1987, with McDonough, 1997). When schools suffer from severe financial constraints and face widespread poverty, their ability to sustain gender-neutral education appears to be significantly compromised.

Similarly, cultural values specific to some nations appear to have at least impeded the spread of gender-neutral values in education. For example, Japan, which has a formal legal structure outlawing gender discrimination, has one of the highest levels of educational attainment in the world, and a comparatively homogeneous population both socially and economically still shows remarkable gender stratification of opportunity in work and higher education. Although Japanese women have experienced remarkable expansion of educational opportunity at the primary, middle, and secondary school levels, tertiary opportunity, particularly in very elite colleges, remains highly stratified by gender.

The Future of Gender and Mathematics Education in the World

Over the past few years, the media have reported on how female athletes are beginning to find their way onto once all-male American football teams. If ever there was a bastion of male-dominated life, American football is it (much like soccer in the rest of the world, except in the female-friendly soccer world of the United States). Young men play a physically violent game of strength, while the public watches and cheers. But now, around the edge of the game, women have begun to play football with men on public teams. What institution has the power to pull off such a major change? Women have not politically agitated for this entrée into football, although some have sued when teams tried to not let them try out because of their gender. There is no shortage of good male players at all levels of the game, and the sport has expanded impressively over the past fifty years. Although the federal Title IX law of 1972 requires schools to equalize funds and programs for girls and boys including sports in schools and colleges, this is for separate-but-equal female and male sports teams, not integrated ones.

The answer, of course, is formal schooling as an institution. In the United States, publicly played sports are an integral part of school and collegiate life, and changes in schooling influence sports. It is an easy jump from the universalistic world of schooling to a universalistic world of sports. In short, schooling, what goes on there, and its message of "a student is a student" regardless of traditional categories of status leave little room for legitimate argument against inclusion of individuals on the basis of categories such as gender. This is not to say that schooling is the only institution reducing the effects of gender; most certainly, women's political movements within the polity had a fundamental role in both legal and ideological shifts. Rather, schooling has been a quieter player in all this, but still its message is pervasive and compelling.

What does this mean for the future of the relationship between people's gender and their schooling experiences? Given what we now know about gender and schooling and the declining effects of gender on mathematics, an easy prediction to make is that gender effects will vanish. Schooling cultivates cognitive activities; its universalism works against traditional status categories of people, so it is not hard to imagine a future world with very low or nonexistent gender differences in mathematics and related topics of science and other technical subjects (Martinez, 2000). Further, if the now-fifty-year-old patterns of expansion of education and greater access to higher-level education for females continue, one could see in the not-too-distant future something close to gender parity at all levels of education, including advanced graduate degrees. The general institutional process now at work is self-reinforcing. More actively structured formal equality and associated norms lead to greater belief in the "naturalness" of gender equality, which in turns leads to more formalized equality, and so forth.

The pace of change, however, is likely to be affected both by national cultural values and by opportunity structures that might vary within nations. We acknowledge that national and regional cultures can block, or significantly modify, some of the force of global institutional change. But in the world of gender and schooling, a world culture of universalism seems too strong for local resistance to last very long. (Obviously, extreme gender inequality as practiced in some Islamic nations will take longer to change.)

Equalization of achievement scores also allows us to question whether or not gender equality varies with measures of schooling (for example, enrollment, achievement, satisfaction). Already female students in many nations have a better graduation rate for all levels of education, have higher average grades, show fewer behavior problems in early grades, and tend to outscore boys in language skills on average. These trends give pause in thinking about the feasibility of the opportunity structure argument we have described. Also, if we are right about the universalistic nature of the grammar of schools, female advantages should not occur; yet they appear to be doing just that.

One could argue that the emerging triumph of females in schooling is a reaction to the lack of opportunity in the past, or even, to some degree, a reaction to the social novelty of increased access. But we doubt anything so simple is at work here. In addition, others have even begun to think about what it is about the operation of schooling, particularly in early grades, that may disadvantage males! Feminists will see a certain irony in this concern about the low performance of some males on the eve of real educational equity across the genders, won after such a long struggle.

Nevertheless the institutional message is that in the future any pronounced gender differences in educational access or performance in any direction will draw concern in large measure because of the norms of universalism and the taboo of illegitimate use of traditional categories that schooling has had such a major role in developing. Any gender differences in education are redefined as a problem of social injustice and inefficiency that needs to be eradicated. These ideas will in the future continue to dominate education programs and policy around issues of gender.

CHAPTER 3

Symbiotic Institutions

CHANGING GLOBAL DYNAMICS BETWEEN

FAMILY AND SCHOOLING

---

with Brian Goesling

THE CHANGING DYNAMIC of the effects of schooling and family resources on youths' mathematics and science achievement over the past thirty years is a revealing story about the symbiotic relationship between the two institutions in modern society mainly concerned with the development of children and youths. In the preceding chapter, we showed how schooling eradicates gender inequality in achievement. Here we describe how a recent surge in the quality of schooling in many nations has done the opposite with students' social background; in other words, it has made the family's influence on achievement more salient. This is an interesting paradox—namely, that the considerable institutional strength and public support of mass schooling has created a situation where ever-smaller differences among family backgrounds play a bigger role than differences among schools in producing variation in student achievement.

The tale here is about the historical shift in the institutional struggle between these two central institutions focused on the socialization, education, and social attainment of children and youths. Instead of concluding that persistent family influences are a consequence of the family's institutional power, we argue just the opposite: that growing family effects on achievement are actually attributable to the continuing institutionalization and homogenization of schooling. At the end of the chapter, we return to why schooling eradicates gender influences, but not family influences on achievement.

It is often noted, somewhat cynically, that after forty years of research on the impact of the quality of schools on mathematics and science achievement we have mostly learned that the factor with the largest impact is the level of family resources of the student, not the quality of the school. Although this is true in a narrow sense, the story is far more complex and is rapidly evolving over time. There is evidence that the dynamic between school quality and family background is undergoing a major transformation worldwide.

Following the rapid and unpredicted growth in enrollment in compulsory schooling in the decades immediately after World War II, it appears that a second educational change, one of quality of schooling, also took place in many nations. Because primary and secondary schooling is ubiquitous in nations like the United States, it is easy to forget that universal enrollment in secondary schooling is just now being completed in the wealthiest of developing nations, and that the poorest of nations still lag behind in enrollment. We know from the history of school expansion among developed nations that after implementing full access to schooling across the primary and secondary levels, developing the overall quality of schooling throughout the national system becomes a major challenge for a government. Even the heavily schooled United States did not have full secondary enrollment until the mid-1960s, and serious educational reform aimed at reaching equitable distribution of resources across schools did not begin in earnest in many wealthy nations until the 1970s.

The same process is unfolding in economically developing nations throughout the world (Baker and Holsinger, 1996). The continued spread and expansion of access to mass schooling is accompanied by inevitable public pressure on governments to provide better-quality schools. Over time, these twin processes (reaching full access and demand for quality) have fundamentally changed the relationship between schools and families worldwide.

A sea change in the relationship between schools and families has profound implications for both theory and policy involving the school and family relationship, and it is likely to influence future debate about the role of schooling in society. But before describing possible futures, we set the stage a bit with a brief history of what we know has already happened in the world, and the attempts scholars have made to interpret these changes.

From the Coleman Report to the Heyneman/Loxley Effect and Back Again

This is a familiar story in educational and sociological circles (Baker and Le-Tendre, 1999). In 1966, the report *Equality of Educational Opportunity* (more simply, the first "Coleman Report") was published. Commissioned by the Johnson administration as part of its War on Poverty and Great Society campaigns, the authors of the report sought to answer policy questions asked about the relations among school funding, poverty, and race (Coleman and others, 1966). The report ended up establishing a central question about schooling for the next several decades: What effect does school quality have on achievement?[1] This question surfaced from the report's unexpected finding that the variation in achievement among students accounted for by their nonschool background (family background, or in the jargon of social sciences the family's socioeconomic status, usually measured as the education level of parents and their economic resources) substantially exceeded a set of school qualities (school resources of various types) in explaining achievement differences. In the parlance of school-effects research, within-school differences in achievement are greater than between-school differences. Even though similar findings would be reported some five years later in a British study (*The Plowden Report*; Peaker, 1971), the Coleman Report was a uniquely American study in its questions, design, and ultimate intellectual impact. The debate on this question has lasted to the present day.

As elsewhere in the economically developed world, by the end of the 1960s American mass schooling had grown to an enviable degree. Institutional developments, often first observed in the United States, would soon be reported throughout the world. The political impetus of the Great Society campaign in initiating the Coleman study was itself the product of the growing institutional power of education accompanying enrollment expansion during the middle of the twentieth century. By 1960, the social "charter" of the school had incorporated the function of improving problems (or equalizing problematic social conditions) that were, strictly speaking, *not* educational problems: urban blight, youth violence, racism, and racial segregation (Meyer, 1977). It was widely thought that raising the quality of basic education for all American youths and helping them learn more would surely solve these problems (Lemann, 1991).

Simplistic as it may sound today, many policy makers at the federal level believed if we could just level the educational playing field basic American values of achievement through merit and hard work would take over. Although this belief in the power of education to drive social change is particularly salient in U.S. history, it also resonated with the hopes and beliefs of people around the world who saw a modern educational system as the golden path to economic prosperity and alleviation of persistent social problems (for example, Rubinson and Browne, 1994; LeTendre and others, 2000).

This is why the basic findings of the Coleman Report so troubled educators, government policy makers, and the public alike. The results seemed not to follow the script everybody had agreed upon, and they flew in the face

1. The Coleman Report went on to a series of important findings about the effect of race on achievement that had a separate impact on educational policy (Riordan, 2003).

of a utilitarian notion of schooling—namely, that if schools educate then differences in school quality should produce dissimilar learning outcomes, and hence by equalizing variation in school resources children would all receive basic education without major disadvantage. In other words, any influence of the level of family resources and position would be eradicated by the mass school system.

But to the contrary, the findings showed that compared to the sizable impact of family background factors on achievement, differences in school resources had less impact and sometimes even no effect. The startling, overly simplistic message taken from the Coleman Report—that school had little effect on achievement—caught the public's attention. As a result of heavy media coverage of the report, this conclusion influenced education policy makers and essentially trapped both policy and research into a decades-long obsession with family background effects.

Of course, this was a mistake—not the finding, but the subsequent interpretation and focus of research and policy debate. Even after many years of discussion, and the "discovery" of the influence of school factors that are often tied to resources such as curricula and instructional quality, one still frequently hears a policy maker or educator state that "schools do not matter as much as the family does in terms of achievement." The misunderstanding stems from blurring the considerable distinction between "school effects" and the "effect of schooling." The latter is the influence on achievement of being schooled *versus* not being schooled, an entirely different matter from the former. The best research on the effects of schooling has not yet been done, but we do have some indication of the massive effects on achievement of going to school versus not going to school, holding constant family background.

The developmental psychologist Stephen Ceci (1991) conducted a comprehensive review of more than fifty studies using various methods to compare schooled and unschooled populations of children over the twentieth century. He concluded that after holding constant the characteristics of children (even initial IQ), each year of schooling imparts a sizable cognitive advantage. Various comparisons estimating the effect size of schooling range from .3 to .6 of an IQ point for every year of school completed beyond what the child started school with; given that IQ tests are made to have a standard deviation of 15 points and that children go to school for many years, this effect is sizable. Importantly, the association between IQ and exposure to formal education is not only due to children with higher measured IQs performing better in school. By comparing similar children (equal on family social background and initial IQ) with differing exposure to schooling, these studies support a causal relationship between attending even a minimal amount of schooling and the development of the individual's intelligence.

Similar results have been obtained in countries with non-Western cultures. For example, Stevenson and others (1978) found that schooling significantly changed the cognitive performance and orientation of Quechua children in rural Peru on a host of measures. This is not to say that schooling teaches what all stakeholders in society would like it to, or that one cognitive orientation is inherently better than another. Rather, these studies illustrate that the technology of mass schooling, as is now found in most of the world, is not trivial in its impact on the individual or how it might influence students beyond merely sorting them for the modern labor market.

Overall, schooling has persistent, positive effects on human cognitive function, as opposed to no schooling. Indeed, modern societies are no longer sustained by traditional forms of apprenticeship learning; reading, writing, and basic math skills are a minimum requirement for a functioning adult in almost every nation in the world, yet we often take these skills and the schooling producing them for granted (Martinez, 2002; Blair, Gamson, Thorne, and Baker, 2005). Schooling clearly influences how students think and learn, and many miss this when they misinterpret the Coleman Report's findings.

But school effects are quite a different matter. The phrase *school effects* is a researcher's shorthand way of referring to the effect on academic achievement of going to one school versus another, usually with differences in resources. School effects research examines if varying the level of resources, or policies, or school climate and so forth from school to school explains achievement differences among students. Of course, the main finding of the Coleman Report was that school effects are minimal. Since then, research on school effects has seen considerable methodological improvements in ways to detect small effects (Riordan, 2003). Regardless, the main point of modest school quality effects still holds in the United States.

The Coleman findings, correctly interpreted, showed that compared to school quality, family socioeconomic status is more saliently associated with academic outcomes. In other words, compared to variation in the quality of schools in a nation, family background translates into achievement level and amplifies social inequality. So it is not that schooling is ineffectual; rather, it is that the variation in school quality seems relatively ineffectual. This dashed the hopes of the Johnson administration's Great Society educational plans to reduce unfair social advantage through a level educational playing field.[2]

Given the cognitive effects of schooling that we have just outlined, how could this be? We need a comparative perspective to answer this question.

2. This idea even found its way into the logic that the George W. Bush administration uses to justify reform of school administrative accountability instead of trying to achieve more equitable resource distribution among school districts.

At the time of the Coleman and UK reports both showing the same pattern, it was generally assumed that small school effects were generic to all schooled societies. Not until a decade and a half after the Coleman Report, however, did anyone actually bother to see if the pattern of family and school effects was the same in all nations. The answer was quite surprising.

In the early 1980s, Stephen Heyneman and William Loxley were working to expand the World Bank's lending policy agenda to include educational development. They undertook a study of the effects of school quality on achievement in twenty-nine countries using data from the 1970s (Heyneman and Loxley, 1982, 1983; Heyneman, 1976). Heyneman and Loxley showed that the "Coleman effect" of larger family background effects and smaller school effects occurred mostly in economically developed nations, while the reverse—smaller family background effects with larger school effects—occurred in less economically developed nations. Specifically, in the 1970s in nations with low gross national product per capita, school quality factors accounted for differences between students in achievement more than did family background. The Heyneman-Loxley effect (hereafter, the "HL effect") challenges the uniformity of the Coleman effect, which had previously been thought of as a consistent pattern across all nations. Also, these studies report another related part of the HL effect: that about one-third of the difference across nations in average mathematics and science academic achievement is associated with a nation's economic development. In other words, compared to poorer nations, wealthier nations in the late 1970s produced more mathematics and science achievement among their youth.

These findings considerably modified the initial conclusions taken from the Coleman and British school-effects findings, in that they contradict the notion that the differences among schools universally have only a modest effect on achievement in mathematics and science. For the first time, Heyneman and Loxley showed clear evidence that variation in school quality (teaching resources, instructional resources, curricular materials, school resources for science and mathematics, and so on) could matter more than variation in family input in producing differences in achievement among students. The HL effect in less wealthy nations, most of which at the time had substantial variation in school quality, illustrates the strength of schooling as a mechanism to distribute human capital. Moreover, the wealth of a nation is related not only to how family and school resources interact to distribute human capital within the population but also to the total amount of human capital produced through schools.

What would produce a situation where the original Coleman effect was the case only in wealthy nations, while the opposite was the case in less developed nations? First, it is important to realize that in economically developed nations almost every child goes to school, and that quality among schools is relatively homogeneous in these national systems (compared to what it was like 130 years ago). So school-effects research undertaken in economically developed nations is really examining the impact of comparatively small differences among schools in resources (Chapter 5 shows that the distribution of educational resources varies across nations).

Conversely, school quality in poorer nations in the late 1970s was unevenly distributed. Many such nations had some schools with resources significantly below a basic level of what is needed to effectively teach students in mathematics and science. Comparative sociologist Bruce Fuller's 1987 review of some sixty school-effects studies in less-developed nations prior to the mid-1980s illustrates the low minimum level of school quality in terms of expenditures on schooling, specific material inputs, quality of teaching stock, classroom practices, pedagogic approach, and school management that produced the HL effect. In the 1970s and 1980s, for example, it was not uncommon to find a significant number of schools in less-developed nations operating with severe textbook and instructional material shortages; in some cases, this meant schools without access to any textbooks. This was by and large because of the overall poverty of these nations, but sometimes inequality of resources was intentional and racially or ethnically motivated.

Not only did many developing nations have limited technical resources during this time; they often had faculties in primary schools with a low level of literacy and numeracy, and the level of school management was often minimal in many nations. At the same time, elsewhere in these nations there were schools with a significantly higher level of resources, and with far better trained faculties. The large amount of internal resource inequality in developing nations no doubt produced the HL effect in the original and subsequent studies.[3]

But since that time there has been both a revolution in spreading access to schooling in less developed nations and, quick on its heels, a revolution in spreading school quality throughout less-developed nations. This begs the question of what has happened to the HL effect as a result of the spread of school quality in many nations since the early 1980s.

With our colleague Brian Goesling, we examined what has happened to the HL effect in the decade and a half after it was first reported and found two interesting results in the 1990s data (Baker, LeTendre, and Goesling, 2002). First, the wealth of nations is still related to the overall level of math-

---

3. Other reasons for the HL effect were speculated on in the original papers, such as the notion that the size and importance of the public labor sector and the civil service in developing countries tend to "tighten" the connections between school achievement at all levels and future employment opportunities.

ematics and science achievement, but the association weakened to almost one-half of what it was in the late 1970s (dropping from an association of about .33 to .15, on a scale of 0 to 1). In other words, even though some of the differences in achievement level among nations is due to national wealth, much less of it is so than was the case fifteen years ago. Second, we find that the HL effect vanished in the mid-1990s; family and school effects are no longer conditioned by the wealth of a nation. The Coleman effect has spread throughout the world; large family effects and small school effects are now the dominant pattern (see also Schiller, Khmelkov, and Wang, 2002).

But we should be clear that among the nations participating in TIMSS there are no extremely poor or politically failing states. Therefore our research applies to school quality development in wealthy and less-wealthy nations and does not rule out the probability that the HL effect is still evident among the poorest of nations, particularly if those nations are too poor to have fully participated in the recent trend of providing resourced schooling throughout the country. The same can be said about nations so chronically beset by civil war or political repression that basic social institutions, including schooling, have eroded to virtually a premodern level. Nevertheless, nations in TIMSS do include a reasonable range of wealth, and a number of the same nations are in both the original HL analysis and ours, and they all show a shift away from the HL effect to the Coleman effect over this time period.

Further evidence that the decline of the HL effect represented a meaningful increase in school quality by the 1990s is presented by the comparative educationalist Abbey Riddell (1989, 1997), who reviewed similar analyses (or did such analyses herself) separately by nation for almost two dozen school effects studies in poorer nations (for example, Botswana, Brazil, Colombia, Egypt, Honduras, India, Jordan, Namibia, Pakistan, the Philippines, Thailand, and Zimbabwe) and found, as we do, a pattern of reversal of the earlier HL effect. The key here is that all of the data used in these analyses reflect the situation in these nations since the 1980s, with most of the data collected at exactly the same period in which the TIMSS data were collected in the mid-1990s. After finding a reversal of the 1970s HL effect in Zimbabwe in 1985 data, for example, Riddell goes on to describe the "unprecedented expansion that had already taken place in the educational system since . . . 1980" and the heavy financial commitment of the government to spend educational resources in ways that would maximize achievement throughout the population of the nation's students.[4]

4. Riddell had a number of technical criticisms of the original HL analysis that led her to reject their findings. But as we discuss in detail in Baker, Goesling, and LeTendre (2002), it is clear that the HL effect did exist in the late 1970s.

Development of Educational Systems and
Influences on School Achievement

The key to understanding the change in family and school effects over the past thirty years—from the Coleman effect to the HL effect and then back again—is in the timing of the revolution in school quality undertaken in many nations around the world. As shown in Figures 3.1 and 3.2, over the past three decades two long-term trends have followed one another among less wealthy nations. First is the expansion of mass education enrollment rate, and second is the growth in public expenditures (in constant dollars) throughout less-developed nations (although developed nations are clearly ahead in these trends).[5] The enrollment revolution in less wealthy nations took off in the 1970s, while the growth in expenditures in these nations did not accelerate until the late 1980s (Fiala and Gordon-Lanford, 1987). An expanding enrollment rate certainly costs a government funds, but (for example, as Riddell observed for a developing nation such as Zimbabwe) so does raising the lowest level of school quality across a national system of schools

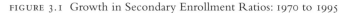

FIGURE 3.1 Growth in Secondary Enrollment Ratios: 1970 to 1995

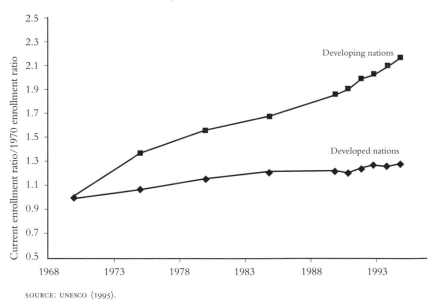

SOURCE: UNESCO (1995).

---

5. Private expenditures are not included here, but the point is that there has been an intensification of national expenditures on education over time (Tsang, 1995).

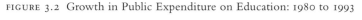

FIGURE 3.2 Growth in Public Expenditure on Education: 1980 to 1993

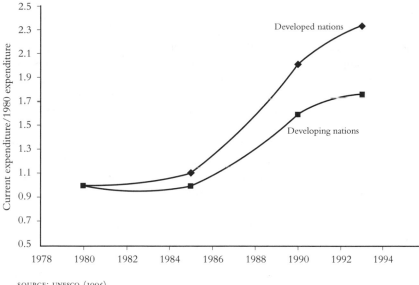

SOURCE: UNESCO (1995).

that greatly vary in resources. Growing expenditures have been used for both of these goals in many developing nations from the late 1980s on (Baker and Holsinger, 1996).

The mechanism behind the shifting relationship between family and school effects may be obvious, but its interpretation is more complex. The national logic of human capital development as a planned and funded governmental project has been promoted throughout developing nations through many mechanisms, including the investment strategies of multilateral development agencies (Chabbott, 2003). Further, for reasons of maximizing human capital production and political justification, the spread of minimal school quality throughout the system has become a standard political objective in these nations. This has led many nations to upgrade the lowest level of school quality and enhance equality among schooling. As many studies of school resources in individual nations show, this process has raised quality in the underresourced schools over a threshold from very ineffective to effective. Learning reading from a teacher who reads at only a second grade level compared to learning from one who reads at an eleventh grade level is likely to be significant and overshadow any family differences in home assistance. But learning reading from a teacher reading at an eleventh grade level rather than from one who reads at a twelfth grade level probably makes far less of a school difference. The same is true for mathematics and other subjects.

If we extend this notion out to an array of other important school resources, we can see that by striving to improve the overall quality of schools nations can reduce extreme differences among schools and hence lower the effect of going to one versus another. This is not to say that school resource differences have or will disappear in most nations. But raising the minimal resource level over a certain threshold lowers the effect of school quality on achievement differences. Our results also suggest that there may be some point at which additional school quality has diminishing returns for achievement. For example, it is well known from American research on school effects that after a certain point resources do not yield proportionally more achievement, so there is likely to be an upper bound to the process.

At the same time, the majority of families try to assist in their children's education, and these families have salient differences in financial resources, educational background, and cultural advantages that make them unequal in terms of how much they can assist in education. If school quality becomes more similar across schools and family differences remain the same, the latter will be a larger force in achievement. The full ramifications of this process have only recently reached a significant portion of developing nations. Over the historical development of a national system of schools, quality differences among schools perhaps do not have a monotonic effect on achievement; rather, there may be larger school effects early in the development of a national system when there are still a significant number of schools operating below a threshold level of resources.

This effect can even be enhanced over time as a significant portion of the population in developing nations receives more education than the preceding generation had. As education expands, new generations of mothers will receive more education, which makes them more familiar with the schooling process and gives them the skills (and perhaps more motivation too) to be involved parents (Lareau, 2000; Pong and Post, 1991; Schaub, 2004). This in turn can stimulate family investment in schooling for children and start a process by which there is more competition over school outcomes and hence greater motivation to use family resources to this end (Collins, 1979).

Qualitative field studies in the United States document the degree to which wealthy families invest in "specialists" who fine-tune minute aspects of college entrance materials (McDonough, 1997). Within the United States, entrance to institutions at the apex of the college system has become an amazingly complex process wherein playing a specific musical instrument or caring for a disabled family member can become salient factors in admission that must be displayed in the correct language to admissions directors (Karen, 1991). As educational systems become more complex, heightened parental involvement can lead to greater inequality, insofar as family resources are un-equal and school resources are more equal. As mass schooling becomes more institutionalized around the world, the mechanics of schooling in terms of curriculum, teaching, and perhaps other resources become more standardized at a minimal level (see Benavot and others, 1991).

The now dominant Coleman effect means that even though the school has supplanted the family in many aspects in directly socializing and educat-ing children, family influences on school outcomes remain. Evidence of the impact of family on schooling continues to challenge the legitimacy of a school system to make achievement depend on merit and not background. For example, some nations, notably South Korea, have extensive policies aimed precisely at eradicating family effects. Others, such as Japan, have a ministry of education that systematically limits collection and access to in-formation that could be used to identify family background effects; they boldly and falsely claim that no such effects exist in the system (LeTendre, Rohlen, and Zeng, 1998).

But our results and others' are clear. In most nations, a higher level of family resources, including plain old-fashioned money capital and all its other forms (social, cultural, and intellectual), causes higher achievement af-ter controlling for anything else about the student and school that re-searchers can think up. School systems are porous, to some degree, to the influence of family resources. Paradoxically, implementation of more equi-table distribution of resources across schools in nations actually enhances the relative influence of family background effects.

Institutionally Weak Family and Strong School

The influence of family background on educational outcomes is often con-sidered from sociological and social policy perspectives as an institutional fail-ure, because it means that schooling is capable of significant "social repro-duction." Social reproduction, in the language of sociology, means passing on to children a family advantage through enhanced merit (achievement and strategies about schooling); conversely, it also means handicapping children's merit through family disadvantage. Similarly, from a policy point of view, governments can find this quality of schooling and families to be an unde-sirable effect.[6] A cornerstone of justification of public-funded mass school-ing is that merit, as expressed through achievement in subjects such as math-ematics and science, will be the sole means by which future educational and occupational opportunities are determined. Furthermore, merit should not be overly enhanced by family background if a society is to achieve a more or

6. Note that in Chapter 4 we discuss the major antishadow-education policies of South Korea as an attempt to lessen social reproductive processes.

less sustainable meritocratic education system and labor market. Of course, never has there been a completely meritocratic society, and probably there never will be. But findings such as those of the Coleman effect (and even the HL effect with its smaller yet persistent family background effects on achievement) challenge this central justification of mass schooling.

Given that throughout this book we are led by a number of trends cross-nationally to speculate on the growing institutional power of schooling, how would we explain the apparent institutional failure evident in social reproduction within the learning of subjects such as mathematics and science?

First, it helps to sketch out other perspectives on educational social reproduction. According to those who see schools as highly reproductive of social class, there are two culprits. One is the school itself, about which there is evidence of intentional and unintentional social class bias (Bowles and Gintis, 1976). The other, of course, is the family, with its constant motivation to mix intimate relationships with children and mobility strategies for their children's life chances, mostly now through investments in schooling. In this more radical view, both institutions work toward a significant degree of social reproduction.

We have another take on this relationship between these two institutions. The spreading of family effects in achievement is ironically an outcome of the simultaneous weakening of the family as an institution to directly intervene in the future welfare of its children and strengthening of education as an institution, particularly in terms of the emphasis on merit indicated by achievement. There are two related processes here.

In most nations now, a child's performance in schooling almost solely determines his or her future educational and occupational chances; the family has been limited in how it can help children for the future and pass on any advantage. In other words, institutionally speaking, families have lost power in ensuring children's future because families are relegated to use mobility strategies through the now-dominant institution of schooling. Simply put, a hundred years ago a prosperous farmer, silversmith, or buggy maker could convey considerable economic advantage to his children by passing on skills, land, or stock via a family-based apprenticeship. Schooling then was a route to success, but only one of several. Further back in history the premodern family, usually in the form of a clan, had significant control over direct mechanisms to ensure children's futures: family inheritance of position, clan status, family-based apprenticeship, and inherited sinecure. Before widespread mass schooling, family effects on social reproduction were large, direct, and mostly unchallenged by any other institutional processes. High-status families directly placed their children into high-status positions, while children from low-status families were usually relegated to low-status positions as adults. This is easily illustrated by the power that European eighteenth-century patrician families had in holding elite positions; hence they could place their children directly into such positions. Not all families had such power, to be sure, but the family as an institution did have considerable power to directly influence the child's future.

The course of social development has changed this. During the historical rise of Western society, particularly during the nineteenth and twentieth centuries, family (along with religion) initially lost institutional power to industrial capitalism, the modern social welfare state, and not long after that to the spread of mass schooling as well.[7] This institutional development sealed the family's institutional fate in modern society. As capitalism, social welfare, and mass education spread worldwide, so did the decline of traditional family strength in social reproduction.

Historically speaking, mass schooling was introduced as part of a radically new social order with its own logic in matching children to futures. The workings of schools, with their emphasis on measurable and public forms of achievement, are a central part of the meritocratic ideology in society today. If schooling as an institution becomes more widespread and holds more control over how we make sense out of rearing children and defining individual merit, then academic achievement takes on even greater importance in the daily lives of children and parents. Schooling, with its meritocratic intentions and widely attributed power to transform children into functioning adults, has become the institutional winner in the battle over direct control of status attainment of children. Mothers and fathers wanting, as always, the best for their children must compete by way of the institution of schooling to pass on advantage to children, and therein lies the mechanism for transmission of social advantage. This means that all of the considerable and intimate emotions, worry, and expectations generated by the modern family regarding children and their future are funneled into the schooling process, particularly aimed at achievement. It is no wonder that even in the most egalitarian school system pressure from families to pass on advantage cannot be completely stopped. Family advantage seeps through the cracks in the school system, like water under heavy pressure through the best of seals.

Interestingly, parents hold little cynicism toward the schooling process. They participate in children's schooling largely by its rules of achievement (parents themselves played the school game for a large part of their youth). Most families in most nations do not try to cheat (or even really game) the education system for their children's advantage; rather, they attempt to turn what resources they have into enhanced achievement through such things as accepted involvement in schooling, activities aimed at cognitive development of children, and acquisition of special educational services. Embracing

7. This occurs with rationality and individualism as well.

and legitimating achievement as the key to access to a child's future is an important aspect of schooling's institutional power.

An interesting example of the power of schooling to transform what parents do with their young children is Maryellen Schaub's social history of the parenting of cognition among young children (2004). She finds considerable growth over the later half of the twentieth century in American parents' awareness and time spent on teaching very young children basic academic skills before they enter school. In the middle of the twentieth century, only a modest proportion of families invested time in the cognitive development of children so young, yet by the turn of the current century almost all families were doing so regularly. They do it not because they are necessarily interested in the general enlightenment of their child, nor for the immediate well-being of children, nor certainly for the child's future in the family business or farm; they do it because of the importance of looming school performance for the child's future.

But what then to make of increasing family effects on educational outcomes, if the family has actually gotten weaker as a direct agent in social reproduction? The answer is found in understanding what creates the situation for family effects in the first place—understanding what causes the shift away from the HL effect toward a uniform Coleman effect in most nations. If our speculation is correct that the recent decline of nations with significantly underfunded (read less institutionalized) systems of education is the reason large between-school differences have vanished, then we need to think about what has caused that on an institutional level. In short, as education became more institutionalized worldwide, the minimal level of acceptable educational quality in all nations rose as a function of it. Though there continues to be variation in school quality within all nations, it is quite likely that greater institutionalization tends to reduce variation at the bottom of the school quality scale. Therefore school quality is spread more evenly within nations, often above the level of basic resources even in many developing nations.

This creates the situation where any influence that family resources have on achievement (parenting of cognitive development, purchase of outside help, influence on school selection, and so on) will rise in prominence compared to the greater homogeneity among school quality within nations. So spreading family effects in achievement does not represent increasing domination of family as an institution; instead, they represent the increasing institutionalization of mass school and its tendency to reduce inequality of school resources within a nation's system of public schooling. We expect that the rise in minimal school quality in many nations is both a consequence of greater demand among families with school-aged children and increased governmental incentive to supply better schooling for assumed future economic and social collective benefits.

This perspective also helps explain why schooling can wipe out, or greatly reduce, gender differences in mathematics achievement but cannot easily wipe out family background influences. Educational gender egalitarianism influences families and their relative investment of time and money in educating daughters and sons, which grows more equal over time and place (Baker and Jones, 1992). But generally a nuclear family does not have children with differing social economic statuses. Family effects become more equal internally according to the gender of the child, but differences persist across families with varying resource levels. It is also true, of course, that siblings do not necessarily receive the same amount of resources within all families (Conley, 2004).

The Future of the Relationship Between the Family and the School

In William Shakespeare's *Romeo and Juliet* the social world of the two competing elite families, the Montagues and the Capulets, is barely recognizable to us today. The tragedy is that lovers, no matter how great their passion, could not in premodern Verona forsake their families (and concomitant social and physical capital) for mere emotions. This was a common theme and made for a well-understood drama in its time. The point is that for Romeo and Juliet the future is made possible only through their respective clans, and as the play shows not even the considerable power of the church can eliminate that all-encompassing bond. It is telling that after the youths' deaths the local lord condemns the two households writ large, not just the parents or individuals in the families.

This major public role of the clan or extended family is lost on the modern reader of the play. It seems antiquated, and indeed it is. Modern audiences resonate with the individuals striving against the oppressive control of the family, but the modern family is nothing like that of the feudal period (whether great or humble). One's family is no longer synonymous with one's social status. In the psychologized vernacular of the United States, the term *family of origin* has become common, even further distancing the individual from his or her family. The myth of meritocratic production of human capital and adult status has won out over family status, estates, and even extreme class reproduction. In Western culture, these ideals are implemented with varying effect in public mass schooling, but it is schooling that has come to be the institution identified with allocation of future life chances.

Given the precipitous decline of the institutional power of the family to influence directly the social status of individuals, and the rapid institutional growth in mass schooling over the past hundred years, the basic contours of the relationship between the two is unlikely to change radically in the future.

They will continue to be symbiotic, with schooling the more dominant of the two in defining and assigning status to children and young adults. But within this overall pattern of the strong school and weak family, what is likely to emerge in the future?

First, schools and public institutions will continue to produce and legitimize the dominant social roles important in the early part of the life course, and this will be mostly about individual achievement in academic subjects such as language arts, mathematics, and science. At the same time, when achievement appears to be disrupted by a family's situation, schools now have power to take sanctions against students and families the system defines as "dysfunctional" or "disruptive." We would expect to see more and more battles around the control of these categories in the name of reducing suppressed achievement of disadvantaged children in the future, with some families able to manipulate these categories to their advantage and others not. For example, the evolving category of "learning disability" is now an actively sought diagnosis that some families use to obtain personalized instruction for their child to enhance achievement (OERI, 1999b). Although this term was virtually unknown in Japan in the 1980s and early 1990s, there are now organized parental groups advocating correct diagnosis, and treatment, for children who are "LD" (OERI, 1998).

Second, we will see continued battles to increase parental control over classrooms and schools waged on a local level. In most nations, "home schooling" (read: family-controlled schooling) of children is illegal, and where it is legal the state usually monitors it closely. There are some indications that the home-schooling movement popular in the United States is now spreading to other countries, but look what has happened in the United States. Although most U.S. parents who adopt home schooling do so in order to preserve family control over values transmission, the enactment of home schooling has come to look very much like "school," with home schoolers following a standard curriculum, banding together to take "classes" from other parents, going on "field trips" to cultural or scientific sites, and even (often successfully) demanding the right to participate in school athletics or use school facilities!

In addition to these future trends, will schooling become more egalitarian or not? Will family influence continue to increase, or decrease? There are two possibilities. In both cases, we assume that schooling will continue to be a dominant institutional form, probably continuing to push into other institutional fields as well (see Storey and Edwards, 1997, on training of managers in banks, supermarket chains, and the like). We also assume that there will be pressure for continuous school quality and its wider distribution across schools as a world norm. Given this, the first possibility for the future is that differences among families will have an increased effect on achievement and hence adult social status. That is, a persistent and strong Coleman effect will continue, and perhaps grow. The second future possibility is that family resources, at least those that seem to matter most to helping children's school achievement, will even out across the majority of families, and hence family and school effects will be roughly equal and modest. There is a case to be made for each future scenario.

The first future scenario suggests that differences in the ability of families to help their children attain school achievement will make a bigger relative impact as school inequality declines because of greater institutionalization by government. Indeed, there is some evidence of this. Comparative sociologists Yossi Shavit and Hans-Peter Blossfeld and their colleagues in 1993 statistically examined the influence of school achievement and family background on one's adult social-occupational status in thirteen economically developed nations where schooling had long been strongly institutionalized. They found, as can be anticipated, that how much schooling the person had has a sizable influence on adult social status (as with occupation); but they also found that families had their largest effect not directly on adult status but indirectly through their influence on school achievement, and this was the same in each country.[8] Researchers such as Blossfeld, Shavit, and others talk about a persistent family SES effect on adult occupation through the influence of family background on school achievement that increasingly controls future opportunities.

Recent evidence suggests that this basic pattern may be intensifying over time. Ingrid Schoon (2003) undertook an interesting comparison of family and school achievement effects on young adults across two cohorts of British children, one born in 1958 and the other in 1970. She reports that compared to the older cohort, schooling in the lives of the younger cohort has expanded in importance and is more institutionalized in its impact on adult status. Further, by the time the youngest cohort was in school, academic achievement took on greater connection to adult status, and these students' family background exerted more of an influence on achievement than among the older cohort (see also Kerckhoff, 1990; and Marshall, Swift, and Roberts, 1997).

The second future scenario suggests that there may be some powerful forces to even out family impact on achievement over time. Greater institutional strength of mass schooling results in pervasive influences that encourage—even force—a wider array of families to invest more resources in their children's schooling success. Social welfare agencies around the world spend considerable time helping disadvantaged families with resources, enticements, and knowledge—and sometimes they even use legal force—to manage the education of their children. Similarly, the growing amount of experience

---

8. This is the standard finding of the huge literature on status attainment in the United States and elsewhere.

with schooling among women over the past one hundred years means that each successive generation of mothers is likely to know more about how school works and better ways to help their own children (Schaub, 2004).

School expansion and the growing length of the school career have also reached down to women from disadvantaged families, and the effect on child rearing over the past century has probably been considerable, if difficult to observe. Even though at the present time in a nation such as the United States, for example, having only eleven years of schooling does not bode well for one's chances in the labor market, on average mothers with eleven years of schooling are more equipped to assist their own children with schooling than mothers with only one or two years of schooling, as was common of poor women's educational background early in the twentieth century.

This scenario does not predict that family effects will disappear altogether, only that they will greatly decline. Wealthy and highly educated parents will continue to have more resources to bring to bear on their children's education in a multitude of ways, but as schooling as an institution becomes more pervasive throughout society relatively less educated parents will also have more ability and motivation to academically assist their children. In much the same way that the lowest level of school quality has risen over time, the lowest level of family assistance in achievement probably has also. Educational opportunity would be stratified, but the mass of people would have, comparatively, more equal opportunity than in the past.

The key issue in these trends for national policy makers appears to be to find ways to minimize the stratification of educational opportunity. If wealthier families continue to spend even more resources on children's education, the gap will not decrease (and family effects will not diminish); hence the future relationship between families and schools could become one of runaway competition between status and education (Collins, 1979). But this may not happen, or at least be somewhat curtailed as a function of greater institutionalization of schooling. Governments continue to enhance education for all children and sometimes openly attempt to limit the impact of family resources, particularly at the top. Also it may be that there are diminishing returns for family effects on achievement after a certain point, although this does not seem to diminish the enthusiasm of families for consuming achievement-tutoring services for their children (see the next chapter on the worldwide growth of shadow education).

Lastly, it is interesting to speculate if educational competition over achievement so enhanced by schooling may simply be reaching a breaking point, where even advantaged families perceive that educational competition is creating negative impacts. We must not ignore the considerable intimate influence of schooling on family psychological well-being. The point is that schools have become the sanctioned institution not only to educate children but to define so much of their world. In countries such as Japan, there has been considerable public backlash against increased educational competition. Public concern over some families' protest by refusing to send children to school prompted the Ministry of Education to reduce the number of days children go to school (Fukuzawa and LeTendre, 2001). The outcome of this particular reform is not yet clear, but it may be that some nations are now reaching the point where educational competition imposes too great a burden on families and students.

For the foreseeable future, schooling will lead the dance with the family, and many other institutions will follow its lead. With no other viable institution to take over socialization and educational functions in national societies, the expansion of schooling over more and more family functions is likely. But the spread will not be without conflict. Both individual families and groups of people have pushed, and will continue to push, for political changes that can affect the institutional structure of schooling. Whether it is home-schooling laws in the United States; outlawing tutoring, as South Korea tried; or a reduced school year in Japan, this dynamic tension between the two institutions will generate further institutional changes that will then spread in the world system.

CHAPTER 4

Demand for Achievement

WITH ITS RELENTLESS focus on academic achievement, schooling deepens the importance for all students to do well to earn grades, educational advancement, and other crucial school credentials. Mastering subjects such as mathematics and science is not just one of the outcomes of schooling; it is the central one that shapes all others. Beyond just practical matters, schooling as an institution makes academic achievement necessary and expected of all children regardless of their abilities and interests, and this has intensified over the history of mass education. As we saw in the preceding chapter, schooling as an institution leads families to funnel what advantages they have through the schooling process. Here we examine a worldwide trend that is a result of this symbiotic relationship between the strong school and the weak family as institutions.

Public mass education around the world has motivated many families to purchase an extensive amount of outside-school tutoring and related services to help their children perform better in subjects such as mathematics and science within school. In a number of nations, these activities are themselves rapidly becoming an institutionalized part of schooling. This massive demand for additional instruction has implications both for the ability of public schools to provide equitable, high-quality education and for future policy making. In this chapter, the story we present is an interesting case of institutional change. Here again, as in the previous chapter, we show how the expansion of mass schooling has had far-reaching (and unintended) consequences for the relationship between public control of schooling and private interests in schooling's consequences.

In the 1980s, as the United States struggled through a major recession and a restructuring of its economy, everything Japanese appeared to be successful. As the Japanese auto industry leapt ahead of the once-dominant and venerable American auto makers, it appeared as if Japan had found some miraculous formula for national well-being. In the opinion of many Americans, a big part of the formula was the effectiveness of Japan's school system in teaching students difficult subjects such as mathematics and science. Spurred on by the widely read Reagan administration's *Nation at Risk,* in which achievement in American schools was unfavorably compared to nations that were also out-competing the United States economically, there was great interest in everything unique about schooling in Japan.

One aspect of Japanese schooling that caught many Americans' attention was the widespread use of after-school tutoring. Japanese terms for these activities—*juku* and *yobiko* (after-school private tutoring done in school-like classes)—became part of many American educators' vocabulary (Rohlen, 1983). It struck Westerners as amazing that after a full day of formal schooling, many Japanese students would go directly to private tutoring classes, where there was additional instruction and drill on subjects presented during the regular school classes.

What was not obvious at that time was that the use of private, after-school educational services was fast becoming a worldwide megatrend among families with children in public school. Families in such nations as Japan, South Korea, and Greece had a long history of using these services. But as we will show here, students in these nations were not alone in using extra lessons and instructional help to master their in-school subjects. The dramatic growth in the supply of out-of-school tutoring services, in varied arrangements, and the growing demand by families with children in public schools to buy the services is an unexpected development that has far-reaching consequences for the future of mass public schooling and its values of universalism. Our tale here is about what has become known as "shadow education"; it tells us about how schooling's power as an institution penetrates the lives of parents, students, and teachers and in so doing may transform itself unpredictably.

More Than a Little Tutoring on the Side: Systems of Shadow Education

Tutoring, whether to help the student who has trouble in a particular subject or to further prepare the student who faces an important and difficult examination, is a timeless activity. For centuries, struggling university students and even teachers themselves have made extra income by selling their services as tutors. Indeed, some of the earliest forms of education were solely based on tutoring; often it was the only route to an education. But the spread of mass schooling changed the role of tutoring from a primary instructional method to a supplement for what happens in school. This supplemental nature of tutoring has strengthened as public schooling expands. In some nations the scale of outside-school private support for learning is so extensive that it would be more accurate to describe it as a system of tutoring that runs parallel to formal schooling. For example, as demonstrated in this chapter, Hong Kong, Singapore, Taiwan, South Korea, Greece, and Turkey have systems of tutoring that parallel formal schooling.

During the fascination with all things Japanese in education in the early 1990s, David Baker and the late David Stevenson coined the term *shadow education* to describe educational activities of this kind (Stevenson and Baker, 1992). Shadow education conveys the image of outside-school learning activities that parallel such features of formal schooling as mastering a curriculum, examinations, and earning grades for learning and skills used by schools to grant students further educational opportunities (Bray, 1999; LeTendre, 1994; Tsukada, 1991).

These activities go well beyond routinely assigned homework; instead they are organized, structured learning opportunities that resemble school-like processes. Most important, from an institutional perspective, these activities are set up to specifically *shadow* the requirements of the public school that the child attends. This is not private schooling, which exists as well in many nations; it is the use of extra, organized learning to augment what is taught in public schools for better achievement. The after-hours cram schools found in some Asian countries (juku in Japan, *hakwon* in Korea) are the most extreme in mimicking in-school forms. There are now hybrids of these extensive educational services popping up in Western nations too. In addition, there are a variety of activities all sharing a similar logic, such as correspondence courses, one-on-one private tutoring, examination preparatory courses, and full-scale preparatory examination schools (the Japanese yobiko). This phenomenon has become so widespread that in 1999 UNESCO commissioned a comparative educationalist, Mark Bray, to chronicle and document these activities worldwide. His report, *The Shadow Education System: Private Tutoring and Its Implications for Planners*, shows both the growth of this kind of activity and the spread across nations.

To give a sense of how large the demand can be for these private shadow education services, in a recent dissertation Ki-Bong Lee (2003) finds that nearly all South Korean primary and secondary school students have used some form of shadow education during their schooling. This translated into huge private spending for these services in South Korea. For example, Lee reports that in 1977 Korean families spent 297 billion Korean *won* (approximately U.S. $386 million) on all forms of shadow education, and by 1998 they spent an astonishing forty times as much in constant won, reaching 12.6 trillion Korean won (about U.S. $16.4 billion). In other words, for every dollar the Korean government spends annually on public elementary and secondary education, Korean families now spend another 80 cents on private shadow education! Obviously South Korean education is extreme in this sense, and it is currently the largest system of shadow education known in the world; but it does illustrate the extent to which shadow education can develop.

Because the interest in shadow education generated wider knowledge among Americans and other Westerners about Japanese education, the TIMSS study in the mid-1990s included questions on use of these services. This was the first time ever that we had comparable, detailed information on the consumption of shadow education across a range of national education systems. With our colleagues Motoko Akiba and Alexander Wiseman, we undertook a detailed analysis of the responses that students gave to these questions. We found some astonishing trends in the what, where, and why of shadow education (Baker, Akiba, LeTendre, and Wiseman, 2001).

How Prevalent Is Shadow Education Worldwide?

We knew about the prevalence of shadow education in many Asian nations, and some Western ones too, but before doing the analysis of the TIMSS data we completely underestimated how extensive the practice is worldwide. If we make the reasonable assumption that the nations participating in TIMSS represent what is occurring in most educational systems worldwide (except for extremely impoverished nations), shadow education is a large worldwide phenomenon. All nations in the sample had an appreciable level of use of shadow education on the part of their students. For example, almost four out of ten seventh and eighth graders participate weekly in tutoring sessions, a cram school, or another form of shadow education activity worldwide. Most weekly participation consists of one hour or less, but one-fifth of the students in these nations who use shadow education activities do so for two or more hours per week. In some nations shadow education is heading toward universality among public school students. In addition to South Korea, more than three-fourths of the seventh and eighth graders in Japan, South Africa, the Philippines, and Colombia participate weekly in shadow education activities. In Japan it has been noted that one main reason students give for participating extensively in shadow education, after the idea of improving their academic performance in school, is that so many of their friends participate that they want to do so for social reasons as well. Keep in mind that these are activities purchased from private sources by families of public school students. At the same time, it is clear that this phenomenon has not equally penetrated education systems everywhere. Figure 4.1 shows the range of shadow

FIGURE 4.1 Shadow Education Participation by Nation
(continued on facing page)

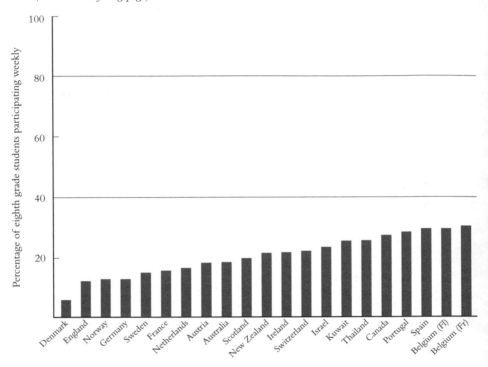

SOURCE: TIMSS 1995. Used with permission by *Educational Evaluation and Policy Analysis.*

education use by nation. Although there are no nations without shadow education, in countries such as England, Norway, and Germany fewer than 20 percent of students participate.

The image of Japanese students attending juku for hours after formal school as a strategy to prepare for secondary school and university examinations dominated the role of shadow education in general—the good student using a private cram school for better examination performance. This was also the primary image of shadow education in the education literature. So before examining the TIMSS data we also thought that use of shadow education would be largely for *strategic enhancement* of achievement, used mostly by students already doing well in mathematics. But this was not the case; in fact, by far the most common use of these activities is on the part of students with poor performance in mathematics, not the successful math students. In other words, shadow education is mostly used for *remedial purposes* to help

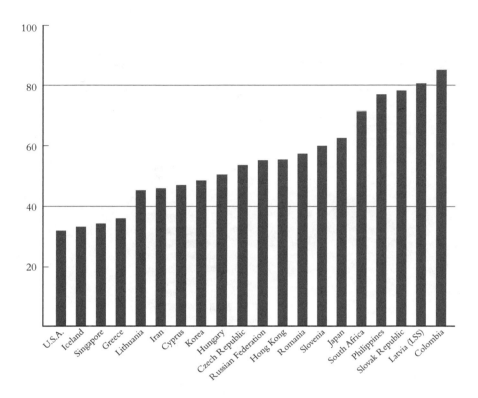

meet the requirements of what is being taught in mathematics in the student's formal school.

Figure 4.2 shows the nations in TIMSS according to whether the nation's students use shadow education mostly for remedial purposes, enhancement purposes, or about an even mixture of both. By and large, shadow education in most nations is a remedial operation (although a share of it could also be for examination performance). In three-fourths of the forty nations in the study, most students use shadow education because they are poor at mathematics. In nations with a substantial amount of shadow education, such as Cyprus, Israel, and Belgium, two or three times as many students with poor mathematics ability are using shadow education as those with high abilities. In other countries the remedial strategy is less dominant, but it is still substantial. For example, in the United States, Germany, and Kuwait about 30 percent more mathematically challenged students use shadow education than

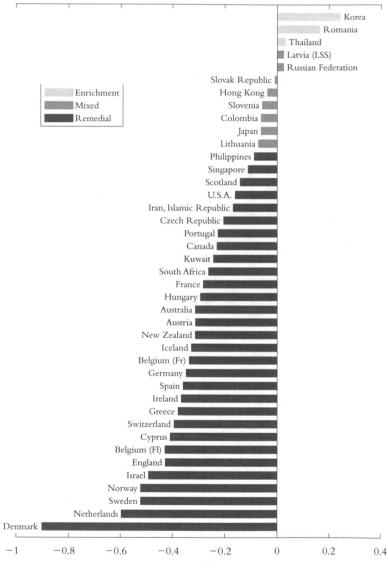

1. Motivation for shadow education. Logit coefficient of effects of math score on shadow education participation, controlling for SES, home language, sex, community, remedial teaching, and the interaction term between SES and math score. Enrichment equals significant (p<.01) positive coefficient; mixed equals nonsignificant coefficient; remedial equals significant (p<.01) negative coefficient.

SOURCE: TIMSS 1995. Used with permission by *Educational Evaluation and Policy Analysis*.

mathematically inclined students. Only in three nations is there primarily an enhancement strategy, that is, use by students doing well in mathematics: Korea, Romania, and Thailand. In the remaining eight countries, there is an equal mix of both strategies; interestingly, these nations—among them Greece, Hong Kong, and Japan—are those that are usually thought to have produced widespread enrichment-oriented shadow education. They do have it, but even here there is a significant level of remedial use.

Which National Factors Influence the Amount and Character of Shadow Education?

Where exactly does the phenomenon of shadow education come from, and why is there considerable variation from one nation to the next in the use of shadow education? An analysis of the cross-national differences in the amount of shadow education, as shown in Figure 4.1, sheds some light. We examined three characteristics of national school systems that vary across nations to see which ones were associated with a high volume of shadow education use for mathematics in the eighth grade.

The first comes from the oft-heard argument that large-scale shadow education is a product of a widely practiced, highly publicized, *enrichment strategy*. This argument suggests that extensive shadow education exists in nations in which there is intense competition for future educational opportunities accompanied by "tight linkage" between academic performance and later life opportunities in higher education and the labor market. This image apparently comes from Japan, where large chains of juku not only provided supplementary exam preparation but actually estimated for students their chance of successfully entering a given university (LeTendre, 1994).

Tight linkage has come to mean a high degree of correspondence between a student's academic performance, usually on a major examination, and later educational and occupational opportunities. In short, the argument is that good students use shadow education as an enrichment strategy when there are clear, high-stakes decision points within the system that are based on exam performance. For example, it is often suggested that qualities such as the tight connection between elite universities and excellent labor market opportunities in Taiwan, use of secondary school certificate examinations in the labor market in Hong Kong, secondary school selection process in Japan, and the examination-based link between secondary schools and the best universities in Greece produce a strong logic for students and families to use extensive shadow education (Bray and Kwok, 2003; Lin, 1983; Mitchell, 1968; Sweeting, 1983; Katsillis and Rubinson, 1990; Stevenson and Baker, 1992). All of these examples revolve around a high-stakes test that is a public gatekeeper to education and labor market opportunities.

The high-stakes-test, shadow-education hypothesis has a lot of logical appeal, and a number of policy makers in nations without such tests (the United States, for example) are fascinated by a possible side benefit of a high-stakes test motivating more study and learning, whether through shadow education or not. Also, as we have shown, nations do vary in their use and timing of high-stakes examination, so the idea appeared as a promising explanation of the varying level of shadow education across nations.

But as we undertook the analysis we had doubts as to this argument's validity on the national level. First, too many nations had extensive use of shadow education, and the idea that this is all related to high-stakes test preparation did not seem reasonable. This is particularly true for those tests that would apply to a smaller proportion of the student population, such as those attempting to enter a top university. Further, the heretofore unknown predominantly remedial character of so much shadow education across most nations just didn't fit the image of good students using it as an enhancement strategy to prepare for high-stakes tests. In fact, our multivariate analysis showed that cross-national variation in the size, prevalence, and role of shadow education is completely unrelated to whether or not a national high-stakes test looms in the future.

A related second argument on generation of shadow education revolves around the notion that some nations (Korea, Singapore, Hong Kong, Japan, and others) have developed systemwide motivation for national achievement in subjects such as mathematics and science through a variety of means, and a high degree of shadow education is a consequence of an explicit *national strategy* to foster national achievement.

As the development of human capital takes on the qualities and responsibilities of a unilateral national mission for successful global competition, educational policies aimed at achievement can be formed from a specific nationalist perspective promoted by the state. This image suggests that national values of this kind can spread through both the faculty and students within a system and enhance motivation for national achievement. In the literature on cross-national differences in schooling and achievement, this argument has been expanded to include cultural scripts for high persistence on academic tasks (see Stevenson, Lummis, Lee, and Stigler, 1990). The notion is that some nations produce a more salient set of cultural and national motivations for students to persist in their efforts toward academic achievement, including taking publicly recognized international tests. Extending this to learning activities outside school leads to the argument that more shadow education activities of either remedial or enrichment purposes will be generated in nations with greater emphasis on student persistence and achievement.

Obviously, measuring the national level of student persistence in mathematics is a challenge. Our colleague and educational psychologist Erling Boe, however, finds that the average student persistence in completing the TIMSS questionnaire is an effective national indicator associated with the national level of achievement. We examined the relationship between average student persistence and shadow education and found that as with high-stakes testing, there is no relationship between the two.

If these more immediate motivating factors are not related to the national level of shadow education, then what is? The problem with the first two arguments is that they are really about why an individual student or family would use shadow education. Certainly students faced with an important test usually study, and if performance on the test controls future possibilities in a clear fashion there is an obvious motivation to use any available and affordable shadow education geared to preparing for the test. The same is true with general motivation to learn mathematics, but again it is an argument mostly about why one student tends to use shadow education and another does not. We suspected that the answer to why there is shadow education, and why it varies across nations, would be revealed from a more institutional perspective. We also realized that extensive remedial use of shadow education held part of that answer.

What is it about schooling as an institution that produces widespread shadow education as a *remedial strategy*, and why would this vary in degree across nations? We reasoned that schooling and one's ability to move through it with at least a minimal level of academic success has become such a central and crucial task for a wide portion of the youth population that prematurely ending a school career takes on extremely severe social consequences for both the individual and society as a whole. As described in Chapter 1, over the past century the widespread use of compulsory mass schooling has made schooling the central, formal institution connecting children and youths to adult status (for example, Fuller and Rubinson, 1992).

Two central messages of schooling are that (1) all children must participate and at least minimally advance and achieve when and where they can; and (2) there are few, if any, traditional routes to adult status left in most modern societies (for instance, status inheritance, sinecure, or blatantly ascriptive status attainment). Individuals are faced with the inevitability of mounting a long formal school career; state policy makers, for a range of issues from economic development to health and social welfare, constantly advance educational solutions to reduce most societal problems. This institutional process makes categories such as school dropout or low achiever into targets for public policy, which is aimed at educational solutions to a host of social problems that frequently turn into calls for yet more schooling, prolonged educational participation across cohorts of youth, and greater scholastic achievement for its ameliorating effects on society.

This central institutional quality of formal schooling is so pervasive and has such a taken-for-granted nature to it that in comparison to more salient features of school systems such as high-stakes tests it is often passed over when thinking about how school dynamics influence students and families. It is also clear that although a mass, compulsory, public school system has become the dominant model worldwide, there is still substantial cross-national variation in the degree to which nations with varying levels of resources are able to implement this model (Baker and Holsinger, 1996). Given this, we thought it reasonable to hypothesize that extensive shadow education is an outgrowth of a more fully implemented model of these qualities of modern schooling within a nation.

We used the enrollment rate (that is, children in school divided by children at school age) and public expenditures as a percentage of the nation's gross domestic product as indicators of national differences in the degree to which school as an institution is incorporated into the society. To our surprise, the hypothesis was wrong—but only partially, and that gave us a clue to correct our argument. Instead of more incorporation of schooling leading to more shadow education, we found the opposite. Both lower public educational expenditures and less-than-full enrollment in the seventh and eighth grades led to more use of shadow education, greater intensity of use, and use by high-achieving students. Nations that do not yet have full access to mass schooling or spend less than the average funds on schooling have more shadow education use by students.

This unexpected finding led us to think more broadly about schooling, society, and shadow education. It may be that underfunding and limited access to schooling in a world where school is globally recognized as the main route to adult status leads families and students to use shadow education as augmentation of subpar schooling. In other words, the value of schooling is seen beyond, and in spite of, lower access and quality of schooling in particular. It could also be that in poorer nations with large shadow education (Latvia, Slovak Republic, Philippines, South Africa, Romania, and others), many of which have undergone massive social, economic, and educational changes recently, vestiges of the more traditional tutoring practice are expanded to meet newly created demands for shadow education by expanding access to some schooling and strengthening the tie between educational credentials and the labor market. We also found that extensive use of shadow education was common among children having difficulty in mathematics in wealthier rather than in poorer nations. This was in line with our original thinking—namely, that in nations with the most incorporated public school systems, school failures take on graver consequences for individuals. An institutionalization argument about the growth of shadow education explains these patterns of shadow education use worldwide, but it is more complex than we originally expected.

Lastly, we turned the issue around and asked to what extent a large system of shadow education influences the national level of mathematics achievement. The policy debate about high-stakes examination and shadow education has always assumed a positive effect on national achievement level. But we found that there is no relationship between the extent of shadow education in a nation and its average mathematics score. Nor is there a relationship between the use of high-stakes testing in a country and the national level of achievement.[1] It appears that the whole policy idea to raise the national level of achievement by using high-stakes examinations to motivate students to study more, with or without shadow education, is not viable.

Shadow Education and Its Future Growth

Many casual observers of the growth of shadow education worldwide will no doubt see it as a sign of private interests interjected into the public good of mass schooling. Some may even go so far as to claim that it is dramatic proof of a crisis of confidence in public schooling, an interpretation popular among neoconservative circles in Western Europe and the United States. Others might conclude only that this is a relatively meaningless by-product of the expansion of schooling. We have a different take on this trend.

The widespread prevalence of shadow education and intensity of its use in the schooling processes by students and families dramatically underscores the degree to which state-supported mass schooling dominates socialization and the ability of families to place children in adult roles and statuses. Instead of seeing the rise of private supplemental activities as a sign of institutional decline or a major shift in institutional configuration, it is more in line with this empirical case to think of shadow education as a likely consequence of a greater institutionalized education system within nations.

As schooling becomes the primary institution for generating and transmitting knowledge to generations of children in the form of achievement, one can expect continued growth in outside-school activities specially aimed at children's performance within school. Homework and the assumption of extensive parental involvement in academics are now common features of the formal educational institution; shadow education takes this same process a step further. Additionally, shadow education itself has been

1. See Bishop (1998) for some counterevidence that high-stakes tests lead to better national achievement.

transformed from an informal one-on-one process by a teacher looking for extra money to an elaborated set of practices, and shadow education continues to evolve.

Canadian sociologists of education Janice Aurini and Scott Davies describe (2004) a remarkable innovation in shadow education in Canada that could represent one future scenario about shadow education and its relationship to public schooling. Demand for shadow education is growing in Canada even though, as our results would support, Canadian education does not have the features that traditionally were thought to create demand such as high-stakes examination for access to universities. What is particularly interesting here is that in addition to the kind of shadow education we have described so far, in Canada there are now corporations that sell franchises to create what are known as "learning centers." It is a huge business. One such company (Sylvan), which is big enough to be publicly traded on the stock market, was recently named the number-one franchise corporation in North America, beating out well-known franchise companies such as McDonald's and Mail Boxes Etc.!

The average Canadian learning center, as described by Aurini and Davies, is a dynamic, locally owned franchise providing a place where customers (students) come and buy a well-thought-out product that can be modified for local demands. These centers bundle together a number of more traditional forms of shadow education such as tutoring and test cramming, but then they add other innovations such as long-term skill building, strategies to learn and manage academic subjects better, and expanded services such as instruction for the preschooler and vocational training for adults. They even develop additional curricula on their own.

Aurini and Davies predict that these could be the wave of the future—some mix of shadow education and private schooling all rolled into one that becomes more of an alternative to than an augmentation of public schooling. We doubt the balance will move too far toward alternative private schooling unless the learning centers can win charters to grant degrees, which in some national systems is politically very difficult to do. But even so, Aurini and Davies have a point about the future.

In Canada the franchising of the shadow education business has helped meet a growing demand and even sparked additional demand; in turn it has morphed into innovative educational services never before brought to the market. Political changes in many nations' public school systems have helped create similar demand, such as a continuous ratcheting up of the academic requirements over time for the same grade level, greater accountability of teaching and learning and standard-setting processes, and increased interest in the cognitive performance of young children on the part of parents. Clearly, shadow education is here to stay globally, is growing in many nations, and will certainly become more prominent as a practice over time.

Another powerful global process in education that will likely increase demand for shadow education is competition over educational opportunities among families. As described in Chapter 3, widespread national efforts to raise school quality continue to homogenize schooling, leaving fewer ways for families to gain educational advantage in the formal school system. In other words, in many nations it is increasingly harder to go to a particular public school that has significantly more instructional resources than other schools. As with private schooling, which is often assumed to provide better education, in many nations shadow education becomes another avenue for families to invest in their children's schooling. A number of studies have already established that in nations with extensive shadow education wealthier families are more likely to buy both more of it and more elaborate forms of it (see Stevenson and Baker, 1992; Lee, 2003).

Once shadow education is established and widely believed to help students, the ability of wealthier families to find more to buy creates a public market, as in Japan where juku publicly advertise their success stories. On the supply side, education systems that are making public education more available, as in an expanding higher education system, draw more of the student population into competition, and if shadow education has been a traditional part of the competition then this fuels more of it.

The greatly expanded shadow education found in South Korea is in large part due to both of these forces acting at the same time, as the government rapidly opened up higher education to the more general population in a system with a tradition of shadow education used by elites (Lee, 2003). An interesting aside is that, outside of Japan, there are virtually no data on the relative effectiveness of different types and varying quality of shadow education for raising achievement, but in many nations the public, policy makers, and the providers of shadow education themselves believe there are real effects of shadow education on achievement. From what we know about school effects in general, we suspect that future studies will find some modest benefit from additional schooling through widespread use of shadow education services (LeTendre, 1996b).

A final force propelling the expansion of shadow education is that, like public schooling, it too takes on expanded functions and in a sense is institutionalized, or at least rides along with the continued institutionalization of schooling itself. Students in nations with extensive shadow education often remark that one reason they attend is because their friends do; in other words, it is what you do after school to be social. The TIMSS case study of Japanese schooling, for example, shows adolescents participating in shadow education in part as a social connection to their peers; it is a vehicle for socializing as well as for study (OERI, 1998). Expanding motivation starts to blur the original narrow intention of using shadow education in hopes of just cramming for a specific exam. Prolific shadow education can become a taken-for-granted part of the overall school experience. We know from the history of schooling that resources and practices thought to alter achievement are themselves rapidly institutionalized in modern society.

Shadow Education and the Future of Public Education

In attempting to raise its populist appeal, the new South Korean military dictatorship, after the 1980 coup and the assassination of President Park, outlawed shadow education with the message that such prohibition would remove unfair private funds of families from educational competition among families. Obviously, from our description earlier in this chapter of the phenomenal size of shadow educational spending in South Korea, the ban did not have much of an effect. Other stronger forces, notably the opening up of higher education for considerably more students and effectively leveling resource differences among elementary and secondary schools, encouraged the use of technically illegal shadow education on a massive scale. This governmental reaction to shadow education was extreme to say the least, but the Korean case raises the interesting questions of what influence extensive use of shadow education might have on public schooling, and how policy makers and observers of educational change should think about this.

Educators must first appreciate the dynamic dimensions of shadow education and its potential to influence formal instruction and management of students and curricula. As we have just described, they must also appreciate the degree to which shadow education might import unwanted inequality into the system.

Second, there is also evidence of long-term influences on what actually happens during school when there is extensive shadow education afterward for many students in the class. For example, shadow education in South Korea and Japan plays an integral role in providing feedback to families and students concerning their chances for admission to select secondary schools and universities. Also, outside-school learning has been shown to reduce the work of Japanese public school teachers through standardizing many students' achievement level in class, and it may even affect the way the Japanese teach in class. The impact of widespread shadow education on teachers and families easily leads to influence on educational policies. In Japan, some educational reform attempts to expand public schooling activities have been stalled because of reliance on shadow education to perform these tasks (LeTendre, 1994).

Third, although these activities are prevalent and potentially a source of influence on formal schooling, the education policy maker and educator should understand that they do not represent a simple route to improving the national level of mathematics production. The notion that tighter links between education and work opportunities, controlled by high-stakes tests, lead to motivation for greater outside-school learning activities, which in turn raise the nation's average level of achievement, is not supported by these data. This is not to say for sure that high-stakes tests do not have national consequences for the improvement of achievement production in schools. Rather, our analyses indicate that if such a process exists, it does not seem to work through the effects of extensive networks of shadow education operating in many national systems. Shadow education probably has some effect on individual students, but either the effects are not intensive enough to change the overall national level of achievement or they are relatively even throughout most of the TIMSS sample of nations. The latter, however, is not likely since, as is shown here, there is considerable cross-national variation in level of participation in shadow education.

Perhaps it is better to think of widespread shadow education not as some simple mechanical addition to formal schooling but as a potential for major institutional change—not revolutionary change, but more along the lines of evolutionary change as a function of greater institutionalization of a preexisting configuration. Mass public schooling sets the stage for the increasing importance of education as an institution, and to the degree that this process creates greater demand for quality schooling than is supplied, augmentation through shadow education is likely. Keep in mind too that no country lacked some measurable level of shadow education, and that many economically well-funded education systems also have extensive shadow education. With mass schooling as a world norm continuing to intensify the importance of schooling, shadow education itself becomes an institutionalized component of mass education that grows and expands. As the Canadian case shows, shadow education is dynamic in its potential to morph into entities not now known. The process is one in which schooling articulates more and more with social and economic chances, hence increasing its own institutional power over meaning and behavior. It would be expected, then, from this interpretation that shadow education activities eventually take on a mixture of short-term and long-term academic (and even some nonacademic) rationales for participation.

As a global institution, mass schooling has greatly legitimized academic achievement, producing a heightened demand for quality schooling, which in turn expanded shadow education to the megatrend that it is today. Shadow education loosens the boundaries between public control of education and private educational activities. Although private educational activities predate the creation of modern public schooling, the latter has ironically produced a modern logic and demand for mass shadow education (read: mass private education services) in many countries. Furthermore, widespread shadow education adds a significant nonpublic component to national school systems without the production of full-scale private schooling. This has the potential to change the governance structure of education by introducing private services to a wider host of families and students, hence merging families, mass schooling, and private educational resources into new institutional arrangements unheard of just a few decades ago.

CHAPTER 5

Rich Land, Poor Schools

INEQUALITY OF NATIONAL EDUCATIONAL RESOURCES

AND ACHIEVEMENT OF DISADVANTAGED STUDENTS

with Brian Goesling

USING BROAD STROKES, one could paint the theme of the politics of schooling in many wealthy nations in the 1960s and 1970s as trying to create school systems with equal educational resources, or what is called "educational equality." The main objective was expanding access to roughly equal educational opportunities for children who were underrepresented in education at the time: females, minorities, and rural children. Gradually shifting away from educational equality, the political agenda in many nations over the past twenty years has been and continues to be on educational quality, where the main objective is raising the basic level of educational achievement. Of course, international information has intensified many nations' focus on international educational competitiveness.

The preceding two chapters explored how a deepening institutionalization of schooling and rising resources in many nations shape how families invest their resources in their children's mathematics and science achievement. In this chapter, we shift attention from differences among families to those among schools in terms of resources dedicated to teaching and learning these two subjects. As we noted in the discussion of the Coleman and Heyneman/Loxley effects in Chapter 3, even though there has been an observable effect of a rising level of quality in many nations, there are still significant differences in access to resources among schools within a given country. Further, as we will show here, nations vary in how much resource inequality among schools their system produces; such educational inequality can have severe negative consequences for the school achievement of poor and disadvantaged students.

Unequal resources among schools can be a result of both intentional education policy and an unintentional consequence of the system. For the most part, modern national systems have tended to reduce both types—the latter as a reflection of greater institutionalization of the idea of the universality of education, and the former as a consequence of political action aimed at alleviation of poverty and social disadvantage. Of course, both kinds of inequality still exist in many nations.

Many national systems intentionally sort children into different kinds of schools, sometimes leading to differences in secondary credentials and rights vis-à-vis higher education. For example, as early as age ten in some parts of Germany or around age fifteen in Japan children are sorted by the kind of school. In Germany, the most academic stream, the Gymnasium, has teachers with more advanced training, accepts only academically talented students, and prepares these students for university entrance. Such a system deliberately creates distinct school types with differing goals and specific resources but tries to equalize resources within each type, thereby legitimizing differences. Similarly in many nations, by law basic physical resources and teacher pay scales are equal; it is rare for a school system to intentionally distribute resources unequally, but there are a number of mechanisms by which this can happen (Oakes, 1985). Sometimes unintended inequalities occur because of variation in the level of educational expenditures across regions, provinces, or state. In the United States, for example, tying local property tax revenues to educational finance has led to discernible differences in resources across school districts in everything from the physical condition of the school to the quality of the teachers (LeTendre, Hofer, and Shimizu, 2003).

Unintended differences in resources continue to frustrate national and local education administrators who hope to attain equality of educational opportunity. By implementing compulsory education for all children over the past century, nations eliminated one major historical source of inequality in access to education, but successful expansion of mass schooling has created a new problem. Implementing mass schooling in most nations meant the rise of expectations about national academic outcomes, and the related goal of lowering (and even doing away with) any unintentional gross differences in the quality of schooling from one school to the next. As schooling becomes more central to so many facets of the future of children and youth, the public's expectations for more equality rise as its tolerance of unintended inequality plummets. The logic of modern schooling emphasizes the general principle that among schools of similar types there should be similar curricula, a similar level of student attainment, and similar basic educational resources. If this is not achieved, it increasingly becomes a political concern and even sometimes a national crisis. We focus here on the amount of unintended resource inequality among schools across nations.

Comparative Savage Inequalities

Twelve years ago, in a richly descriptive and aptly titled book, *Savage Inequalities*, Jonathan Kozol (1993) presented haunting stories of the failure of U.S. public schools to educate the nation's most socially and economically disadvantaged students. The American case of educational inequality is particularly telling about how institutional values of universalism and considerable inequalities coexist in one national context.

Public education in America, as elsewhere, has always been held up as one of the key paths to a socially just and prosperous society. As we have seen, wealthy nations invest considerably in education, and in general this pays off in a higher average level of achievement. Yet the United States, economically dynamic and the most politically powerful nation in the world, has a poor record in establishing a fair and level educational playing field. Evidence continues to show a disproportionately high number of educational problems (low achievement, low attainment, and premature ending of schooling) among economically, racially, and ethnically disadvantaged youths (Farkas, 1996). At the same time, there is growing evidence that the human costs of educational failure for both individuals and society continue to increase over time (Rubinson and Browne, 1994). Simply put, educational inequality creates problems that drain social resources over a long period of time.

Scholars and reformers in the United States have been aware of this problem for quite a while. Over the last thirty years, unequal distribution of basic educational resources has garnered considerable attention and significant academic studies and policy ideas (see, for example, Coleman and others, 1966; Hanusek, 1994; Hedges, Laine, and Greenwald, 1994; Mosteller and Moynihan, 1972). Much of the empirical work centers on the large differences in per-pupil expenditures that appear when comparing schools, districts, and states. These funding disparities have been linked with differences in the quality of schools and instruction; political attempts to change resource inequalities between schools have resulted in litigation challenging school finance systems within almost all U.S. states and have even been linked to vigorous debate on tracking and social inequality (Lucas, 1999; Loveless, 1999).

The ongoing debates and failed attempts to eliminate between-school resource inequality led us to explore what the situation in the United States looked like from a comparative perspective. Is this really an "American" problem, or can we identify global patterns and factors that might help us clarify the situation in the United States? We asked two questions about how savage inequalities look from a global perspective. First, are American disadvantaged students comparatively more at risk of educational failure than similarly disadvantaged students in other wealthy nations? Second, what is the consequence of educational performance among disadvantaged students for the overall international educational competitiveness of the nation?

With the TIMSS data, we examine how well American schools educate students with several types of disadvantaged background and compared these results with findings from other nations. For this chapter, we focus only on high schools, but readers can find the results of an analysis of the eighth grade in Baker (2002). We used two indicators of social and economic disadvantage: low education of the student's mother and living in a single-parent home. The proportion of students with mothers having less than a high school degree and single-parent homes in the U.S. twelfth grade TIMSS sample is 11 percent and 15 percent respectively; international averages for students in all wealthy nations are 29 percent and 11 percent.[1] Although these family characteristics do not create a disadvantaged home in every case, they significantly increase the risk that children will have a disadvantaged home life, which can lead to less-than-full academic achievement for a number of reasons.

Are disadvantaged American students more at risk of educational failure? As shown in Table 5.1, the answer is clearly yes. American disadvantaged students learn considerably less general mathematics than similarly disadvantaged students in other nations. Among the thirteen wealthiest nations in the TIMSS twelfth grade sample, the average American mathematics knowledge for both students with mothers having less than a high school education and from single-parent homes is strikingly low. Overall, American twelfth graders did not perform well, so on the one hand it is not a surprise that disadvantaged students in the United States also performed poorly. But on the other hand, it is true that although the American overall eighth grade sample did as well as that in a number of other wealthy nations, American eighth grade disadvantaged students also finished last compared to similar students in other wealthy nations (Baker, LeTendre, and Goesling, 2002). This suggests that the most disadvantaged students in the United States are not just affected at one level of the school system; they fail to achieve across the span of compulsory schooling.

The consequences of low educational performance in human terms are pervasive and complex, and we can judge the impact of low educational performance by recalculating the overall American mean mathematics knowl-

1. Although the United States has a high dropout rate by age eighteen, it offers a number of other ways to obtain a high school diploma such that it has one of the highest high school completion rates in the world in cohorts aged twenty-four to twenty-eight.

edge to see what would happen if the United States educated its disadvantaged students as well as other wealthy nations do. If the United States were as successful as, say, Sweden in educating youths with mothers without a high school degree, then it would improve its overall national mean by fourteen points in twelfth grade mathematics. If we add doing as well as Sweden does with youths whose mothers have just a high school degree, the

TABLE 5.1

Comparative Analysis of Educating Disadvantaged Students

Students with Mothers Without a High School Degree ($\bar{x}$ Proportion in Nation = 29%)	Mean Math Achievement	Students from Single-Parent Homes ($\bar{x}$ Proportion in Nation = 11%)
Netherlands	560	Netherlands
Sweden		
Denmark	550	
		Iceland
Iceland	540	Sweden
New Zealand		
Austria, Norway	530	Switzerland
Switzerland		Australia
International mean	520	Norway, Denmark
France, Australia		
Canada	510	
		New Zealand
	500	
	490	
	480	
		Germany
	470	
Germany		
	460	
	450	
United States		
	440	
	430	**United States**
	420	

SOURCE: TIMSS 12th 1995.

improvement in the U.S. TIMSS mathematics average score would place the country above five wealthy nations that currently outperform it.[2]

This is a simple exercise that can be done with any proportion of a distribution, but the message is clear. Because the United States (as well as other nations) fails to educate its most disadvantaged students, it lowers the overall cross-national standing. Receiving a subpar education significantly adds to the risk of entering the ranks of the underclass, and coming from a disadvantaged home in the United States places a youth at greater risk of poor educational performance than in many other wealthy nations.

These findings should also be disturbing for American policy makers because they show that school systems in other nations somehow have found ways to lessen the impact of disadvantaged background on school achievement. This is not to say that what is done in these nations is perfect, or that the negative impact of disadvantaged families has been completely ameliorated, but these findings suggest there may be social and educational policies at work in other nations that might serve as a model for the United States in meeting the educational challenge of students from disadvantaged families. We know that disadvantaged students are more at risk of lower educational performance, and that in nations like the United States the overall effect substantially lowers the national mean achievement.

But what have nations done to address this issue? The school has been the central institution used to prevent social problems in most nations, and it is often thought that reducing resource inequality across schools is a key to lessening the impact of disadvantaged families on achievement. Has any country devised a mass education system that significantly lowers, or even eradicates, differences in basic educational resources across schools?

Educational Resource Inequality Among Schools Worldwide

To answer this question, we analyzed how well national school systems distribute basic educational resources equitably across schools. With our colleague Brian Goesling, we estimated the degree of resource inequality among schools with eighth graders in fifty-two nations by combining the 1994 and 1999 TIMSS data (Baker, LeTendre, and Goesling, 2002). We developed a measure of inequality for basic educational resources, including instructional resources such as budget for teaching materials, supplies, libraries, heating and lighting, and other physical plant resources; instructional space; computer hardware and software; professional experience of teachers; and student-to-teacher ratio (class size). We also restricted the analysis to middle grade schools in order to lessen the chance of including

2. Similar results are found for other indicators of student disadvantage.

some intentional resource differences across curricular streams in upper secondary schools.

When we estimated the degree of inequality of educational resources across schools, we found that all TIMSS nations have some level of between-school resource inequality (*between-school* is the research shorthand for saying resource differences among schools). As shown in Table 5.2, although mass schooling is predicated on equality in basic resources in practice this is just not the case. There is considerable cross-national variation in educational resource inequality, and like cross-national differences in mathematics and science achievement the national level of between-school inequality clusters into three distinct groups. The first, with the highest estimated level of between-school inequality, includes South Africa, the Philippines, Latvia, Chile, and sixteen other nations. The seventeen nations in the second group are roughly equal to the international mean; notable in this group are Greece, France, the United States, and South Korea. The nineteen nations with less between-school inequality include Sweden, Germany, Japan, and Kuwait. Most wealthy nations have less inequality in basic resources across schools than the United States does, and this surely has some consequences for its overall educational competitiveness as well as persistent poverty across generations.

When we examined which nations had high and low levels of between-school inequality, the results were as we expected, with one surprise. First, wealthier nations tend to have less inequality in resources across schools, although there are a few interesting exceptions, among them the United States. Second, nations with a lower level of inequality tend to produce a higher level of overall mathematics and science achievement. The positive impact of having more equal resources among schools is about the same in magnitude as the impact of national wealth on average national achievement, discussed in Chapter 3. Last, contrary to what many think, the degree to which education governance is centralized is not associated with less or more resource inequality.

The first two findings make sense intuitively. Wealthier nations have more to spend on education, more sophisticated consumers of education (that is, better-educated parents), more professionalized administration, and better-trained teachers; these are all factors that go into the political process to reduce gross inequality in distributing resources across a set of schools in the nation. Also, as we have already shown, education resource inequality deprives socially disadvantaged students, which in turn causes considerable damage to a nation's overall efforts to raise the national level of achievement. In other words, in a highly inequitable system it is probably the case that those students who most need instructional resources (to make up for the detrimental effects of a poorer family background) do not receive them.

TABLE 5.2

Basic Resource Inequality Across Nations

Nations with Significant Levels of Inequality	Nations with Average Levels of Inequality	Nations with Low Levels of Inequality
South Africa	Moldova	Sweden
Philippines	Greece	Hong Kong
Colombia	Malaysia	Italy
Macedonia	Bulgaria	Germany
Morocco	Lithuania	Iceland
Iran	Slovenia	Australia
Romania	Israel	Spain
Portugal	France	Cyprus
Turkey	Chinese Taipei	New Zealand
Russian	Slovak Republic	Japan
Federation	Canada	Finland
Latvia	Ireland	Singapore
Thailand	*International average*	Norway
Denmark	Tunisia	Austria
Jordan	United States	Netherlands
Chile	Korea	Czech Republic
Indonesia	England	Belgium (Flemish)
	Hungary	Switzerland
		Kuwait

SOURCE: TIMSS 1995.

NOTE: Within boxes, national levels of inequality are not statistically different from one another.

This compounds educational disadvantage, leading to potentially severe and lasting social disadvantage. Although wealthier nations have, on average, lower resource inequality, academic failure in these nations probably has more dire ramifications because of their complex labor markets and the domination of educational credentials. Compared to individuals in developing economies, less-educated individuals in highly developed economies have few ways to compete in the labor market, and since that fact is compounded by attending schools with lower resources this can result in large communities of impoverished, undereducated adults.

The lack of association between administrative style in nations and level of resource inequality is not so surprising in light of the rather ambiguous state of centralized versus decentralized government structures that many nations now find themselves in as a reaction to the "devolution revolution" in educational governance (see Chapter 9).

The numbers behind Table 5.2 representing educational resource inequality within these mass systems of education are abstract compared to the tragic human stories of educational failure in the United States found in Kozol's book. But they are in reality one and the same, and they give us a way to measure the extent to which poorly implemented mass education can contribute to the creation of savage inequalities in some nations (see early estimates of inequality in Heyneman, 1982). Similar to what we find about school violence in Chapter 6, these results show that resource inequality is not only an "American" problem; it occurs in other nations as well. How can our institutional perspective of the widespread strength of schooling take into account persistent inequality in school resources within a nation?

National Politics and Educational Inequality

These results show problems in many nations in the implementation of mass schooling. Returning to some basic institutional assumptions, we know that around the world mass schooling is legitimated by (among other values) the commonly held ideal that schooling should operate in a meritocratic fashion with achievement as its main currency. This means opportunity should be linked primarily to performance, not social status, family background, or other nonacademic aspects of the student. It also means that one's ability to learn specific curricula is connected to the opportunities with which one is presented at school. So to orchestrate a meritocratic process, schools should have at least equal resources. Some would argue that schools serving disadvantaged communities should even have more resources to compensate for poor family background, to put each student at the same starting line academically; as an example, this is what Japan actually implements.[3]

But why doesn't this happen in more nations? Why can't a country like the United States, which seems to value mass education so highly and spends a substantial amount on schooling, do away with its resource differences that reproduce across generations an unfair amount of low achievement and limited future educational opportunities, and all the concomitant social problems faced by children of poor families?

The usual answers to this question are particularistic and mechanical, not institutional. One such answer goes that U.S. governmental policy and its resulting programs aimed at poverty are comparatively weaker than social and economic welfare systems in many other wealthy nations. In other words, the United States has comparatively less progressive income transfer policies in its tax system, which combined with the variation in state-to-state policies and resources to assist families in poverty both add up to making the American disadvantaged experience a greater economic deprivation than that for similar people in other developed nations.

3. Our technical measures of resource inequality could not pull out this kind of ameliorative distribution, so for some nations the overall measure of inequality is a bit inflated.

Another frequent answer concerns the uniquely American practice of running public schooling through its system of locally administered, property-tax-funded school districts (some fourteen thousand of them). This, the argument goes, causes many districts in poorer urban and rural communities serving a geographically concentrated population of students from disadvantaged families to suffer severely deficient financial and managerial support for schools.

But politically neither factor is insurmountable; there are obvious ways to fix them toward more educational equity. In fact, they really are such flimsy barriers to more educational equality that many frustrated advocates for American disadvantaged children turn to almost paranoiac images of planned, sustained, systematic racism and social classism in educational policy. Kozol's otherwise moving account of educational inequality in the United States is a classic example of this, suffering from an unrealistic image of an officially unstated yet systematic and oppressive educational policy presumably blessed by an uncaring American majority.

Certainly racism and social classism have had some influence on education inequality in the United States, but as the preceding chapters have shown the production of inequality of educational outcomes such as mathematics and science achievement in many nations is more a product of informal forces acting through the family. For example, some U.S. states have tried to equalize resources among numerous local districts that heretofore were captives (or winners) of differing property values (tax base) between communities. As welcome as this expression of equal resources is in some quarters, stories abound about how upper-middle-class families conspire to provide direct financial support to enhance school resources beyond a state-imposed limit. Probably on the whole these families do not see themselves in some grand social-class or racial struggle, but rather as families with considerable resources attempting to improve their own kids' school for all the obvious benefits.

The same is true in nations such as Chile, where all of the upper and middle class buy out of the public system with its generally lower resource level and uses private schooling directly because of a belief in higher educational quality (among other benefits). For the same reasons given in Chapter 4 about the growth in consumption of shadow education, as schooling becomes the main (and virtually only) game by which to pass on social status to children, pressure for better implementation of meritocratic processes in schools is met by counterpressure from families competing to secure better education for their own children.

But in and of itself this does not explain the persistence of resource inequality among schools in so many nations. Undoubtedly, as we have just done for the United States and Chile, we could pick through each national case and piece together particular mechanisms that lead to some degree of inequality within the system. But that does not really get to the question at hand of why so many nations implement mass public schooling with some degree of resource inequality present that has a detrimental effect on disadvantaged students. What is missed in much discussion of educational inequality is that organizational barriers to more equity in most nations are by themselves relatively easily overcome, but at the same time the institutional values that education weaves into modern society strongly reinforce even the weakest technical barriers to more equity.

Toward an Institutional Explanation of Educational Inequalities

Among scholars of social inequality, the most popular image of schooling holds that unequal resources and unequal access to quality schools reflect (and hence reproduce in the next generation) underlying social power differences among groups within a society. Wealthier groups demand and find ways to secure the best schooling for their children regardless of children's ability to achieve, and in some systems this comes at a price of lower school quality for less wealthy and less politically powerful families.

Correspondence between schooling and its role in social inequality has been a central notion in social stratification research at least since the late 1920s, when sociologist Pitirim Sorokin and others first wrote about "social mobility," a term meaning how easy or difficult it is for children to attain a higher social position than their parents. This image also motivated some of the earliest comparative analysis of schooling and national patterns of social mobility, as found in Turner's now-classic article (1960) about how "sponsored" and "contest" mobility processes differentiate the education systems of England and the United States.

In the same spirit, sociologist Richard Rubinson (1986) argues, in an award-winning article, that implementation of mass schooling is shaped by the specific social class struggles within a nation. So, for example, the nineteenth-century American working class won greater access to public schooling from a fragmented capitalist class that was more involved in internecine competition than consolidating its own power, compared to the working class in Western Europe at the same time. His larger point is that schooling is porous and penetrable to political interests; the relative power of these political interests shapes educational access and inequalities. In this image of schooling and society, institutionalization of mass schooling and its organizational implementation is constrained by national politics (see also Buchmann and Hannum, 2001).

We don't disagree with the basic idea of mass schooling being porous to political interests, or that those interests can be motivated by social class competition or even racial or ethnic bigotry. There have been many sad chapters in the development of schooling in which it was used for bad purposes by political interests. Also, mass schooling's long-term development by national governments certainly attests to the major role of political action in the organization of schooling. But we would add that now, in many nations, the holes through which political interests of specific groups seep into schooling are small, and probably becoming even smaller with greater incorporation of common values about education that the world culture seems to interweave so thoroughly into national systems of schooling.

We predict this first of all because of the impression the TIMSS data give of the relatively modest absolute amount of inequality in mass education found across nations. Even though inequalities persist in real systems of schooling, in a matter of minutes anyone can dream up a far more effective *elite-serving* inequitable education system than is actually operating in most developed nations in the world today, including the United States (Werum and Baker, 2004). Indeed, there is historical evidence that although many nations initially constructed schooling with intentional resource inequalities built in, from the early part of the nineteenth century onward they systematically dismantled such intentional inequalities to a significant degree. There are, of course, nations such as Germany with remnants of a highly stratified nineteenth-century secondary system still operating with unequal educational secondary school degrees built in. But also in Germany (as in other nations of Western Europe) basic resource equality among schools is legally prescribed and organizationally achieved to a large degree (see Table 5.2). The point is, even with clear cross-national differences as we describe here, mass public systems in developed nations are not hugely unequal in resource distribution, certainly not to the degree implied by more conspiratorial images of the role of schooling in social reproduction.

Secondly, we predict a lessening of inequality of resources in the future because as an institution mass schooling gains considerable legitimation from developing and maintaining a meritocracy process based on achievement, even though this is rarely, if ever, perfectly implemented. Mass schooling works to spread the belief that individuals should be evaluated and promoted on the basis of merit, which is reflected in their achievement. (Chapter 2 describes the impact that this institutional value has had on gender and achievement.) Further, for a number of reasons outlined in the introductory chapter, national governments have bought into this idea to a considerable degree. Of course, state apparatuses are open to group political interests, but the ideas of human capital investment and its universal acceptance have proven powerful enough for the development of schooling generally to occur with little partisan difference in beliefs in these basic institutional values. This is reflected in the public expectation of mass schooling as a way to break the cycle of enduring poverty and social disadvantage across generations. Of course, implementation of these ideas can be on a partisan level, as is seen in the divergent emphasis that political parties of the left and right put on certain educational policies, but the point is they all think mass formal education is the key.

The ideas of merit and cognitive achievement are attractive to the modern mind; compared to a century or so ago, now highly schooled populations in many nations help to create and maintain these ideals. Even overt differentiation of future educational opportunity at a relatively young age in national systems such as in Germany and Japan are legitimized by the same basic ideal of meritocracy that pervades schooling throughout the world. The ideas of merit and academic achievement may even trump more local cultural beliefs about when and to what degree school performance should result in differing opportunities, and even about what causes ability in students (LeTendre, Hofer, and Shimizu, 2003). They certainly have already trumped more traditional conservative ideologies about schooling as maintaining a "natural, hierarchical" social order, or confirming the individual's natural place in that order.

Perhaps, then, the best way to think about the origin of educational inequality in mass schooling is as a result of two institutional characteristics that mass schooling itself simultaneously produces: meritocratic opportunities to learn and the increased social and economic relevance of school performance and credentials for adult status and well-being. These institutional characteristics per se are not contradictory; they are highly complementary and together increase the overall institutional stature of schooling (Meyer, 1977). But they lead to differing behavior on the part of school systems and families. The former (the school) attempts to ratchet up meritocratic functions on the basis of cognitive performance within schooling, while the latter (the family) is highly motivated to create as much educational opportunity for children as it can. This not only includes things done within families but also more collective action taken by similar families acting as interest groups. Schooling as an institution increases the motivation for successful cognitive achievement, particularly in subjects such as mathematics that are deemed highly applicable to further achievement; at the same time it attempts better and better implementation of meritocratic processes around such achievement.

Certainly not every individual school does this, but for better or worse the overall trend in the operation of mass schooling in many nations increasingly turns on cognitive achievement and the idea of merit according to mastery of a few highly valued academic subjects. On top of this is the fact that the prominence of schooling in society as the main avenue to adult success makes this a powerful set of values. Therefore in the United States the problem is not a socially uncaring upper-middle class of families; instead the problem is that as a group the upper-middle class have supercharged motivations and significant resources to assist their own children to better educational achievement. The paradox is that, as an institution, schooling produces both forces. The holes that make schooling porous to political interests may indeed become smaller in the future, but the pressure behind the political interests attempting to find those holes intensifies as education determines more and more of children's future.

Of course, the government in many nations mediates raw political interests in the education arena, and nations differ partly in the degree to which the government is a buffer. The United States, compared to France, has less governmental buffering of local interests, for example. This is also not to say that since inequality always tends to exist national systems can do nothing to address it. Our simple yet compelling evidence here about cross-national differences in achievement among socially disadvantaged students suggests that some nations buffer students from social inequalities educationally more than others. A nation like the United States, with its considerable wealth, certainly can and should do far more for its disadvantaged students.

But our larger point is that the powers unleashed by institutionalization of the belief in merit and the primacy of educational achievement for attaining a successful future inevitably create a dynamic tension between the efforts of schools to focus on more equity in the conditions for achievement and private interests to focus on educational advantages for their children.

By and large, our discussion about educational resource inequality has been limited to wealthier nations, but what about poorer ones? As our results showed, they tend to produce greater inequality than in wealthier nations. What is happening on the level of schools and families of the students who attend them also happens on an international level as well. Educational inequality among nations, as well as within them, is a major challenge to national economic and social development. In a world increasingly dominated by the drive for human capital enrichment, substandard education systems that produce large inequality along the lines of social disadvantage are at risk of national disadvantage as well. Continued educational expansion and its recent revolution in quality (and, we would add, the growing trend toward less unintended inequality of educational resources) ups the human-capital stakes for poorer nations.

Particularly troubling are nations that—through poverty, internal corruption, and external exploitation—have in recent times failed to develop effective systems of mass education, public health delivery, and economic development. Called "failed states" by some scholars, these countries (notably Angola, Afghanistan, and the Congo) have been beset by civil war and a host of terrifying social problems. In such nations, expansion of mass schooling is effectively disrupted and the equalizing effects are lost. We know very little about how severe the impact has been in these states, but it is clear that significant international resources are needed to stabilize such nations or regions and restart mass schooling. Many other nations are still struggling with basic educational and developmental issues (examples are Cameroon and Niger). If these nations and regions continue to find themselves stalled in equalizing access to education and developing quality schooling for at least a large portion of children, then their inhabitants will be forced to endure long-term deprivation and social instability—a scenario that has serious implications for all nations.

CHAPTER 6

Safe Schools, Dangerous Nations

THE PARADOX OF SCHOOL VIOLENCE

with Motoko Akiba

IN THIS CHAPTER we turn from issues of families, inequality, and institutionalization of achievement in schools to explore violence and related disruption in mathematics classrooms and schools in many nations. This subject has received little cross-national analysis, even though in a number of nations it is a major educational concern.

School violence is currently the subject of intense study and national prevention efforts in the United States. During the 1990s many Americans came to wonder if the public schools could ever be truly safe. Horrific incidents in Columbine, Colorado, and Santee, California, left the nation shaken and worried. Because schools are such an important part of our society, these tragedies make us wonder about what is happening to our society. If the school—the institution that is legally and morally charged with educating and socializing our children—is unsafe, can any place in society ever be safe?

It will probably come as a shock to many readers to learn that the rate of school violence in the United States is not among the highest in the world. In fact, compared to a number of nations, U.S. schools appear quite safe. Why does this paradox exist? Partly it is because of the role the media plays in focusing our attention on horrific, but relatively rare, events. Partly it is because of the level of violence and easy access to firearms in some other nations. Unfortunately, by focusing on the most terrifying acts of violence in our own schools, we lose sight of the fact that school violence is a serious, everyday, and *global* problem that has a wide range of effects on students. Public attention is fixed on the acts that happen rarely, not on the kind of acts (such as getting punched in the hall between classes) that are much more common. These daily forms of violence affect tens of thousands in many nations but receive little media attention.

This chapter is an overview of how much school violence exists in the world; it examines what social factors are likely to predict the national level of school violence. We show that, like inequity in educational resources, school violence is a problem affecting all school systems and in turn affected by transnational forces. Much to our own surprise, we found that national patterns of school violence are not predicted by the amount of violence among adults in a country but instead are strongly related to the quality of the educational system. Violence in schools appears to be connected to production of gross inequity in educational achievement, and our study demonstrates that school violence must be studied separately from juvenile delinquency. National indicators of crime or juvenile delinquency are poor predictors of everyday forms of violence in schools cross-nationally. Policy makers and educational reformers have lacked an international perspective of what generates school violence, thereby limiting the types of reforms used to increase school safety.

We show that if a nation really wants to lower the rate of violence in school, it must put substantial effort into improving the quality and equality of schools, which means addressing the same problems of resource distribution we raised in Chapters 2 and 4. A nation cannot rely on drastic punishment of violent students as in the now-popular American term "zero tolerance" policies alone. If policy makers want schools to be a safe and productive place for students to study, they need to provide higher-quality instruction and more equitable distribution of the opportunity to learn, not just more metal detectors.

Setting aside media reports, we know U.S. students and teachers are afraid of school violence (Maguire and Pastore, 1995; Hinds, 2000). These fears have increased, even though there is some evidence that violence has actually decreased, since the early 1990s (U.S. Department of Education and U.S. Department of Justice, 2000). Fear of violence, especially weapons, is a major motivating factor in the spread of zero-tolerance policies around the country, which include extreme school (and sometimes legal) punishments for even the smallest infraction of school rules about interpersonal conduct. Now applied to drugs, alcohol, profanity, and a host of other things, zero-tolerance policies are associated with on-campus police officers, metal detectors, surveillance cameras, locker searches, and other security measures that have become commonplace in schools around the United States and have spread to some other nations. The actual effectiveness of these various programs in preventing violence is a matter of debate, but they certainly have not eliminated teacher, student, or parent fears.

Yet Americans are not alone in worrying about the safety of their children at school. A student murderer in Kobe in the late 1990s shocked the
Japanese public, and the Japanese Minister of Education actually made a
public appeal to *elementary school* students to stop carrying knives to school!
A horrific school shooting in Erfurt, Germany, shook that nation. In many
other nations, people have had to endure acts that Americans tend to think
of as an "American" problem. But beyond this, violence in schools is a
worldwide phenomenon and daily problem in the form of aggression, bullying, harassment, assault, and intimidation. With the exception of a few
studies on bullying, everyday school violence has rarely been considered
globally.

How much school violence is there among the nations of the world? Are
we undergoing a worldwide crime spree in the classroom? Can any school
ever be "safe?" With Motoko Akiba, we undertook an analysis of the TIMSS
data to answer these questions (Akiba, LeTendre, Baker, and Goesling, 2002).

How Common Is School Violence Cross-Nationally?

What we have found is that by far students in school are *not* likely to be exposed to extreme violence. However, those who are may carry the trauma
with them for years. This means that student perceptions or worries about
violence impose a separate but equally valid barrier to educational achievement. If students (or teachers) do not perceive themselves to be safe in
school, it is unlikely they can work to their full potential. So we must consider violence (actual reports of being victimized) as well as perceptions of
violence (beliefs about the threat of violence) as separate factors that affect
what students and teachers do in school.

Figures 6.1, 6.2, and 6.3 show the national rate of school violence for
three questions asked of students and teachers in the TIMSS nations, organized from the lowest to the highest nations in each graph. Because defining violence cross-culturally presents several difficulties, here we focus on
victimization data, the best common measure of violence in schools around
the world. Using this common measure, we conclude that school violence
is a major global problem, no school system is immune from it, and some
nations have an extremely high rate of violence.

The victimization rate is a conservative indicator of the impact of violence because it records only the percentage of students who have actually
encountered violence, not the wider range of people influenced by an act
of violence. It is a better indicator than official data because most nations
collect statistics only on juvenile crime, meaning that records are generated
only if the police are called in. In many cases, low-level violence is never reported. One long-term study of school violence in Germany, for example,

found that even teachers were often unaware of the level of violence that went on in schools (Leithaeuser and others, 2002).

The victimization rates in Figure 6.1 show that there is considerable variation in school violence around the world. The majority of students in Hungary, Romania, and the Philippines reported being the victim of violence during school in the previous month. Even in countries with a peaceful image, such as New Zealand and Canada, more students are reported being the victim of violence than in the United States! Cultural perceptions of violence might partly explain the extremely high rate in Hungary or Romania, but they are unlikely to explain why so many New Zealand or Canadian students report being the victims of violence. We must consider the explanation that, although some American schools suffer from much violence, most U.S. schools appear to have less violence than is found in such other countries as Korea, Spain, or Australia, at least from the viewpoint of the students themselves.

Looking at the U.S. position relative to the other nations, we find that the United States falls below the international mean for school violence. This means that U.S. students in the seventh and eighth grades report less violence than their average peers around the globe. Of course, other measures can be used, but student reports of victimization are an excellent measure for looking at how much day-to-day violence occurs in classrooms, bathrooms, hallways, and gyms. The United States may have a higher rate of violence outside the school for this age group, but from the students' point of view U.S. schools are about in the middle of the international pack. Young adolescents in the United States do not appear to be either more or less likely to be victims of school violence than their peers around the world.

Self-reports of victimization are the best cross-national indicator we have on school violence, but they may underrepresent the overall level of violence in schools, because one act of violence can have multiple effects. As many parents will attest, seeing a best friend get beaten up by a class bully can have a serious effect on a child bystander. To get at this broader aspect of violence, we looked at what students said happened to their peers. Figure 6.2 shows the national rates for the percentage of students whose friends were victims of violence in the past month. This measure is less precise, since it relies on student perceptions of what has happened to others, and some students may have large or small peer networks; but it is likely to catch a wider range of violence as well as get at how many students are indirectly affected by school violence.

In about half the nations in the study, one out of two students at the seventh and eighth grade levels reported that a friend had been a victim of violence in the past month. Hungary, Romania, and the Philippines led the world, but even Denmark and Hong Kong had a significant rate of reported

FIGURE 6.1   National Rates of School Violence Among Seventh and Eighth Graders *(continued on facing page)*

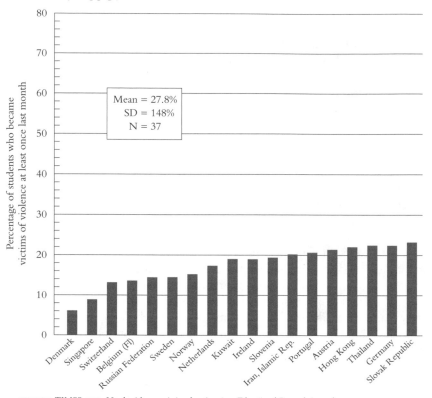

SOURCE: TIMSS 1995. Used with permission by *American Educational Research Journal*.

violence to peers. From the student point of view, school violence is common the world over.

Everyday school violence is a problem of global proportions, and not just in developed countries. A study by the International Bureau of Education, *Violence in Schools*, showed that school violence is a serious and increasing problem in such developing nations as Guatemala, Nicaragua, and Ethiopia; researchers also identified school factors as its major cause. These data help us get a more objective assessment of where the United States stands compared to the rest of the world. If we look at the range reported, we see substantial variation in the world: 80 percent of Hungarian students but only just over 15 percent of Singaporean students reported that a friend was a victim of violence in school. On average, close to 30 percent of seventh and eighth grade students in the United States reported that their peers had been hurt in school. These rates place the United States well below the

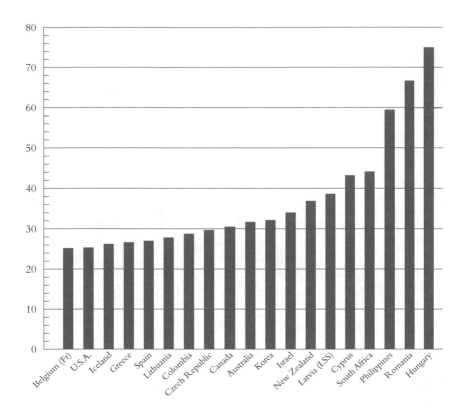

international mean. This in no way lessens the seriousness of the problem, but it is strong evidence that we cannot simply assume that because the United States has a relatively high level of adult violence and widespread availability of firearms this creates school violence.

Before we end this overview of the trend, we note that we don't have a great deal of information on how knowledge of violence affects students. Just how much worry about in-school violence influences students around the world is an important question that future researchers need to address, but evidence from the TIMSS case study suggests that students may vary greatly in how they deal with the prospect of violence in their school. An excerpt from interviews with two teenage German students shows that for some of them violence in school falls into the category of "hearsay," while for others it is a rigorous danger that profoundly affects student perception of school.

FIGURE 6.2   Rates of School Violence Among Peers
(continued on facing page)

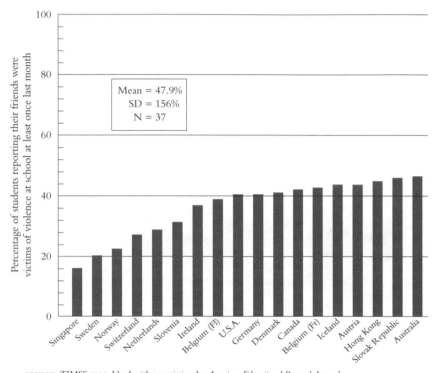

Mean = 47.9%
SD = 156%
N = 37

SOURCE: TIMSS 1995. Used with permission by *American Educational Research Journal.*

In regards to the question of violence in school, Marta said it was much worse at her last school in Central City. For example, she said, "there was one kid who always wanted to fight. But that's because he was different from us, he didn't fit in. He had a knife and would threaten people with it. Finally, he was kicked out of school and everyone was happy about it."

"Her cousin," Hanna said, "goes to a Hauptschule and told her that the kids there attacked a teacher with a knife." Hanna said "she is not sure if that's really true or if her cousin was making it up to impress her." "In any case," she said, "at my school, there is not a big problem with violence." [Authors' note: the Hauptschule is academically the lowest secondary school among three kinds.]

These girls' statements exemplify several pertinent facts about school violence: (1) it is widespread around the world, (2) a single incident of school violence can affect an individual or individual's peer group for a long period, (3) perceptions about risk of violence affect attitude, (4) violence is not evenly distributed within a nation, and (5) individual students vary greatly in

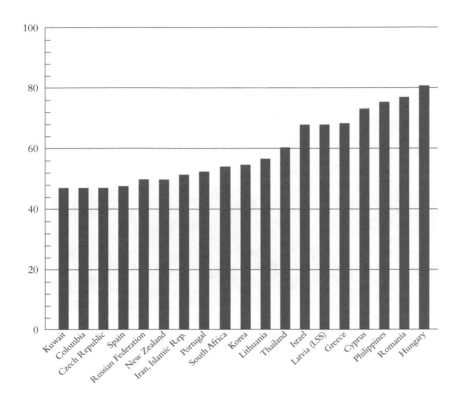

their reaction to reports of violence. For some students—those who go to a school in an affluent neighborhood and sit in a safe classroom—violence may be a distant worry. For others, it may be a constant foreboding. Some, like Hanna, are skeptical even though they hear about incidents of violence.

Violence in school does not affect just students. Teachers are sometimes the target of violence, and their effectiveness as educators may be hampered by violence disrupting the instructional period. From previous cross-national studies, we know that teachers around the world reported a high level of classroom disruption for violence and less serious misbehavior (see Anderson, Ryan, and Shapiro, 1989). Although the obstreperous student may not pose a danger to teachers or other students, as shown in Figure 6.3 teachers in the TIMSS study certainly see that student as affecting the classroom learning environment.

In many nations, four out of ten teachers or more thought their teaching was quite limited by student disruption in the classroom. They ranged from

FIGURE 6.3 National Rates of Problems in the Classroom
(continued on facing page)

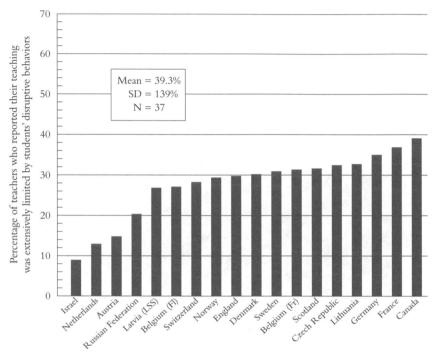

SOURCE: TIMSS 1995. Used with permission by *American Educational Research Journal*.

Israel, where fewer than 10 percent of teachers thought their teaching was limited, to South Korea, where more than 65 percent of teachers noted disruption as a strong limiting factor. In this case, U.S. teachers were above the international mean in their perception of classroom disruption.

Again, though, a disruptive student is not necessarily a violent one. A class clown can have a devastating effect on instruction but may not cause students or teachers to worry about their safety. On the other hand, disruption, even when it is nonviolent, can initiate more dramatic behavior. Fooling around can lead to hurt feelings, escalating tempers, and threats (if not actual incidents) of violence. One American high school student told TIMSS observers, that "as long as schools are schools, there will be problems, rivalries between classes, name calling, and disruptions in class caused by those kids who are unhappy." Teachers, then, are understandably concerned with maintaining a respectful, orderly classroom climate. For the United States to be above the international mean on this measure means that teachers are dealing with classes they find hard to control, and students are sitting in

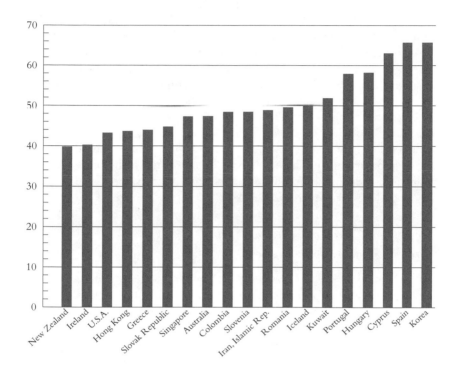

classes that may often be disrupted. This kind of low-level disruption eats away at the time the teacher and class can use to concentrate on academic material, and it is likely to increase concern about violence.

The TIMSS survey also queried teachers on how threats to their own and students' safety limited their teaching. This question, in contrast to the one on general disruption, is a more direct measure of the degree to which teachers see violence affecting the classroom and the learning process. Here, in stark contrast to student experience with and perception of violence, we find that teachers around the world do not perceive a threat to their own or students' safety as limiting their teaching. Fewer than 5 percent of teachers in the Netherlands reported such limitations. Even in Romania, with its high rate of victimization among students, fewer than 50 percent of teachers thought threats of violence limited their teaching. Again, U.S. teachers fell below the international average for perceived threats to self and student safety, with fewer than 10 percent of teachers responding that threats to their or their students' safety imposed a strong limitation on their teaching.

Many educators would agree that a single incident can undermine the educational process; however, the effect of such an incident may be more limited than we thought. One U.S. high school administrator noted: "Recently there was a gun incident at our school, so for a brief period of time, they [*the students*] were worried about that. Their well-being. Students worry about grades, their safety" (emphasis added). This principal did not think that a single incident left a lasting mark on the school, and it is interesting to note that he mentions "worry about grades" in the same sentence with concern about safety. Are we missing part of the puzzle of understanding school violence? Could it be that academic stress or competition is as great a factor in student consciousness as fear of violence? Could academic competition actually produce violence? To answer these questions, we added more measures and examined what national factors are associated with school violence at the national level.

Finding the Causes of Cross-National Levels of Student Violence

To put the next analyses in content, it is useful to describe a little of the history behind how social scientists have come to think about school violence. In the past, the study of school violence was a small part of the large field of research on what causes juvenile deviance and delinquency. Previous studies did not differentiate between violence that occurs specifically within schools and overall juvenile delinquency that occurs anywhere (see review in Lawrence, 1998). Consequently, the theories used to explain school violence were drawn from research on general juvenile delinquency. These theories assumed that (1) the psychosocial causes of violence in school are the same as those for other delinquent or deviant acts and (2) the causal factors have the same relative effect across the range of social institutions that an adolescent might encounter on a given day (home and family, street corner and gang, classroom and peers or teacher).

What these theories say is likely to cause delinquency, and by extension school violence? There are three major theoretical perspectives: (1) strain theory, (2) labeling theory, and (3) control theory. Strain theory argues that school can produce strain on students that in turn promotes delinquent behavior. Cohen (1955) specifically emphasized that students from lower social classes may be frustrated in school and respond to this frustration by acting out with disruptive behavior, truancy, or even forming a delinquent subculture.[1] Labeling theory states that "academic tracking" stigmatizes low-

1. For more on adolescent subcultures of violence and resistance, see Polk and Pink (1972). Polk, Frease, and Richmond (1974) found that school failure (but not social class) was directly related to delinquency; they emphasized the "gate-keeping" function of schools, by

achieving students, increasing the likelihood of delinquency (Schafer, Olexa, and Polk, 1972; Kelly, 1977; Kelly and Grove, 1981).[2] Finally, control theory identifies the strength of the bond between students and their schools and teachers as an important barrier in deviating toward delinquency. That is, students who do not like school or teachers are more likely to report delinquency than those who are more strongly attached to their teachers and school (Hirschi, 1969).

The problem with these studies, for our purposes, is that they focus on individual-level issues, not on how national conditions of schooling influence rates of crime, delinquency, and violence within schools. Cross-national studies of overall crime, such as homicide (see Newman, 1999), do analyze the effect of national conditions, and from these studies three major factors can be drawn: a large number of poor, a large number of youths in a nation's population, and a lack of overall social integration. All three are strong predictors of national rates of crime and violence. We decided to use these national factors to see if they were related to school violence specifically. We also included national characteristics of the public educational system because we knew from previous studies (Baker, Akiba, LeTendre, and Wiseman, 2001; LeTendre and others, 2001) that these factors affect a range of educational phenomena. Our suspicions were correct, but we were still surprised at how distinct a social phenomenon everyday school violence is in a number of nations.

Crime and Delinquency Versus School Violence

Let's begin by looking at the statistical association between overall crime and school violence. We used the homicide rate (per 100,000 population) from U.N. data and INTERPOL data, as well as U.N. data on assault, rape, and robbery—all good indicators of adult violence reported by nation. It has been generally considered that the level of school violence and other juvenile delinquencies are a reflection of the crime rate in society (Lawrence, 1998), but our findings did not support this for violence in school. *None* of the indicators of everyday school violence was related to the national crime rate.

---

which elite positions and credentials are conferred on some students while others are assigned lower status and lower credentials. Strain theory also resembles resistance theory (see Giroux, 1983, for review) in using a concept of "delinquent subcultures" that evolve in response to systematic imposition of lower-class status via the educational system. Evidence of delinquent subcultures has been empirically documented in the United States and the United Kingdom (Willis, 1977). Whether strain leads to delinquent behavior or produces subcultures or resistance regarded as delinquency is a question that remains to be definitively answered.

2. Data from Holland (Nijboer and Dijksterhuis, 1983) also showed that poor achievers in school are often labeled as failures, resulting in negative student attitude toward school and eventually rebellion against school.

It is also possible that juvenile crime and deviance occurring outside school are distinct from crime or deviant acts committed in school. We took this idea as a working hypothesis. Because schools are so highly institutionalized, with such clear and powerful social roles, it may be that social interactions on the order of violence follow different patterns and have their own causes from social interaction occurring outside of school. If so, this would mean that to find truly effective remedies for school violence we cannot rely on data that mix together in-school and out-of-school violence. We would need to look at the effect of in-school factors on in-school violence.

For example, following some of the original ideas of the delinquency theorists, we would expect that severe gatekeeping mechanisms (such as high-stakes tests) or systems that produce a large number of academic failures should produce more violence. We tested a number of factors, assessing the association between characteristics of the school system and school violence measured by self-reports of victimization. The clarity of these results surprised us; school system factors such as overall academic effectiveness (measured by national mean math score), creation of winners and losers (coefficient of variation of math score), and the level of academic competition (size of shadow education) are all associated with cross-national rates of in-school violence. Specifically, nations that have lower overall achievement scores, greater variation in mathematics scores, or more use of shadow education tend to have a higher rate of in-school violence. Although the general level of crime and violence in a nation is unrelated to everyday school violence, a number of factors associated with schooling within nations are related.

We pushed the analysis further and examined national-level factors previously identified as associated with the national rates of juvenile delinquency and deviance. Nations with lower economic development (GDP per capita) have more in-school violence, but the level of income inequality within a nation (the Gini coefficient of income inequality) is unrelated to the rate of in-school violence. Also, nations with a large portion of youth age fifteen to twenty-nine also have a higher rate of school violence (a large youth population has been linked with social problems such as adolescent suicide), but indicators measuring the level of social integration of the nation (divorce rate, percentage of linguistic minority) are unrelated. The picture was becoming somewhat clearer; certain national characteristics influence both school violence and juvenile delinquency or juvenile problems, but other characteristics have no association with school violence.

We also knew that school quality and general social equality have been shown to be associated with national development indicators such as GDP and a proportionally large young population (Heyneman and Loxley, 1982;

Baker, LeTendre, and Goesling, 2002). The question remained as to whether national conditions of schooling really have an independent effect on violence, or if the conditions of schooling just transmit the impact of larger social conditions. For example, poorer nations could be less able to provide quality schooling and also develop more school violence because of a large impoverished segment of the population.

The answer to this question was surprising. We expected the association between economic conditions of a nation and the rate of in-school violence to be unchanged by conditions in the school system. But we were wrong; for both the economic and demographic factors when school-system-level variables are introduced into the statistical models, these social factors are no longer related to school violence. Not only is the adult violence level unrelated to school violence, but also economic conditions and even the demographic effect of a young population are unrelated, as soon as national school factors are considered. In the end, only mean math achievement, variation in math achievement, and the size of the shadow education system are predictors of the national rate of school violence.

What this means is that we have to look to factors within the school system if we are to gain a greater understanding of school violence. We tested our analyses in a variety of statistical ways, and the same results held true: when school-system variables are added to the equation, social variables become nonsignificant. There is still a lot of work to be done in understanding what causes cross-national variation in school violence, but the best evidence to date suggests that the conditions of a nation's schools are a prime factor in generating school violence.

Unanswered Questions

School violence, in one form or another, is indeed an international problem, to which no country is immune. Many times our attention is focused on a terrible act of school violence—the kind of mass shooting that has happened in the United States or Germany, for instance—but these incidents are quite rare. Rather, teachers and students are more concerned about less dramatic but far more pervasive forms of violence.

How much do these "lesser" forms of violence affect students and what they do at school? We have seen that students obviously perceive the situation differently from how their teachers do, and that students themselves can differ widely in their reaction to violence. If we are to seriously reduce school violence, we need to know more about how students themselves perceive school and school violence. What questions do we need to ask to understand school violence better?

If we look at what students in the United States, Germany, and Japan said about their school life, then we must consider bullying and gangs as the two pervasive forms of harassment or intimidation faced by these students. The simple presence of gangs or bullying is not violence per se, but both are strongly linked with fear of violence in the minds of students and parents. One Japanese mother lamented: "My daughter seems to lack a sense of rivalry and willingness to study hard. I don't see them in her at all. She was very quiet in elementary school, so she was an object of bullying there. . . . She suffered a lot, I think."

This parent notes the pain and anguish caused by bullying, but she also makes the interesting link between academic competition and bullying. Does academic competition create the kind of classroom climate that encourages violence? Does the stress and strain of having to constantly worry about grades drive students to become aggressive? These are serious questions that face all nations and deserve considerable attention in the future.

Another unanswered question is how much local factors—such as the level of poverty in the local community—affect violence in a specific school. Some teachers and administrators would argue that schools have little control over what goes on in the classroom because they may believe that the causes of student disruption come from home. In Germany, a TIMSS observer watched a student disrupt class; later he asked the teacher about it. The teacher noted the boy was "hungry for attention and acknowledgment" and "will get it by disrupting class if needed." The teacher also said he (the boy) "comes from a family which ignores him, he is unwanted at home and doesn't receive any affection or guidance." The way many teachers see it, a student's home life or community environment drives behavior in class.

School shootings brought to our attention the unanswered question of how we deal with the aftermath of violence. This is a significant question, one we must not lose sight of. Some U.S. schools face a local environment replete with violence. Such schools have to work to provide a safe haven for students, but also to deal with the aftereffects of violence on student performance, motivation, and sense of safety. One U.S. high school administrator noted:

I have a school that is considered by many as a school of last resort. I accept students from all over the city who have been discarded, thrown out—illegally in some cases, some who did not attend school during the last years of elementary school. I get undiagnosed crack babies, I get students with what I call a multitude of negativisms. They have been raped, been in jail, been on drugs, and been drug dealing. I've got kids who have been shot. Even as they go through the metal detectors, they go off because the students still have bullets in them that the doctor couldn't take out.

How do we begin to reconnect such students to the process of schooling? We know that if our schools continue to produce a huge gap in academic achievement, then we will have to accept the persistence of one source of school violence. From the standpoint of yet another U.S. administrator, the schools now face more and more severe problems than in the past:

The kids come to school with far more problems than they used to. Everything ranging from a very poor home life where they are not being nurtured, to sometimes very extreme cases of drug abuse, physical abuse, psychological problems. It used to be that the deans would concern themselves with kids being tardy and just ditching class. Now that is much lower on the priority list because they are dealing with kids who are violently aggressive.

The link between community environment and school environment is clearly the most important area for future studies. Some anecdotal evidence suggests that a school can be a haven of safety in a violent neighborhood, but we still know little about the factors affecting these phenomena. Rather than looking broadly, nations need to begin looking more closely at internal differences in communities and schools. We should also extend this research to dealing with the aftermath of violence, both in school and in the community.

Other factors must also be kept in view. Some of our analyses showed that the size of shadow education was significantly related with a high level of school violence in a country. It is possible in many countries that low-achieving students who are taking outside-school lessons are more likely to involve themselves in violence than the low-achieving students who are not taking outside-school lessons. Future studies would do well to attempt to control for the presence of a large number of students in educational tracks that divert them from college entrance. The presence of such a track may have a powerful relationship with the overall rate of violence in a system with significant academic competition.

Finally, we have to admit that we know little about how violence varies with the level of schooling. The TIMSS data let us compare only middle grade schooling, but are the middle grades really the time when all forms of school violence are at their peak? In Japan, for example, middle schools are considered to have more violence than high schools—a belief that is supported by national reports of crime. If we considered high school violence alone, would the United States move above the international mean? More important than any ranking, not only the amount but the nature of violence may change with the level of schooling. Late elementary and middle school may see the onset of extremely violent crime (rape, assault with a weapon) that could substantially alter student and teacher perceptions of their safety and ability to study. It could also be the time when widespread sexual harassment makes school a harsh place for girls and gay and lesbian students. We need to know a great deal more about what goes on inside the classrooms and corridors of the world's schools.

What Do We Need to Do?

What does all this mean on a practical level? In one model, after controlling for a range of factors, we found that an increase in the variation of achievement in math was associated with an increase in the percentage of students who became victims of violence at school. This means that the more school systems create a set of academic winners and losers, the more likely they are to produce more in-school violence. This does not mean that nations should stop trying to raise test scores, but as we argued in our last chapter they should be careful to try to raise the level of performance among *all* students. Persistent inequality in national resources produces both long-term and immediate problems for nations. The most pressing one may be school violence.

The message we have for policy makers and educational reformers is clear. Effective reduction of school violence requires better knowledge and monitoring of school conditions, so that reforms and programs aimed at addressing basic differences in opportunity to learn can work to decrease the factors that are linked with violence. Zero tolerance policies—banning weapons or ejecting violent students—has an immediate emotional appeal to parents worried about their children's safety, but it does not address the causes of violence. If we do not make serious efforts to decrease or eliminate factors that cause school violence, and instead attempt only to suppress its expression, we will never be able to ensure the safety of our schools.

First, we need to understand more specifically and qualitatively how violence in school is similar to or different from violence outside of school. Do certain kinds of violence in school (for example, sexual assault) more closely resemble community violence in terms of frequency of occurrence than other forms of violence (such as physical assault)? Second, we need to understand how different or similar student, teacher, and principal perceptions of violence are in order to account for seeming discrepancies in the reporting of violence and in terms of increasing the efficacy of violence prevention. Third, we need to look more closely at the difference between violence and perception of violence, understanding that student actions may be motivated by perception of the chance of violence that are not congruent with the actual probability of encountering violent behavior. Fourth, we need to look more closely at the role that poor instruction plays in promoting violent behavior. Fifth, we need to understand how specific organizational mechanisms (such as tracking) operate in various systems and how they may be related to production of violent behavior.

Our data show that one in three to four students perceive themselves as victims or potential victims of violence in school within a month across the thirty-seven nations in TIMSS. School violence is a major problem affecting students' learning environment around the world. With mass education systems institutionalized globally, it is clear that further investigation into the nature and correlates of school violence must be conducted if policy makers are to substantially improve school environments. School violence needs to be addressed by paying close attention to the qualities of the school system as well as relationships between schools and the communities they serve.

CHAPTER 7

The Universal Math Teacher?

THE TEACHER IS the heart of the school. Around the world, parents are anxious to have their children be placed with a good teacher. In the most advanced studies of how schools influence educational outcome, researchers have argued that it is the quality of instruction in the classroom that is the most crucial element (U.S. Department of Education, 1999). Nothing short of national educational success is claimed to ride on the overall quality of a nation's teaching corps (Stigler and Hiebert, 1999).

When researchers find differences in teaching style or instructional practice of American teachers compared to teachers in Japan and Germany or elsewhere, they often claim the differences stem from deeply rooted cultures of teaching in those nations (Stevenson and Stigler, 1992; Stevenson, Lummis, Lee, and Stigler, 1990; Bennett, 1987). Probably the best example is how a video image of an eighth grade Japanese mathematics teacher, made as part of the TIMSS study, took on almost mythical qualities of effectiveness in the American debate over how to improve the country's allegedly ineffective faculty. It was claimed that the Japanese teacher's command of the flow of the classroom, lesson preparation, and textbook structure was a model of educational achievement (Kinney, 1997–98).

When the initial TIMSS results were released in the United States by the federal government, what caught the attention of American education policy makers and the public the most was this videotape showing one eighth grade mathematics teacher each from America, Japan, and Germany, all teaching the same topic.[1] To many who watched this tape, the images seemed

1. Although the public video showed only one teacher from each country, conclusions were drawn from a large video study of numerous teachers.

to confirm the idea that there are national differences in instruction. Unlike the videotaped American teacher, the Japanese and German teachers used conceptual challenges, encouraging students to explore, investigate, and solve problems with greater insight into the mathematical principles at work. What more dramatic evidence could there be of comparative differences in teaching than the three teachers right there on the screen? Certainly, many American educators thought, there is some national recipe or script for effective teaching that must be part of the answer for why some nations do better than others in mathematics and science achievement.

Although there are cultural differences from nation to nation that affect teaching around the world, in a detailed analysis of American, Japanese, and German teachers with our colleagues Motoko Akiba, Brian Goesling, and Alex Wiseman we have found that this emphasis on "national cultures" of teaching is too simplistic (LeTendre and others, 2001). The idea that, for a whole nation, teaching at all levels in all schools follows a single "national script" is directly contradicted by the pattern of similarities we find in the very nations represented on the released TIMSS teaching video. National rules, policies, and laws affect the way teachers organize their day, but in many ways the work of teachers not only in Japan, Germany, and the United States but also probably in Chile, Spain, or Taiwan is quite similar. There is a global model of teaching that has expanded around the world with the global institutionalization of schooling, even though there are also national and regional forces that affect teachers' working lives.

This chapter describes how the forces pushing and pulling teachers' working lives across highly contrasting nations creates a tapestry with many commonalities but only a few striking differences. This is because teachers work in schools that make up an institution that runs across national borders and that has been subjected to the extreme isomorphic force of a world culture making the core curriculum and basic instructional practices essentially homogeneous around the globe. At the same time, the cultural role of the teacher was highly developed in many nations before widespread modern mass schooling, and before many national governments created their systems of education. These nation-specific cultural values and legal structures continue to produce some variation in the working lives of teachers.

Teaching in Three Countries

To better compare how teachers in U.S. middle grade mathematics classrooms go about the business of teaching, we constructed national profiles that reflect the *range* of instructional activities teachers use. The TIMSS contains information as to what mathematics teachers believe and value about teaching, students, and learning as well as their actual classroom practices.[2] We combine the TIMSS survey data with the open-ended interviews and observations from the extensive TIMSS case study component to capture a representative picture of the worklife and values of teachers.

The picture these data reveal helps us identify specific organizational features in national systems of education that affect the working lives of teachers around the world. Because the organizational features of schooling vary significantly across these three nations, it can be said that on balance a teacher's workday depends highly upon which nation the teacher works in, but there are many common tasks to deal with. We also found a fair amount of conflict between teacher beliefs and ideals within a given nation, suggesting that national patterns of beliefs about teaching are in flux. This, we argue, reflects conflict in the real world among teachers' stated ideals, the organizational environments, educational policies, and student or parent expectations. But upon further analysis, this picture becomes more complicated as we find substantial cross-national similarities in the beliefs and values about education that teachers hold and use to make professional decisions about students and teaching. First, let us take a look at the basic working lives of American, German, and Japanese eighth grade mathematics teachers.

The Average Work Week

One striking difference in teachers' lives is the number of hours they spend in the classroom. Japanese teachers, on average, spend only about sixteen periods per week teaching, compared to about twenty in Germany and 18.5 in the United States. Japanese teachers have fewer classes to prepare for than their American and German counterparts (a significant benefit, in the opinion of teachers in any nation). A lower average number of teaching periods is a good indication that Japanese teachers can more carefully craft each lesson.

Another crucial dimension is the range of pupils teachers have to deal with. In this regard, German teachers seem at a disadvantage. They spread their teaching out over more grades. About 65 percent of German teachers teach three or more grades, compared to about 13 percent of American teachers and about 6 percent of Japanese teachers doing so. Again, this is a rough measure of the degree to which teachers can tailor or specialize their teaching.

Finally, teachers are sometimes required to teach more than one subject. For many of them, teaching outside their subject of focus can be a painful

2. For a number of technical reasons, it is easier in the TIMSS data set to make conclusions about the sampled mathematics teachers and their classrooms than the science teachers. So here we focus only on the former, though we strongly suspect similar results would be found for the latter.

experience. Even when teachers relish teaching other subjects, it requires extra preparation on their part if they are to display the same mastery as in the subjects in which they have been trained. Teaching in the subject area is perhaps the best measure we have of teacher specialization, and here Japanese math teachers are clearly at an advantage. Japanese teachers trained as mathematics instructors were actually conducting math classes 90 percent of the time, as opposed to 61 percent among the Americans and only 52 percent for the Germans. In addition to teaching more periods and across more grades, mathematics teachers in Germany and America spend a lot of their time teaching other subjects. This all adds up to a significant advantage for Japanese teachers, at least in terms of specialization within the subject (see Ingersoll and Smith, 2003, on the United States). Of course, being a subject specialist is not the same thing as being a good teacher, but considered nationally this difference is likely to have an impact on the overall quality and consistency of math instruction.

These basic differences in working conditions afford Japanese teachers some substantial advantages—that are not necessarily a cultural product per se but derive from policy choices about the staffing of schools. In addition, the national textbook selection process in Japan means that there are only a few texts available and that the content and quality of these texts is remarkably similar. Of course, there is also a strong cultural value among Japanese teachers to carefully "polish" each lesson (Stigler and Hiebert, 1999). But the Japanese have the "organizational space" to actively pursue their values and create lessons, which appear to be of high quality and fairly standardized across the nation (OERI, 1998).

Similar standardization (and implementation of a higher quality) of teaching practice and texts could be obtained in the United States and Germany, but this would require some major revisions of the school system itself. Both the United States and Germany have federal systems that grant considerable autonomy to the states. In America, local school boards themselves can make significant decisions about which texts to use. In both America and Germany, teachers in some districts help select the textbooks; virtually all of the U.S. teachers interviewed for the TIMSS spend a great deal of time creating supplementary lessons in order to tailor them for each class. German and U.S. teachers work hard, but they face differing organization environments from those of their Japanese counterparts.

Teaching conditions in Japan allow teachers to concentrate on a single subject, and Japanese teachers appear more likely to teach the subject in an ideal way than American or German teachers; the result is a picture of remarkable homogeneity across the country. The lean and organized math and science lessons observed in the TIMSS video studies of eighth grade Japanese classrooms are not just the product of a different culture of teaching; they

reflect basic contrasts in educational policy and school organization that affect how teachers are allowed to organize their time. Cultural values or ideals
can affect educational policy and choices about school organization; there is
no "deep" cultural barrier preventing adoption of policies in U.S. districts
that would implement similar work patterns.

However, not all educators agree that the "specialist" model of the
teacher is appropriate (or "ideal") for teaching young adolescents in a middle grade school. Given sufficient planning time, teachers can teach several
subjects yet attain a high quality of implementation in all. This leads us to
discuss another finding from the survey and case study data. The wide variation of work schedules in the United States and the lack of overall coordi-
nation of schedules often prevent U.S. teachers from providing highly pol-
ished lessons.

The TIMSS survey data show that, comparatively, American and German
teachers get less common planning time than their Japanese counterparts in
eighth grade classrooms do. We found that teachers in the United States reported meeting with their colleagues to discuss curriculum or teaching issues less frequently than in Japan or Germany, with 45 percent of teachers
in Japan saying they met at least once a week with peers as opposed to 37
percent in the United States and only 30 percent in Germany.

This basic difference in the number of assigned instructional periods has
significant ramifications for how teachers organize their week. American
teachers tended to report a workweek that was significantly affected by
planning for (and adjusting to changes in) nonteaching work. One U.S. middle school teacher described her day in this way:

> A: OK, well we must be here by 7:30 and I'm usually [here] between 7:15 and
> 7:30, earlier I guess this week because I have duty, cafeteria duty, all this week.
> Q: Does that happen very often?
> A: Well, it does to me for this nine weeks because I do not have an elective, I'm
> not teaching an elective, whereas the next nine weeks, yes, I will, so I have
> first and second periods free, so I have two planning periods in essence. . . .
> There are several other people who don't also [have an elective], and we take
> care of the normal bus duty or the morning cafeteria duty, excuse me, or for
> the poor people who are in the ISS teacher . . . she has no planning, she has
> no break all day long unless somebody goes in there and stays with her kids
> so one week . . . I would say that every single teacher has some kind of duty
> at least for a couple of weeks out of the year. That's pretty typical.

American teachers reported a significant range of differences in the number of assigned periods they had each week, with individual teachers in the
same school having drastically differing schedules. More equal distribution of
planning time, and more planning time overall, is a reasonable reform goal
for the U.S. middle grades—a goal that is not dictated by cultural beliefs.

When we look at what teachers reported about their working lives and the impact of their teaching load, planning time and control over planning time appear correlated with other important facets of work environment. Meeting with other teachers to plan lessons and discuss ideas for teaching is a salient aspect of a teacher's professional life. For many decades, we have known the isolation many American classroom teachers feel when they close the door and face a period alone with a group of students. The National Middle School Association has repeatedly called for common prep periods for teachers in the middle grades, for teachers to be able to rely on their colleagues' expertise and common pool of knowledge.

The most striking feature of planning in the United States was again the variation in how much time teachers had to prepare. The interviews from the case study database suggest that teachers in some districts are supported by their schools through extensive planning periods, while in other schools—like the one with the ISS teacher just mentioned—they have no time to plan, and other teachers have frequently scheduled meetings. Some U.S. teachers described a plethora of meeting opportunities.

> Q: Do you have much opportunity to interact with the teachers here?
>
> A: Just with my team. I mean in the department, I guess, interdepartmental meetings, grade levels, we do try to interact on a grade level setting. . . . Usually toward the beginning of the year we all sort of get together and discuss how we will go about teaching the curriculum and then we do have monthly meetings with our math department and since it is just the two-member team we have team meetings . . . at least two or three times a week.

Finally, teachers have many other duties besides teaching that affect their working lives. In the TIMSS teacher survey, they were asked to list for how many total periods they were formally assigned such tasks as supervision, counseling, and other administrative tasks. The most significant difference appears in administrative functions, where American teachers reported about six scheduled hours per week compared to the Japanese, who had about two. When asked, "How many periods are you scheduled altogether per week?" American teachers logged a far higher average number of scheduled periods.

The higher number of periods of scheduled work (teaching and non-teaching) for U.S. teachers may or may not reflect actual differences in total time spent on work, since teachers do not just do the work they are scheduled for but a great deal of extra work in addition. What this points to is (compared to German and Japanese middle grade teachers) U.S. teachers having a more highly scheduled work week—a fact that suggests teachers in the United States have less autonomy to control the flow of work in a given day or week.

In both the United States and Japan, at least, work norms for teachers include a host of extra duties that teachers perform without receiving extra pay or for which they are paid a nominal sum. As one U.S. middle school teacher reported:

[At] 2:30 we escort the children out, and then at that point, most teachers come back and prepare for the next day. Some teachers like myself have a social center where there is an after-school program that goes from 2:40 to 3:40, which for me occurs on Tuesdays to Thursday.

I have pom pom. There's different, teachers have their own after-school program and it's just basically to keep the kids off the street, you know, to introduce them to something different, there's sewing going on, there's art going on, there's all-star sports going on, there's band, there's a lot of different activities that occur after school for the children.

If we break down the time that teachers reported in outside school tasks, we find that both Japanese and German teachers spend more of their outside-of-school time planning lessons than American teachers. U.S. and German teachers, however, spend much more time meeting with parents than their Japanese counterparts, and they also spend more time preparing tests.

Teachers in both the United States and Japan work hard to provide a range of extracurricular experiences for middle school students. In Japan, teachers often try to encourage low-achieving students by spending a fair amount of time engaging in club activities, preparing school events, or just cleaning with the students. The fact that admission to high school in Japan is constrained by an entrance exam significantly limits what middle school teachers can do in the classroom, and the pace of instruction they can keep. This leads to inevitable conflict between the ideals of teaching and the reality of instruction. Many Japanese teachers are frustrated with the system; one replied to a question:

Q: If you could change something about the Japanese educational system, what part would you want to change?
A: The third year of junior high school; here everyone goes on to more school, but at other schools, there are children who don't want to study more. And we really force them to go on. . . .
   Even in Central City, there are children who don't want to study, and during classes they just goof off. And they get in the way of the children who want to study. And coming to school for those who don't want to study is just anguish.

Beliefs About Math

Teachers, in any nation, are not completely free to organize their own work environment. Furthermore, teachers differ in what they hold as an ideal of teaching, and what they think are the realities of teaching. Overemphasis on cultural ideals, however, ignores the fact that individuals may vary considerably in the degree to which they evince belief in general cultural values. Every teacher, as an individual, is aware of what is actually feasible in the classroom as well as being aware of the expectations of others. These differences are important for educational reform, because we need to know what teachers believe should be taught in the best of all possible worlds as well as what they see as the current state of affairs.

The survey portion of the TIMSS reveals some surprising contradictions with previous studies. In numerous ways, American, Japanese, and German teachers expressed many of the same concerns about what hinders their teaching, and the same beliefs in what they think gives students an edge in mathematics.

For example, some cultural analyses suggest that Japanese teachers downplay the nature of individual ability differences and consider it as a benefit of teaching (Stigler and Hiebert, 1998). However, when teachers were asked to agree to various sets of statements on the order of "some students have a natural talent for mathematics and others do not," we found that 21 percent of American teachers disagreed or strongly disagreed with this statement, as opposed to about 28 percent of Japanese and only about 11 percent of German teachers. Virtually identical percentages of Japanese and American teachers agreed with this statement.

The responses on this question do not invalidate the idea that Japanese teachers have a stronger ideal that individual differences should not be a factor in affecting mathematics achievement, but they do show that the real world of teacher beliefs is far more complex than the simplified notion of cultural ideals would suggest. Many Japanese teachers do think there are innate differences in math ability and that they are a major factor affecting student achievement. The case study data show that the Japanese have several indigenous terms for labeling individual ability differences (to cite examples, *saino*, talent or giftedness, and *soshitsu*, innate abilities or gifts; OERI, 1998).

Japanese teachers recognize that effort is an essential ingredient in developing these gifts, and they tend to emphasize effort in a cultural way that most American teachers do not. Nevertheless, many Japanese recognize these differences. One Japanese teacher listed four elements in individual ability difference that are recognized by the majority of Japanese teachers: (1) genetic disposition, (2) education and support from parents, (3) classroom environment and atmosphere, and (4) acknowledgment in school.

Rather than finding individual differences to be helpful to their instructional practice, many Japanese teachers actually think of them as a barrier. In the TIMSS survey, teachers were asked: "Is your teaching limited by students with different academic abilities?" Teachers in Japan were just as likely to see differing academic ability as an obstacle in teaching as their German and American counterparts.

Japanese classroom instruction in the middle grades is influenced by the high school entrance examination system. Since most teachers wish to send as many students as possible to the best high school in the community, they closely follow the national curriculum that public high school entrance examinations are based on. Teachers feel responsible to give all classes the same opportunity to succeed in the exam. Teachers believe there are individual ability differences, but they also believe there are comparable differences in effort. In balancing the equation of effort and ability, teachers tend to favor ability.

Here cultural ideals and beliefs collide in Japan. Many Japanese teachers apparently believe they can change student ability by encouraging better study habits and increasing student effort on task—a belief not widespread in the United States (OERI, 1998). In Germany, many teachers still believe that through accurate assessment, students' abilities can be measured fairly well in the fourth grade and appropriate academic placements made. Japanese teachers face what might be called a cultural contradiction. The ideal of the teacher being able to adjust ability conflicts with the reality of a strict entrance examination system that demands that the teacher give all students an equal opportunity to learn the curriculum—another cultural ideal. When asked about grouping students by ability level in class, one Japanese teacher responded: "I don't think that's acceptable. I don't think it's a very democratic way of handing the situation."

Contradiction between cultural ideals usually produces stress or strain on the individuals of a society. Japanese teachers find themselves in a quandary when faced with multiple-ability levels in the same classroom ("Do I spend more time on the 'slower' students or pump up the 'fast' ones?"). This exchange between a TIMSS researcher and a middle school science teacher in Japan clearly demonstrates the conflict Japanese teachers face:

Q: Do you divide your students into groups according to ability?
A: No, I don't do that. In Japan, that will never work positively because students would feel ashamed.
Q: Are you, then, doing anything special to cope with individual differences?
A: I give them *hoshu* [extra work]. I first give them a handout on a certain lesson, and tell them that if they don't understand, they could attend hoshu after school.
Q: To what level of students are you giving hoshu?

A: I am hoping that the students who are below average would come to hoshu. Those who do well can solve problems on their own. So hoshu is aimed at the students who are having a hard time trying to find out the way to solve problems. But we cannot provide hoshu everyday, so I know it isn't enough.

This Japanese teacher faces a dilemma. It arises in part from contradictions between cultural ideals, but also from the working conditions of teachers in a modern, democratic nation. This teacher's dilemma is immediately familiar to most American educators. Despite the cultural and historical differences among the United States, Germany, and Japan, teachers in these three nations often face quite similar conditions and problems. Providing adequate instruction to a class made up of students with heterogeneous ability levels is not determined by, or solved by, cultural beliefs. All over the world, not just in these three countries, educators face significant problems in trying to grant equal access to the curriculum for all while simultaneously working to maximize each student's individual potential.

National Culture and Institutional Forces

Deep cultural beliefs about the nature of the teaching and learning process do indeed exist between the United States and Japan (LeTendre and Rohlen, 2000). These cultural beliefs are not static and do not exist in a vacuum. Some of what is considered "Japanese" about Japanese schooling is actually attributable to reforms introduced by the American occupation after World War II (see Wray, 1991). Researchers such as Stigler and Hiebert (1999) and Tobin, Wu, and Davidson (1989) have identified national scripts of teaching (and variants thereof) that are dominant or preferred styles of classroom interaction. Without a doubt, we can observe cultural differences among German, Japanese, and American classrooms. But we need to be careful not to focus too much on these differences, and not to assume that these patterns are stable across time. All cultures are in flux, and the expansion of schooling has affected basic cultural dynamics around the family and gender around the world. The same expansion is affecting teachers' lives as well.

Going back to one of our original premises—that modern schooling is much more homogeneous than premodern schooling—even a casual observer from the United States would recognize many features or routines used in lessons. Despite the "Japaneseness" of the lesson, most of the subject format, flow, behavioral sequences, and even some of the noninstructional behavior would be immediately familiar to anyone, from any country, who has completed compulsory education. The purported impact of "Confucian values" or other nation-specific cultural values about education or achievement have to be contextualized in a broader historical and cultural setting.

These cultural values exist in an institutional environment that is highly homogeneous throughout the world.

This is why we found that for core instructional behaviors most of the variation occurred within nations, not between nations (LeTendre and others, 2001). This means that in some key aspects U.S. teachers are likely to differ from one another more than from average Japanese or German teachers. For example, when it comes to basic practices such as lecturing and using textbooks, there is great variation within each nation. Although Japanese teachers, on balance, have a more fluid concept of intelligence than Americans, and although the concept of effort is significantly different in the two nations, the organizational realities of a modern, comprehensive, public school system ensure that teachers in all three nations face many of the same problems and use the same solutions as they carry out their day.

It is not altogether clear whether the few cross-national variations are the result of cultural beliefs, nation-specific organizational patterns, or a mixture of both. It is not possible at this time to truly disentangle the effects of beliefs from the effects of organizational factors. Do American teachers have so many more classes than Japanese because of cultural beliefs? Or is it because of historical trends in the professionalization of teaching? The most reasonable answer is that it is probably both. In either case, teachers are working inside an organization that continues to expand across the early life course, and that continues to disseminate values of individual achievement, meritocracy, and human capital development.

In the modern world system, diverse nations and cultural groups are experiencing similar challenges and trends: transition from an industrial economy to an information economy, an aging workforce, increased demand for education, and so forth. Schools are organizations that are continuously subject to the impact of political, economic, and social trends that occur locally and globally. National governments often respond to these pressures by instituting measures that dramatically shape teachers' lives. For example, responding in part to negative comments on the length of the school day that appeared in non-Japanese media, the Japanese Ministry of Education implemented a large-scale reform designed to reduce the number of days in the school year. Although this change met with some resistance and has had unintended consequences, it clearly demonstrates the extent to which the most basic aspects of an educational system can be changed when affected by global economic or political forces.[3]

Similarly, numerous reforms motivated by international comparisons have hit the average U.S. school in the last ten years and profoundly changed the

3. The reduction of the school day has been linked by scholars and Japanese newspaper reporters to continued criticism from inside and outside Japan of the negative effects of the long hours of school and work on students and employees.

working environment of teachers here. Since the publication of *A Nation at Risk* (U.S. Department of Education, 1983), there has been widespread pressure to increase student performance, emphasize traditional academic work, and set higher levels for teacher certification standards. The recent No Child Left Behind legislation has only added to that pressure, affecting classroom instruction on a national level. In many American states, teachers are now required to attain a certain level of proficiency on the Praxis test, and the National Council for Accreditation of Teacher Education is working with the Educational Testing Service to develop a second test that is aligned with NCATE standards for teacher professional development.[4]

In Germany, special measures for foreign children have been implemented, among them an extra six hours of instruction in German as a second language and the hiring of school social workers or part-time school psychologists (OERI, 1999). In response to changing populations and international pressure, both German and U.S. teachers have experienced significant changes in their working conditions.

The working conditions of the teacher are most affected by global institutional forces in the core tasks—classroom instruction, curriculum choice, patterns of assessment—and felt the most impact from national forces in terms of the work environment—the number of instructional hours required, rotation between schools, and professional development. Cultural beliefs appear to have their strongest effect on noncore behaviors, aspects of the teacher-student relationship that are not dictated by direct instructional needs. These forces do not remain static, as nations strive to reform their educational systems.

If current trends continue, we should expect to see continued standardization of core teaching practices within academic subjects around the world. The curriculum in core subjects is already highly standardized, and measures of assessment are following close at hand. In fact, the increasing regularity with which cross-national studies of schooling are carried out will itself standardize measures of educational achievement across many countries. It will also tend to produce a difference between nations that can attain high standards of teacher training and those that cannot; for example, we are likely to continue to see more differences in the quality of instruction between the very poorest of nations and those in the middle and upper spheres.

National differences may continue in the aspects of teaching that are not closely linked to classroom instruction. Working as coaches, counseling students, supervising lunch rooms, carrying out administrative tasks, or taking part in drug prevention programs are all tasks that teachers around the world busy themselves with every day. National differences in these tasks are

4. (http://www.ncate.org/specfoc/etsoct99.htm).

likely to persist, although we expect that as schooling takes over more and more aspects of socialization of children schools around the world will be expected not only to teach math but also to encourage healthy lifestyles. Further, policy makers in many nations will continue to debate the extent to which teachers will need to be specialists or generalists.

In many respects, the world culture of schooling is paving the way for ever-growing similarities among teachers' jobs. The universal math teacher may not be here yet, but a close approximation of it is just around the corner.

CHAPTER 8

Schoolwork at Home?

LOW-QUALITY SCHOOLING AND HOMEWORK

with Motoko Akiba

WE TURN FROM WHAT teachers do and think about their jobs to what they expect students to do at home to learn mathematics and science. Homework—defined simply as assignment of academic work by teachers to be completed outside of school—has been widely practiced after the fifth grade in American schools since the 1800s (Gill and Schlossman, 1996). The history of homework shows that there has been significant political controversy since its inception. In the United States, by the late 1890s, general public support for homework had declined, and many progressive educators even agitated for the elimination of homework. This antihomework sentiment continued until at least 1941, but it has largely been replaced by a prohomework sentiment in the 1980s, especially in the years following the release of *A Nation at Risk*, when a national "consensus" supporting homework emerged (Gill and Schlossman, 2003b). There are basically two sides to the homework debate in the United States. One claims that it is important for the mastery of mathematics and science, even leading to such grandiose benefits as making workers who can compete better in the global economy; the other claims homework has dubious academic benefit and can even be harmful to family life and other aspects important to the child's development (Kralovec and Buell, 2000).

For most people, homework is perhaps the most prosaic of tasks—a list of vocabulary words to memorize, or ten math problems from the end of the chapter to complete. Yet there is enormous range in the homework teachers can give, from simple drills to complex, long-term research projects that require students to meet and work with peers outside of school. Just how teachers use the results of homework also varies enormously. Some teachers do not even check to see if a student has done the homework, perhaps assuming that students who fail to do the work will suffer on subsequent tests. Other teachers not only collect and grade the homework but also offer students extensive feedback. Homework differs in type and amount, with subject and year, from one school to another, from nation to nation (LeTendre and others, 2002).

Internationally, homework has enjoyed a resurgence of interest since the 1980s, but that interest has not always been positive. The popularity of homework in the United States seen in the 1980s has eroded over the past few years, and once again educators, families, and school reformers are raising concerns that children have too much homework. Similar debates and trends in homework go on in other nations as well. For example, many Japanese elementary schools in the late 1990s issued "no homework" policies. Homework, such a seemingly simple task, is more complicated than at first glance (Corno, 1996).

Despite the fact that homework is ubiquitous in some nations (and appears to be a popular topic among policy makers), it has not garnered the detailed cross-national study that other teaching practices have. An exception is a study by Larson and Verma (1999), who reviewed several national case studies of homework and found that the average amount of homework assigned varied markedly by nation, with a significantly higher level of homework being reported in Asian nations compared to the United States. Perhaps because of the common assumption that homework is a kind of afterthought to instructional practice (a way to tidy up a few bits of the lesson plan that weren't covered in class), its global significance has been largely ignored in the cross-national literature.

Proponents of homework in the United States argue that it can be a major factor in student academic success (Goldman and McDermott, 1987; Corno, 1996). Homework, for our research, is particularly interesting because it is the most obvious way that school inserts itself into the home. The institutional dance between school and family may be something scholars charted over the last century, but most parents are more concerned with the dance they have to do with their children to get tomorrow's spelling words memorized. Mundane as it is, homework is a direct insertion of school authority, with its emphasis on a culture of cognitive achievement, into the daily lives of families in many nations, often opening up a kind of direct communication link between the classroom and the home (Gill and Schlossman, 2003a; Goldman and McDermott, 1987).

But how does this interaction play out? If homework is like other core instructional practices, we would expect it to be used to a similar extent and to similar ends by teachers around the world. Like shadow education, we'd also expect it to be chiefly a remedial strategy. If so, this would call into question the implicit assumption we often encounter in the policy world's discussion of achievement differences across nations—namely, that more homework done among a nation's students means better national test scores. A cross-national examination of homework also gives us some understanding of just how much schools can insert themselves into the family's daily routine across nations.

Not a Simple Matter

Even though in some nations nightly trials and tribulations over homework are one of the most obvious ways parents are pulled into the institutional logic of schooling, homework is perhaps the neglected stepchild of educational studies. A lot of folks have tried to study it, but it is not often considered a core instructional practice—rather, an "add-on task." Still, homework varies along many dimensions. How do you compare a worksheet of addition problems that is checked but does not affect the child's grade with a semester-long science report that counts for 25 percent of the grade? Both tasks can be homework.

TIMSS has information from mathematics teachers in their use of homework, so we created definitions of homework that would measure some of the major dimensions in its use. First, we measured the amount of homework in terms of the number of minutes or hours teachers said they assigned (a rough estimate at best, given the range of time it can take any child to finish his or her homework). Second, we quantified the type of homework, distinguishing among worksheets or problems from texts and more extensive tasks such as group projects. The use of homework refers to what pedagogical ends teachers use homework: did they check it, provide feedback, or let other students provide feedback? Finally, we measured the impact of homework on the student and family as to whether or not homework completion actually affected a student's grade (see LeTendre and others, 2002).

We also reviewed studies of homework to derive some hypotheses (for example, the more teachers use homework in grading, the more homework produces learning gains) about homework that we could test with TIMSS data. Here we ran into a problem similar to our work on cross-national school violence. Homework has been almost exclusively studied at the classroom level, not across nations. It is a far different thing to measure the effect of ten pages of reading per night on students in Mr. Smith's English class instead of measuring what effect increasing the national average of homework by ten minutes a week has on national mean test scores. We realized that, as with school violence, educational policy makers were probably not getting the right information they needed to make decisions about homework and the performance of national school systems.

Does making kids study more each night result in higher test scores? Already national educational debate seems to be locked into such an unexplored logic. If studying more each night helps Mr. Smith's class do better on their Friday test, can't we apply that strategy to countries as a whole? Our answer is clearly "No, we cannot." The function of homework in the global institution of schooling is affected by factors that may or may not play themselves out in the same way at the classroom level. To understand what nations, and not Mr. Smith, should do about homework, we need first to know how (or at what level) homework has become institutionalized within the global system.

To tell the global story of homework, we begin by comparing how much and what kind of homework teachers around the world assign in their mathematics classes. Then we consider what national factors, such as the quality of the public school system, affect homework usage. The global story of homework (with the exception of one nation, Israel) shows the same strong tendencies toward isomorphism that we have found in other chapters. As with core instructional practices, there isn't much variation in how teachers give out or use homework. Like shadow education, we find that national homework patterns in math are largely driven by the quality of the educational system. Even though Mr. Smith may find that more homework helps his class, overall it is the case that systems with a lot of homework appear to be systems with low overall educational achievement.

How Much Homework Do Teachers Assign?

Nations vary considerably in terms of how much homework gets assigned, as shown in Figure 8.1. Unfortunately for American students, across all the measures of homework phenomena as a whole the United States is among the most homework-intensive countries in the world for seventh and eighth grade math classes. U.S. math teachers on average assigned more than two hours of mathematics homework per week in 1994–95. Contrary to our expectations, one of the lowest levels was recorded in Japan (about one hour a week). We were quite suspicious of these numbers at first, and we even had our colleague check the original language questionnaires in Japanese. In the end, we could find no flaw in them. These figures challenge many previous stereotypes about the lackadaisical American adolescent and the diligent Japanese teen (although the latter is more likely to be doing shadow education after school than the former; see Chapter 4). These findings also call into question the common assumption that increasing national homework levels somehow improves the level of national educational performance.

Just by looking at Figure 8.1, we can see that many nations with very high scoring students—Japan, the Czech Republic, even Denmark—don't have teachers who assign much homework. At the other end of the spectrum, countries with very low average scores—Thailand, Greece, Iran—have teachers who assign a great deal of homework. Simply looking at this table, it almost seems as though the more homework a nation's teachers assign the worse the nation's students do.

Of course, the relationship is not perfect. A few high-scoring nations also have teachers who give out a lot of homework. For example, teachers in Singapore assigned more than three hours per week on average. In Romania—which appears to win the title of "homework country of the world"—teachers were dishing out more than five hours of homework in math alone! Although the United States falls slightly above the mean, it really is not very different from the international average. In Korea (one of the top performers in math) teachers give out only slightly less homework than in the United States. There are obviously other factors at play.

Clearly, it takes a lot more than simply increasing the amount of homework to bring up student national scores in a given subject. Indeed, the range of time assigned to homework should give policy makers (and teachers) cause to think. Is assigning more homework really productive? How many minutes (or hours) are needed just to gain a few points on a test? Do students really do the homework that is assigned? If there isn't a strong relationship between more homework and better performance, what other factors should be considered? Could it be that homework works better at some grade levels than others (Cooper, 1989)?

We know that some nations have already enacted homework strategies that differ with the level of schooling. In Japan the no-homework policy does not typically apply to middle school and high school students (OERI, 1998). At this level, almost everyone in Japan recognizes that teachers will send some work home in order to meet the goals set by the Ministry of Education. By contrast, at the elementary school level no-homework policies appear to have become more common in Japan. The rationale most commonly heard for these policies is that young children need time outside of school to play and learn other activities. The policies also appear to be a reaction to the widespread use of cram school studying (shadow education) and examination preparation, which many Japanese believe undermines their educational system (OERI, 1998).

Setting aside the acrimonious debate about the problems facing Japanese education, most Japanese children take after-school nonacademic lessons (swimming, calligraphy, music), and apparently a majority of parents and teachers feel that these lessons are more important than drilling for academic subjects. Many parents around the world would probably agree. For the elementary school ages, children probably profit more from engaging in a range of after-school activities with considerable kinesthetic learning components

FIGURE 8.1 The Amount of Math Homework Teachers Give per Week in Thirty-Nine Nations *(continued on facing page)*

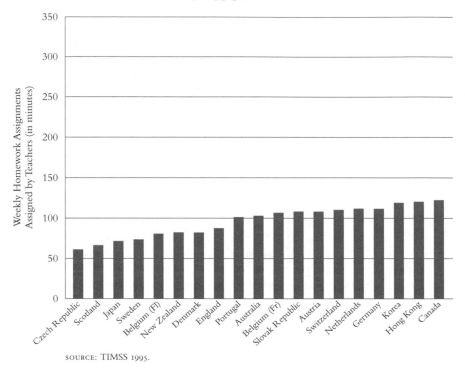

SOURCE: TIMSS 1995.

(that is, doing something) than from sitting and memorizing, particularly if we consider the overall cognitive and emotional development of the child. Does this mean the type of homework should differ by age?

Also, what if the national goals of school systems differ? What if homework were less about academic preparation and more about personal growth and investigation? Would schools need a no-homework policy if homework involved working on a community project, or spending time looking for platyhelminths in a local pond? It seems that the kind of homework used has a large effect on how homework is viewed within a given nation. So in the next section we look at what kinds of homework teachers tend to give.

What Kinds of Homework Do Teachers Give?

Most of us remember being asked to do math problems from the back of the textbook chapter, or to review a list of vocabulary words as part of our routine homework assignments. As we grew older, they probably changed to reading assignments or even more involved projects, such as collecting

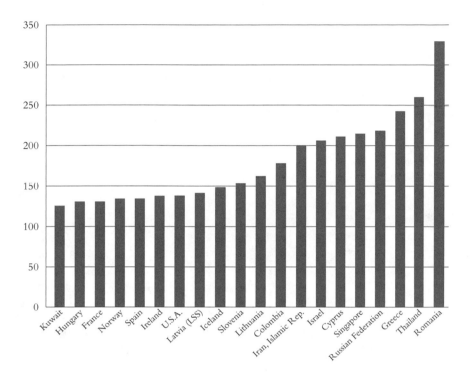

data on household purchases or interviewing family members about the family history. We tend to think of only a small set of activities as homework, but in reality teachers can assign a range of activities. In the TIMSS questionnaire, teachers were asked how often they used a range of homework assignments that included textbooks, worksheets, reading, writing, small groups, individual projects, oral reports, journals, and more.

Despite the possibility for much variation (and creative usage by individual teachers), we found that among teachers who assigned homework assigning textbook problems is by far the most common type of homework teachers use, closely followed by worksheets. Indeed, textbooks and worksheets combined were the dominant form in virtually all countries—with the single exception of Israel, which has a long tradition of group work and group assignments; almost 60 percent of Israeli teachers said they always use small-group investigation for homework in math.

But Israel is an anomaly, and although it is a cipher for scholars expecting global homogenization the fact is that in about half the countries in TIMSS more than half the teachers said they *always* assign problems from

FIGURE 8.2 Most Common Types of Homework
(continued on facing page)

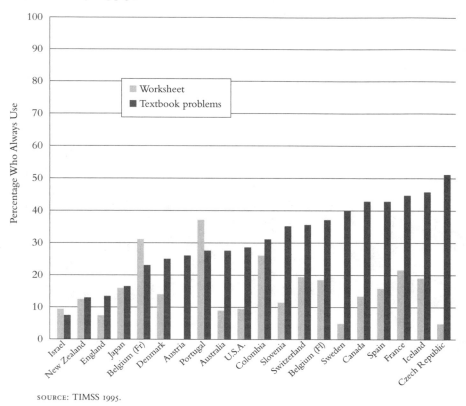

SOURCE: TIMSS 1995.

the textbook for homework. Of course, given the subject area (math), this is not that surprising. We might expect to find more variation in type of homework in subjects such as social studies. What is surprising is that although textbook problems and worksheets are the dominant form of homework, in some countries not many teachers followed this practice.

Figure 8.2 shows the percentage of teachers who always use a given type of homework. We didn't find much variation in the dominant type of homework across nations, but we did find a lot of variation in how similar homework assignments are within a nation. In Japan and England, teachers appear to vary their homework, rarely using just one type. In Cyprus, the practice seems almost universal. This aspect of homework suggests that some nations have much more institutionalized patterns in the kind of homework given than others. This variation may be, in the future, an alternative way to look at standardization of practice—what range of instructional pattern teachers

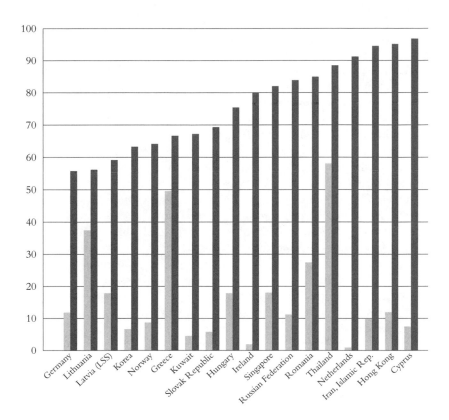

are using. In this regard, U.S. teachers clearly have more diverse homework assignment patterns than in many other nations.

This suggests that homework (at least in seventh or eighth grade math) is a kind of backup. It is something teachers use if they can't cover all of the lesson in one period, or to furnish more drill for students, hoping to push them on to a higher level. Later on we will consider how teachers use homework, which permits some insight into this question, but first let's look at homework in another way.

Let us consider further the cognitive goal of homework. Teachers can use homework as drill and memorization, a form that seems dominant in the world in middle grade math classes, or they can use homework to stimulate "higher-order thinking." That is, teachers can give students open-ended tasks or group assignments that require them to apply the skills they have learned in class to after-school tasks or projects. In terms of homework assignment, we might be more familiar with social studies projects or science reports where students are required to collect data, analyze them, and then present an in-class report. The same kind of process can be used in math. In only a handful of countries, however (with Israel by far outpacing any other), do teachers apply this strategy.

These data allow us to formulate a more complicated picture of homework. Overall, time assigned by teachers may not be a very good measure of *effective* use of homework. In fact, it may be the poorest teachers who assign the most homework. Effective teachers may cover all the material in class without the need to assign a large amount of homework, especially drill and memorization assignments. Other explanations also seem plausible. Teachers who have a specific plan about how to use homework may be more effective than teachers who just load on the material. What is clear is that there is tremendous variation in some countries in the kind of homework teachers assign—which signals that in some countries, at least, reform of homework would not run into strongly institutionalized practices. Policy makers might do well to look more at what kinds of tasks teachers are assigning, rather than how much work they are giving if they want to find practices that effectively raise student academic achievement.

What seems a simple phenomenon (homework) is actually a complex set of practices. It is hard to see clear patterns, other than the interesting one that suggests more homework doesn't line up well with better test scores at the cross-national level. We are now going to make the puzzle even more complex. What if the amount and type of homework weren't the dominant factors affecting student performance? Perhaps what really matters is how teachers respond to homework and incorporate it into the classroom process or grading.

How Do Teachers Use Homework?

We start from the premise that how teachers use homework does have an impact on student performance. For example, if a teacher never checks or corrects homework (and this happens more than many teachers care to admit), students may simply learn that failing to complete homework assignments has no real impact on their lives. We find a lot of variation; in nations such as the Slovak Republic, fewer than 30 percent of teachers always record homework assignments, compared with more than 82 percent of teachers in the United States. Again, Israel was a significant outlier, with only 7 percent of teachers always recording homework, but 92 percent of teachers there always have students correct each other's homework.

Even if teachers check homework but do not make it a large part of grading, students too might be unlikely to complete their assignments. This is a tricky argument, however, because some researchers have argued that the most effective use of homework is not for grading but to give teachers insight into which skills students need to develop (Cooper, 1989). It may be that teachers who use homework to identify skill deficits—and then provide feedback to students about how to build up their skills—are using homework in the most effective way. This would mean that the amount or type of homework assigned is an irrelevant measure, because we do not know if teachers are using homework effectively or ineffectively.

We do not have a way to measure this exact aspect, but we do have measures of how teachers use homework. Unfortunately, the story is not turning out too tidy. There is considerable variation in whether or not teachers give students feedback on homework (with Colombia and the United States among the world leaders and Japan and Korea among the lowest). The United States is relatively high in terms of percentage of teachers giving students feedback on homework, although only a little more than half of American teachers actually do give students such feedback. Globally, we see that teachers really aren't using homework to help students understand their faults or strengths in mathematics. In the United States, teachers are expected to check homework, but it is less clear that they are expected to provide a great deal of feedback on homework.

But U.S. teachers do lead the world in using homework in grading. Figure 8.3 displays the percentage of teachers in each nation who give students feedback on the homework they complete. Almost 70 percent of U.S. teachers use homework assignments to calculate student grades, compared for instance with Switzerland, where fewer than 5 percent of teachers use grades. Clearly, U.S. teachers are trying to get the most they can out of homework. It would seem that, compared to teachers in other nations, U.S. teachers have been influenced by homework research and do indeed check and grade homework.

But this leads us to an unappealing situation. U.S. teachers appear to be doing what the researchers have suggested: giving more homework, checking it, and grading it. The United States even has rather a high level of feedback to students. Why, then, are U.S. students not doing better in mathematics? Recall that most theories of homework are based on studies of the classroom. Could the relationship between homework and achievement in national systems be different? Perhaps homework has already become institutionalized as a kind of catch-up or make-work category. We undertook a few more tests to see what the relationship might be.

Does Homework Improve National Student Achievement?

The results we produced should give teachers and national administrators pause. Not only did we fail to find any positive relationships, the overall

FIGURE 8.3 Percentage of Teachers Who Use Homework in Grading
(continued on facing page)

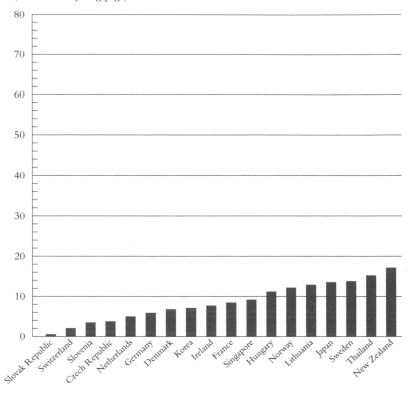

SOURCE: TIMSS 1995.

correlations between national average student achievement and national averages in the frequency, total amount, and percentage of teachers who used
homework in grading are all *negative!* If these data can be extrapolated to
other subjects—a research topic that warrants immediate study, in our opinion—then countries that try to improve their standing in the world rankings of student achievement by raising the amount of homework might actually be undermining their own success.

How could things have gotten so turned around? Some readers might
immediately assume that the measures in TIMSS and other studies are
flawed. Certainly, researchers have identified better measures of homework,
such as time journals (Gill and Schlossman, 2003b). More precise measures
of homework (especially type and usage) would allow us to see more of
what is going on in individual countries, but we do not think the overall

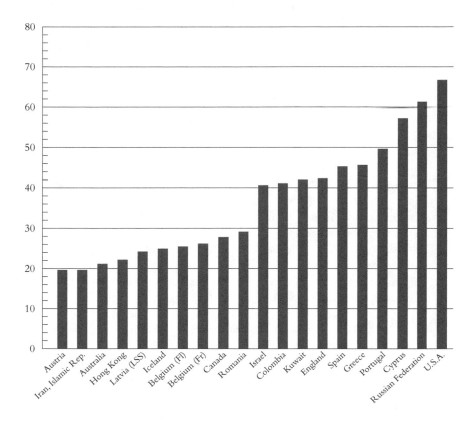

picture would change much. The problem, we argue, lies in the kind of research that educational reformers and planners have been using to guide national systems. As we said before, the best studies (Cooper, 1989; Corno, 1996) found that most research on homework is done at the classroom level. Indeed, such studies often compare classrooms that get homework with classrooms that don't. This is an entirely different kind of study from one that looks at national patterns of homework and student achievement.

In highly controlled classroom studies, positive effects may be found that have little to do with national patterns of usage. In her review of homework, Corno (1996) finds that homework is often misused by teachers, that parents can resent too much homework, and that regular use of homework may not produce better achievement results. We suggest that homework has largely come to be institutionalized as a remedial or catch-up form of education.

Throughout the world, homework appears to be rarely used in a way that would build cognitive skills or give students accurate knowledge of the skills and concepts they needed to work on.

Summary

Homework is an afterthought for most national planners and reformers, except perhaps in the United States. Indeed, it seems to be an afterthought for most teachers, a way to finish up material not covered in class. We see considerable national variation in some aspects of homework assignment, type, and usage, but overall it looks as if homework is not used effectively by most teachers in the world. There are significant differences in the average amount of homework in math that students receive around the world. Students in Japan and Scotland spend little time doing math homework, while students in Romania and Thailand spend several hours per week. Nevertheless, the global story of homework is one of a remedial exercise.

The relationship between national patterns of homework and national achievement suggest that rather than a simple and effective tool for increasing national achievement, more homework may actually undermine national achievement. Homework, perhaps more than any other aspect of schooling we have addressed, highlights how critical it is for national policy makers, teachers, and law makers to understand the global patterns and forces that affect modern education. We still need to know a good deal more about homework in national systems before we begin using homework (or no-homework) policies as a national mechanism to increase student achievement. Several points related to policy and research need to be addressed.

First and foremost, it appears that for most of the world teachers are not using homework in an effective manner. Lots of homework is assigned, but mostly as drill. Educational policy makers and reformers need to consider the overall quality of homework given in a nation as much as they need to consider quantity. We found some global variations in homework that (as with aspects of teacher work roles; see Chapter 7) are likely linked with cultural preferences among the world's national teaching forces. For example, in the Slovak Republic it appears that most teachers don't really care about homework completion. Perhaps they don't see it as their job to check up on whether students do homework or not. Overall, though, teachers around the world do not seem to be using homework in ways that could make it more effective. Rather than the amount assigned, we need to look at type and usage of homework, as well as whether or not students are actually doing the work.

This brings us to our second point: homework policies should be age-specific. Parents of early adolescents or teenagers are likely to react differently to homework than parents of small children. LeTendre (1999) noted that some parents of middle school students with younger siblings were highly critical of homework for first through third graders. At the opposite end, Gill and Schlossman's work (2003a) shows that in upper grades students may simply ignore homework assignments. If a nation is going to implement homework policies, it needs to carefully delineate and consider the age of the students in question.

Our third point is that an undue focus on homework as a national quick fix, rather than a focus on issues of instructional quality and equity of access to opportunity to learn, may lead a country into wasted expenditures of time and energy. In response to the intense focus on studies of mediocre U.S. student performance and media stories of long-studying Japanese students in the early 1980s, many schools and teachers in the United States apparently increased the homework they assigned (at least to younger children). Ironically, this was at the same time that the Japanese were trying to give children more free time away from the rigors of studying. But neither reform appears to have had an impact on overall national achievement level. This may be hard for policy makers to swallow, but American students appear to do as much homework as their peers overseas (or more) but still only score around the international average. All that time spent on homework may have been wasted effort in terms of overall national achievement, something few policy makers or reformers would like to admit.

But given the empirical evidence, we must face the fact that increasing homework is unlikely to have a positive effect on the national achievement level. We need also to consider the findings of researchers such as Gill and Schlossman (2003b), who find little lasting change in the homework level among U.S. high school students over the past fifty years. They note that homework has increased where researchers believe it matters least for academic achievement (Cooper, 1989), and where there is the least public consensus that more is a good thing.

Which brings us to our final point, concerning the relationship of the school and family. Gill and Schlossman (2003a) and other scholars argue that parents often want their children to do homework, and that monitoring homework can be an effective way for parents to communicate with and understand the schooling process. We do not deny their point but would counter that the kind of homework teachers send out is likely to receive quite another response from parents. We do not question the importance of drill as one essential tool in increasing cognitive competence, but homework may not be the ideal time to use such a tool.

Consider the assumption behind such usage. Assigning textbook or worksheet questions as a drill assumes that the child has the kind of home environment conducive to supporting drill and memorization practice. How realistic is this expectation for the majority of parents in the world today? Even in affluent nations, parents are extremely busy with work and household chores (not to mention chauffeuring kids to various meets and practice sessions). Especially for small children, are parents likely to enthusiastically drill their kids every night? Or might many feel that the school as an institution is trying to insert its routines of drill and memorization into family time?

We think that the interaction between parents and teachers over homework is conditioned by social background factors. Most homework appears to be remedial, which means that most parents are able to understand their child's homework through the end of the period of compulsory education. But since teacher usage of homework varies so much, parents who have better communication with the school or who can "read" the teacher better will be more effective in guiding their child's efforts. Similar to Lareau's arguments, we expect that higher-SES parents will be more skilled in dealing with homework and more likely to see it as an opportunity rather than an imposition (Lareau, 2000).

In poorer households, families where parents tend to have less education and linguistic barriers in some nations, or in single-parent families, homework may be less welcome (Goldman and McDermott, 1987). Indeed, an unintended consequence may be that those children who need extra work and drill the most are the ones least likely to get it. The relationship we have outlined indicates that more homework is likely to increase family background effects, thereby generating more inequality and essentially eroding the quality of education overall. If the school expects the family to make up what it cannot furnish in instruction, then educators must face that fact that families are unequal in what they can provide, and there will be severe differences in what students receive.

If this line of reasoning is correct (and it best fits the data that we currently have), then simply increasing the overall amount of homework will most likely increase disparities in educational performance and undermine the overall achievement level. Those families that are better able to marshal resources to support outside school learning will likely gain disproportionate advantage.

Should national educational policy makers just join the "abolish homework" bandwagon? No, and perhaps they should avoid sweeping homework policies altogether. Policy makers and educators need to understand that homework is only one facet of schooling, and that like shadow education it plays a largely remedial role around the world. As such, homework is not a good target as a primary focus of reform. Instead, attention should be paid to quality of instruction and equity of access to quality schooling, with perhaps subsequent attention paid to the type and usage patterns of homework over the course of schooling. Since homework can be a vehicle for parental control over the schooling process, policy makers and researchers might be well served by future studies of which kinds of homework best engage both student and parent. Given the tendency for families to try to foster advantage for their offspring, increasing transparency or clarity in the school's homework policies might be a simple but effective policy tool that could help reduce inequalities between families and how they deal with homework.

CHAPTER 9

Slouching Toward a Global Ideology

THE DEVOLUTION REVOLUTION

IN EDUCATION GOVERNANCE

with M. Fernanda Astiz and Alex Wiseman

THE PAST TWO decades have witnessed a sea change in thinking on how best to run schools across many nations, through a virtual revolution in decentralizing and the devolution of central educational authority around the world. But the switch to less centralized school administration has had some interesting unintended consequences that have left nations with paradoxical governmental structures. Most changed their administration, but much less so than the widely acclaimed ideology of devolution called for. From an institutional perspective, this trend is an excellent case from which to consider what happens when new ideas about education spreading globally encounter local organizational constraints and invested political interests.

Prior to the mid-1970s, the reigning managerial formula for educational efficiency, performance, and equality of opportunity in most nations was *centralized control*. Three decades later, the reigning managerial formula in many nations is exactly the opposite: *decentralized control*. Decentralization, devolution, localization, and even the marketization of public services have become part of a new way to think about how public schools are managed. Our tale in this chapter is about what this dramatic change in the institutional culture of public management means for the functioning of public schools throughout the world.

With all of the rhetorical and political push toward administrative devolution (that is, the transfer of authority from national to subnational units) of such public services as health, social welfare, and education throughout the world, in most nations the actual day-to-day administration of schooling has only gone part of the way toward decentralization. Further, some formally decentralized national systems of education have instituted more centralized control of key educational operations during this worldwide love affair with devolution. In many interesting ways, the United States falls into this latter category of nations. Governance of schooling in many nations now functions under a previously nonexistent, and paradoxical, combination of centralized and decentralized processes coexisting in a kind of administrative truce. There is clear evidence of a global institutional trend toward decentralization among nations, but the actual operational outcome is in reality far more complex than anything predicted from a simple notion of globalization of decentralization.

But what exactly *is* decentralization of educational authority? If an educational system invests most of its authority over key decisions about what is taught, who teaches, and how they teach at the state or provincial level (as in the American states), is this more decentralized than when key decisions are controlled at the national level? What about a highly centralized province or even a large (urban) centralized school district within a system where there is little national centralized control? Which example is more or less decentralized is difficult to say. Obviously the notion of decentralization is relative, and somewhat slippery to define.[1]

Those who have thought the most about decentralization of administrative authority of schools agree on a few basics. First, centralization and decentralization form a continuum, with authority over decision making in schools resting within a central national agency at one extreme and authority spread across many local units at the other end. Second, although there may be some exceptions within a nation, in general one can summarize a national set of schools along this basic continuum. In the actual practice of comparing nations' educational structures, this boils down to determining the degree to which operational decisions about school are controlled by a central national ministry or provincial ministries, or by local units as with school districts in the United States. Regardless of its precise definition, decentralization of school authority is part of a sizable world trend toward a new way of thinking about the nation-state's responsibility to provide social services and how best to do so.

Evolution of Devolution of Public Services

The sweeping neoconservative (or neoliberal, in Europe) political movement of the past several decades changed the political ideological landscape in many nations. In the late 1970s and early 1980s, a group of influential

1. See the special issue of *Comparative Educational Review* on globalization and education, edited by Martin Carnoy and Diane Rhoten, 2002, vol. 46.

politicians, public policy strategists, and intellectuals in the UK and the United States began to think differently about the role of government in its public administration of such services as social welfare, health, and education. The change was based on a shift in the philosophy about the role of government in the economy, from a Keynesian nation-state actively managing economic competition to a laissez-faire nation-state allowing a Freedmanian perfect market of economic competition. Following the lead, there was a similar change in ideas about how to improve public administration, which shifted the role of the government from providing social welfare to coordinating a market-driven system of public services. Exactly what it meant to make public services market-driven, however, ended up being based more on vague neoliberal principles than clear operational formulae. Even the economics of neoclassical markets, to whose principles proponents of incorporation of marketlike processes into public services liked to refer, never really addressed the intellectual issue of markets and public administration (Burlamaqui, Castro, and Chang, 2000).

Recent historical change in thinking about the best ways to manage public education has traveled the same path. From the immediate post–World War II period until the mid-1970s, to centralize educational services of all kinds was to modernize for national success. In many nations during that time period, centralized public services (including and in particular the running of schools) were assumed to be a key strategy to buffer national development objectives from harmful hijacking by local interests and incompetence. This philosophy was particularly evident in the advice (and models of practice) given to (and in some cases forced on) many new nations established during the postcolonial period. Either dominating nations from the colonial period left a culture of centralized public administration or national development agencies presented and pushed the centralized model onto new nations in the name of modernizing public administration. Either way, centrally controlled education was widely seen as a crucial strategy for nation building in relatively new nations facing the immense challenges of integrating traditional groups with different customs, languages, and in some cases long-term violent animosity among competing subnational religious and ethnic groups.

In just the last two decades, the initial interest in national central control over schooling has completely reversed. Propelled by the irresistible promises of greater administrative efficiency, lower costs, and the greater democratic participation of citizenry, national governments and those who advise them have turned to the image of devolving more power and administrative responsibility to local governments. A river of rhetoric about this issue has flowed from wealthy nations such as the United States to many developing nations. Additionally—and with some irony, given early positions on centralized authority—powerful international agencies such as the World Bank—that can shift the terms of educational policy in many regions of the world—strongly advocated (and reinforced in their conditions for loans for educational improvement) more local control of schooling. The message now is that developing nations must adopt decentralization, at least in principle, in order to receive significant national loans for education improvement, and thereby overcoming what many international agencies see as cripplingly inefficient central bureaucracies in many of these nations.

But why haven't all nations' educational systems become decentralized in their management? Even cursory observation of educational governance cross-nationally suggests not all nations have followed the decentralizing trend, even though there is somewhat of an administrative revolution under-foot in education that regards more traditional forms of centralized authority as obsolete. This raises a number of interesting questions about where this world trend in educational administration is going. What impact have these political and ideological trends had on how schools are managed on the ground across the world? Can we find real decentralization of authority oc-curring within school districts and provinces in nations, or only centrally planned decentralized façades, a "slouching posture" toward decentralized ed-ucational authority?

How Decentralized Is Educational Administration in Nations?

To answer this question, we focus on one key area of the operation of schooling: control of the curriculum. Control over the content of school curricula and methods of curricular implementation within classrooms is an administrative issue in the decentralizing movement. Curricula are the ma-jor technical input to the schooling process, and they are often regarded as the corpus of valid cultural knowledge. In short, curriculum is at the opera-tional center of schooling, yet it is a complex matter that takes considerable management. Certainly, if any area of school governance reflects recent consequences of an ideology of decentralization, curricular policy and its implementation do.

In a technical study of this topic with our colleagues M. Fernanda Astiz and Alex Wiseman, we examined to what degree decentralized educational governance has progressed across schools in TIMSS nations (Astiz, Wiseman, and Baker, 2002). In a series of questions about the management of their schools, principals, and headmasters indicated the degree to which various centralized (national ministry), less centralized (provincial ministry), and de-centralized (school or local district) authorities are involved in decisions about school curricula. From responses to these questions, we constructed a ratio of the degree of centralized to decentralized management for each nation. This we call the measure of "operational decentralization"; it is displayed in Table 9.1, adopted from our study. These ratios have the advantage of illustrating an actual mix of decentralized and centralized governance meeting at the school door. If a nation's principals experience extensive decentralized (local) influences, the ratio is zero; if the opposite is true and there is extensive centralized control of a nation's principals, the ratio climbs significantly above 1.0; and if there are many principals reporting equally extensive influence of both types of governance, the ratio is at or near 1.0.

The ratios illustrate one of the main points of the trend in governance we find cross-nationally. There is a continuum among these nations' operational governance, but even so there is considerable mixing of both forms of governance of curricula. Almost two-thirds of the nations have ratios between .65 and 1.97, indicating a significant mix of both influential centralized and decentralized administration of mathematics curriculum operating at the same time; many of these nations actually have an equal amount of both modes of governance. The fact that a large number of nations fall into this administratively mixed group suggests that this may now be a widely used managerial approach. England, Norway, Japan, and a number of other nations operate their public schools with a considerable mix of centralized and decentralized control.

Our second main point is illustrated by the second column of Table 9.1, where there are official indications of each nation's level of administrative decentralization. These were taken from official accounts of systems in the late 1980s and early 1990s, provided by experts from each nation; a 1 is decentralized, as in the highly localized U.S. system, while a 5 is centralized, as in the quite nationally controlled French system. Comparing this column with the operational measure shows that many officially centralized administrations actually run, according to a representative sample of principals, with considerable decentralized components in their administration.[2] We doubt that the discrepancy is due to a lack of understanding of the system on the part of principals or experts. Rather, in many nations the "official" measure is not so much a result of inaccurate documents as it is out-of-date documents, perhaps from a time before the full impact of the current round of global pressure to decentralize government services. Our point here is that in the trenches of managing schools there is considerable global movement among nations toward some form of decentralization. Globalization through administrative rhetoric and strategies has caused real changes in the way curricula are managed.

2. Technically, these are principals from a representative sample of schools where eighth grade mathematics and science are taught, not necessarily a fully representative sample of a nation's principals; probably the difference is slight.

TABLE 9.1

Comparison of Level of Curricular Control

		Measure of Level of Operational Centralization	Measure of Level of "Official" Centralization
Mostly decentralized	U.S.A.	0	1
	Canada	0	3
	Portugal	0	5
	Netherlands	0.03	1
	Australia	0.21	3
	Sweden	0.49	5
	Mean	*0.12*	*3.00*
	Std. dev.	*0.20*	*1.79*
	Czech Republic	0.65	5
	Spain	0.67	5
	Switzerland	0.70	3
	Hungary	0.88	4
	Denmark	0.94	4
	Belgium (French)	1.01	4
	Norway	1.01	4
	Scotland	1.01	4
	Kuwait	1.01	5
	England	1.01	5
	Iceland	1.04	5
	Japan	1.05	5
	Ireland	1.10	5
	Lithuania	1.15	5
	Colombia	1.17	5
	Russian Federation	1.25	2
	Germany	1.35	3
	Korea	1.40	5
	Singapore	1.42	5
	Iran	1.59	5
	Austria	1.69	5
	Thailand	1.73	5
	Belgium (Flemish)	1.94	4
	New Zealand	1.97	5
	Mean	*1.20*	*4.46*
	Std. dev.	*0.37*	*0.83*
	Hong Kong	2.40	5
	Israel	2.42	4
	Latvia	2.78	5
	Slovenia	4.70	5
	Slovak Republic	7.45	5
	Greece	10.29	5
	Romania	11.06	4
Mostly centralized	France	12.50	5
	Cyprus	25.46	5
	Mean	*8.78*	*4.78*
	Std. dev.	*7.37*	*0.44*
	International mean	*2.24*	*4.25*
	International std. dev.	*4.77*	*1.10*

SOURCE: TIMSS 1995.

Is more decentralization mixed in with centralized process better for educational efficiency, effectiveness, and access? It is hard to say, and a question well beyond the scope of our tale here. But our study did show some implications of the forms of decentralization on what actually happens to curricula in classrooms. Past studies from the early 1980s reported a consistent and significant association between cross-national variation in the level of centralized administration of mathematics curricula and the consistency and amount of curricula implemented by mathematics teachers in classrooms (Stevenson and Baker, 1996; Westbury and Hsu, 1996). These studies demonstrate a connection between the degree of centralization of governance and the quality and consistency of delivery of curricular material at the point of instruction; some analysts think this connection could explain cross-national differences in achievement (for example, Spillane and Thompson, 1997). But this cross-national research was done with data reflecting education in nations before the great wave of global decentralization in the late 1980s and 1990s. So an interesting question is, with the more recent mixing of decentralizing and centralizing governance process as a function of globalization is there still evidence of the association between administration process and classroom implementation of curricula?

Decentralized management has been supported because it spreads decision-making power to a wider set of actors, presumably ensuring more accountability within the system. At the same time, opponents of decentralization have been concerned about its ability to furnish enough quality control throughout national sets of schools. One such area of concern has been the consistency of curricula taught across classrooms. For example, one of the main complaints about the highly decentralized American system is that there is too much inconsistency in content of mathematics and science curricula presented across the nation's classrooms (see Chapter 10). Our analysis examined if, compared to more centralized management, systems with more decentralized management had less consistency in what was taught in eighth grade classrooms.

The answer is yes. Decentralization comes at a cost of less curricular consistency among a nation's classrooms. Further, many more local factors, such as the academic level of the students, the teacher's work experience, and qualities of the school tend to influence the pace and content of curricula in classrooms in systems with more decentralized management. These findings are the same as reported in the studies using data from the early 1980s (Stevenson and Baker, 1996), the effect of types of administrative control continues to influence what happens in classrooms into the mid-1990s, during the major worldwide push for decentralization of school management (Astiz, Wiseman, and Baker, 2002).

The point here is not to debate the pros and cons of consistency in classroom implementation of curriculum. Rather, our point is that this world trend in managerial philosophy and practice has real repercussions for what happens in schools and classrooms. The mixing in of decentralization authority probably comes with a certain amount of inconsistency in curricula across classrooms, but that may be good or bad depending on how schools and teachers make their decisions.

So far our tale is a story of global movement toward decentralization of schooling as part of a larger trend in the devolution of public services. But we do not want to paint a picture of simple convergence on one model. Indeed, one of our main messages here is how a global trend has so far produced considerable mixing of both modes of administration within systems when that was not the intention of proponents of devolution. Further, not all nations are equally decentralized, and some have even added centralized features (consider the move for a voluntary national curriculum in the United States). As shown in Table 9.1, some nations continue to be predominantly centralized or decentralized in curricular governance; 15 percent of these nations are completely or mostly decentralized and 23 percent are mostly centralized.

Our study also examines four national cases to show how the mixing of decentralized and centralized process occurred and to show that the degree to which various differences in the political and historical paths nations have taken in developing public schooling produces a variety of responses to world institutional trends, such as the push for decentralization of public services. Each illustrates a part of the overall trend that we think is occurring in the "governance revolution" in education.

United States: Administrative Exceptionalism and Extreme Localism

The federal government in the United States has little formal control over educational administration and policy. With its fifty separate state departments of education and approximately fourteen thousand semiautonomous school districts, it is one of the most localized systems in the world today. This localized administrative structure has deep cultural roots in the American experience. Localism, profound ambivalence toward a national state apparatus, and a celebration of grassroots democracy have always been the hallmarks of "American Exceptionalism" (Skowronek, 1982). Over time, this has led to a largely unplanned, but highly legitimated, public administrative system of schooling that some refer to as ultradecentralized. Across various public sectors, Americans tolerate a fairly high degree of administrative chaos and inefficiency from this system. If the French educational system exhibits reflexively centralizing tendencies, then the American system is equally reflexive in decentralizing. It is not surprising, for example, that considerable intellectual support for the general notion of deregulated, marketlike public services, and decentralization arose out of the American neo-conservative movement of the 1980s and 1990s.

The U.S. systems for health care, transportation, public health, law enforcement, and certainly education have historically been most legitimated as local services, with centralized control and authority emerging through considerable political and cultural conflict. The extreme nature of its local control has meant that reforms were often defined as an attempt to constitute more centralized authority; hence they were often championed by national forces, including both the federal government and nongovernment national groups of educational experts. For example, early in its history the American public school system underwent some centralization and homogenization at the direction of professionally led reform movements within the nation (Tyack, 1974).

Yet even in the extremely decentralized U.S. educational system, there exist centralizing and decentralizing countertrends that create a number of paradoxes in administrative reform and implementation. Over the past two decades, there have been two contrasting forces in U.S. educational reform in terms of the locus of policy generation and administrative control of the curricula and related educational topics. On the one hand are reforms aimed at centralizing national curricular goals and standards (for example, *Goals 2000*, national voluntary standards for curriculum and instruction, and the most recent accountability laws passed in the George W. Bush administration). On the other hand, there is an equally strong goal of greater local control over curricular implementation and quality of instruction with the rise of charter schools and movements toward a voucher system for private schools (Elmore and Fuhrman, 1994). Global trends toward education reform that are based on economic competition have influenced American policy makers to want to increase central (that is, national) control over curricular content as well as decentralize large, underperforming urban school districts.

It is interesting to note that currently, as in the past, international competition (often with nations having far more centralized administrations of education) has driven interest among American educators in creating more central policy. A well-known example of this is the so-called Sputnik crisis, which led to the National Defense Act in 1958, increasing federal funding and proposing more centralized policy about mathematics and science development through the National Science Foundation (Cross, 2003). Another example is how the economic downturn in the early 1980s and the United States' highly publicized mediocre international test scores mixed together to set the stage for another round of centralized curricular reforms with some decentralized components of implementation as well. Governors and several presidents took a leading role in establishing more common state and national objectives for educational change; but these objectives could only be achieved through local educational units. At the same time, neoconservative political trends within the American polity have pushed decentralized policies on local districts, some of which are internally quite centralized.

Comparatively, the United States represents a mirror image of many other nations in its response to global trends—moving from extreme decentralized authority to some more federal involvement in the operation of the classroom—yet as a case it confirms the general process of coexistence of both centralization and decentralization processes noted in other nations. The United States just approaches this from the other end. In America, a historically weak policy center is coupled with an extremely localized administration that often leads to the mixing of managerial reforms, simultaneously aiming for both more national centralization and more local control! The tension between these political cultures continues to play out to this day. A frequently heard quip about the recent political battles over national standards and tests is that "it will never happen—the American left wing hates the notion of standards, while the right wing hates the notion of national!"[3]

We turn next to the other extreme in this trend: France.

France: Cracks in the Wall of Centralized Curricular Authority

The old joke goes like this: the French minister of education can look at his watch and then tell you what page of the textbook students in all the nation's classrooms are currently reading. This satirical image of a centralized authority of schooling is amusing precisely because, in the past, educational governance in France came close to attaining that level of integration. French centralized government and its administration of public services was often seen as the complete antithesis of decentralization, yet even here there have been some telling reactions to the global movement toward an ideology of decentralization.

The socialist government in the early to middle 1980s surprised both intellectuals and civil servants alike with its attempts to implement decentralizing reforms throughout the government. The reforms had some effect, but out of all the governmental sectors education was the most resistant to change and remains the most centralized.

3. American political lore attributes this statement originally to Chester Finn, former deputy secretary of education in the 1988 Bush administration, although it is often repeated without attribution.

The organization exercising this centralized control is the Ministry of National Education, which was established officially in 1932 but has been in operation for more than one hundred years. Its size and centralized bureaucracy are legendary. In the 1980s, for example, five thousand ministry administrators in Paris oversaw more than one million employees across twenty-seven regions. As one former minister of education said in the 1970s, "The Ministry of National Education is the largest organization in Europe except for the Red Army" (Baumgartner, 1989). Modeled on late-nineteenth-century governmental central bureaucratic authority, the ministry issues regulations, conducts evaluations, and exercises supervision throughout the entire educational system. It even determines the number of hours that must be spent annually on certain areas of study in primary and high schools, producing lists of approved texts and subjects. The National Program Committee designs curricular programs for elementary and secondary schools at the national level and is composed of experts appointed by the minister. This has clear consequences, even to the point of some absurdity. For example, students from geographical regions as diverse as the Alpine and ocean coasts are all expected to be equally proficient in the physical education curricular areas of skiing and sailing (Baumgartner, 1989). The driving goal here is educational (and societal) equality through uniform access to a homogenized curriculum. In this way, the centralized authority, even though applied excessively, achieved a high degree of legitimacy.

Even though the Ministry of Education maintains a remarkably strong commitment toward centralized administration, since the 1970s France has experienced several political attempts to decentralize in order to respond to local and regional educational problems (V. A. Schmidt, 1990). Among these problems were the rise in ethnic diversity of students, as well as expansion of education and subsequent pressures on the highly restricted and selective system of higher education. Long-term conflict over support for public versus Catholic education was reinvigorated in the early 1980s. Throughout the decade several reforms were enacted that attempted to increase local control over the curriculum. The efforts to decentralize in 1982 and 1983 made use of regulations transferring educational administration and some educational responsibilities to local departments, regions, and municipalities.

Nevertheless, the political, administrative, and ideological barriers to significant decentralization remain formidable. From a massive and politically integrated set of teacher and educator labor unions to regional demands and the sheer complexity of the centralized bureaucracy, real decentralization has been slow to come to education in France (Botrel, 1996). Although more localized control of the physical plant of schools and janitorial services is being decentralized, curricular authority at the heart of the educational enterprise has seen only modest decentralizing. For example, at the local level, greater freedom to maneuver in terms of curricular content was given to the schools, particularly to the head teachers. *Collèges* and *lycées* became local public education establishments enjoying financial autonomy. They also acquired some (though hardly full) curricular autonomy as each school draws up an "institutional project" setting out how it will implement the national curricular objectives. But the reasons for minimal decentralization go beyond just the technical realpolitik of France.

The worldwide interest in decentralization meets some considerable institutional resistance in France, where a centralized government is seen as the guarantor and protector of a free and equal public education for all (Botrel, 1996). Unlike in the United States, where localism has historically been equated with homegrown democracy, much the opposite is true in France. To the degree that decentralization is seen as creating inequality in education, the culture of the French national system has some deep-seated reasons to be slow to embrace it.

The French case illustrates several important things about how managerial and administrational trends spread (or in this case barely spread). Although privatization, performance accountability, and greater responsiveness through decentralized control form a powerful message for managerial change in education, nations like France have not been greatly influenced. Two factors have slowed the organizational change sweeping over most other nations. The first is the lingering effect of historical decisions about the legal and organizational structure of public education. Entrenched political and organizational interests help such structures resist change. The second is that social norms (cultural values) affect which changes can easily gain social legitimacy and thus affect a nation's receptivity to a new trend.

The French case of minor decentralization amid a growing trend is a clear example of the action of the two factors. Historical choices created a highly centralized system, which certain groups (both administrators and teachers) wish to maintain. The structure has strong social legitimacy because it satisfies certain expectations widely held within the local culture. But at the same time, a highly developed economy and a central position in the core of nations that set standards for multilateral agencies (such as UNESCO, which is based in Paris) puts the French system under a spotlight, and the world is increasingly seeing an exception rather than the norm. Witness the struggles that the system is now having with integrating a sizable Muslim student population, and with a central ruling that no students, including female Muslims, can wear religiously motivated clothing such as headscarves (and local school officials must determine which articles of clothing this rule applies to). The French case neatly illustrates how over time a nation that was once well within the world norm in governance of education has become an exception.

Spain: Mixing Modes of Administration

Spain and the Colombia case described later are good examples of paradox involved in "centrally controlled decentralized" educational administration. The combination of large-scale political change toward more democratic processes and a world trend toward decentralization led to an administrative mix in the case of Spain. During the last period of Franco's era, under secessionist pressures and increasing demands for more stable democratic institutions, the Spanish central government started a process of decentralization that included education. After Franco's death in 1975, democracy was reestablished in Spain, and a decentralizing state was seen as a way to continue democratic development.

Unlike in France, the Spanish experienced the kind of political upheaval that can break apart entrenched interests and overcome former cultural ideological models of governmental administration. The new constitution of 1979 organized the country into seventeen autonomous communities, devolving central functions to those regional units. Each community received all governmental functions and services, including education (Hanson, 1995). Some of those regional communities, with strong cultural and linguistic traditions, questioned the central government authority claiming even wider powers in education (Boyd-Barrett, 1995). One important example of the claim was incorporation of languages other than Spanish into the curricula, as well as use of those local languages as means of instruction.

After many years of political debate about exactly how a decentralized administration would work, a school-based management system was established under which school councils comprising parents, teachers, and students would run local schools. This school council was thought to be more responsive to local needs and allow more rapid decision making. Council authority included the right to elect school principals while the Ministry of Education retained control over hiring teachers and granting degrees. The ministry also set and maintained "minimum requirements" governing the school-year schedule and curricular content, especially those courses associated with national concerns such as Spanish history, Spanish language, mathematics, and science. At the same time, the autonomous communities retained control over the amount of time during the school day allotted to pursue their own academic programs.

A process of decentralization over the curriculum was incorporated within the context of national control over a core curriculum. This coexistence of centralized and decentralized practices shows the tension between the commitment to increase the ability of communities and individual schools to modify the curriculum in light of local and individual needs while keeping unity through curricular control in a fragmented and recently democratized nation.

Colombia: Decentralization as Savior of the Nation

By the end of the 1980s Colombia suffered political, social, and economic anarchy. Drug cartels along with leftist and rightist guerrilla armies dismantled the political capacity of the government, thereby eroding its legitimacy (Fiske, 1996). The first step in reestablishing government legitimacy was a decentralization policy geared toward most government processes and services. In 1989, the Colombian Congress passed legislation, which in 1991 gained constitutional legality, giving municipalities responsibility for administration of public education, among other services. The idea was to shift power from the central government, which had exercised control since the 1970s over the political, economic, and other institutions, to the periphery. This transfer of authority was a form of devolution because the National Ministry of Education could not assume responsibilities after the transference (Hanson, 1995). Only in the case of a significant breakdown at the local county or municipal level could the ministry intervene.

The reform made a radical change in the role of the Ministry of Education, particularly in terms of curricular control. The ministry now is responsible for nationwide policy formation, planning, evaluation, and training. It retains centralized authority over curricular frameworks, but not over specific curricular content. This change was made under the supposition that decision making close to the school level will better adapt the curriculum to local settings and thus yield a greater sense of ownership, improve student and teacher motivation, and increase community participation (Hanson, 1995).

This decentralizing process culminated in 1992 in a draft by the National Planning Department and the ministries of education and finance to implement municipalization of school autonomy, private-sector participation in education, and a voucher system in education for poor students at the secondary level. This law met with considerable resistance from the national teachers' union. As a consequence, a new law was adopted two years later showing some political compromise. The terms of the compromise clearly illustrate the coexistence of centralized and decentralized structures. The responsibilities devolved to municipalities were limited; schools did not have the autonomy to select, hire, and sanction personnel. The design of the core curriculum and its assessment remained centralized to increase efficiency and quality through administrative control; however, certain adaptation is done at the local level. Finally, the Congress did not grant approval for complete municipalization of basic education or for school autonomy.

In Colombia's case, decentralization succeeded in part because it bestowed legitimacy on the government and limited the power of the teachers' union.

The Future of an Administrative Revolution

More than any other service provided by national governments, public education is a mixture of the administrative minutiae of long-term education for the whole population and the political symbolism associated with educating the nation's future. The mundane and the lofty are imbued within every aspect of schooling. All public organizations combine these qualities, but schools seem to filter them down to every part of their operation. The coolness of administration and the hotness of public politics meet at the classroom door and blow in together. Therefore changes in administrative process cannot be dismissed as just quibbling over organizational detail; they are not easily severed from political implications and grand educational objectives. The administrative form publicly symbolizes political and philosophical meanings about education and society. Education is one area of public life where it is easy to see the forces of culture interacting to create new institutional forms.

Anthropological studies suggest that considerable "creolization" of public policy takes place at the school and classroom levels (see Anderson-Levitt, 2001). Nation-states react to an environment dominated by multilateral agencies and multinational corporations. Legal and organizational history, as well as cultural values about education, can alter how countries change or the pace of change. However, in the case of smaller, more economically peripheral countries (such as Colombia), the scope and pace of change is significantly affected by multilateral agencies (the World Bank, the IMF, and others). Pressure from these agencies to adopt certain forms of educational administration, such as decentralized forms of authority, often drives national reform for economically marginalized nations. The eventual outcome of the implementation of these reforms mixes together national conditions, national history, and the position of the nation within the global system.

Many administrators and agents of multilateral agencies would prefer to characterize global change in educational administration as a march toward decentralization. The reality is that the nature and pace of adopting decentralized governance in many nations is more slouch than march. Global change in educational administration is not being driven in a single direction but is moving in different directions with continuing tension between tendencies toward centralization and decentralization. How else can one think about the creation of a centrally controlled decentralized administration? In many nations the allure of decentralized public education is as great as the expectations for its successful impact on education and society. Not only is administrative devolution seen as a road to greater technical efficiency and performance of schools; it is often expected to have quite a remarkable impact on strengthening democracy—all the same promises made four decades ago about the wonders of more centralized authority over education!

What is the future of this trend? Is the mixed model of centralized and decentralized administration of education a temporary transformation to more of the latter and less of the former? As a number of our tales in this book suggest, educational phenomena are highly susceptible to institutional forces. Slouching toward devolution in school governance is an excellent example of how open the technical core of schooling is to world ideological trends (Meyer and Scott, 1994). As our empirical study shows, there are clear organizational consequences of this process for the functioning of schools worldwide. Attempts by nations to reconcile decentralized administration and control of public education with older forms of administration illustrate what happens to various operational parts of public organizations (such as schools) when powerful institutional environments change. So one likely scenario is that this mixing of decentralized and centralized will continue for many nations well into the future.

But there is some reason to take pause before making this prediction. Unlike profit-seeking private firms, public organizations operate in a visible environment and dedicate significant effort to maintaining the form of the organization within socially acceptable boundaries for the particular sector. This is what we mean when we say that cultural forces are often most visible in the educational sector. Even partial devolution of authority means that work roles among school administrators and teachers will significantly change. Since these work roles often have elements idiosyncratic to the nation, there can be significant resistance to change. For example, in countries where the top school administrator is a "head teacher," the prospect of a more administrative work role may appear more odious than liberating or empowering.

Finally, many nations find themselves caught up in an international seesaw of global policy trends. From centralization to decentralization—but will the pendulum swing back again? Faced with a history of such change in the dictates of multilateral agencies, it is only prudent that national administrators (especially in nations with limited resources) be cautious about wholeheartedly adopting the newest educational policy line coming out of New York, Washington, or Paris. Institutional trends in education and the political interests that represent them tend to run from wealthier nations to poorer ones, not the other way around. The history of what the world thinks is a good administrative structure for national school systems is a fine example of this.

CHAPTER 10

Nation Versus Nation

THE RACE TO BE THE FIRST IN THE WORLD

THIS CHAPTER leaves the world of how schools operate and turns to the politics of how schools change across nations. Public reaction to results from international school achievement tests in many nations has heightened awareness about educational competition with other nations. For example, in the mid-1990s, after the first set of TIMSS results became public, the United States went into a kind of soul searching about its mathematics and science curricula nationwide. The release of the more recent international study on OECD nations called PISA led Germany into a national education crisis. Around the world, countries are using the results of international tests as a kind of academic Olympiad, serving as a referendum on their school system's performance. Even though these tests were never designed to assess the overall performance of an entire school system, nations and even subnational educational authorities now regularly use them for competitive assessment.

The story here is about why there is so much focus on educational problems, inventing of solutions, and implementing them across systems of schooling in nations. As with our other tales, we find a common trend among nations, one of constantly tinkering and adjusting schooling to improve achievement, social fairness, and satisfy the numerous stakeholders in formal education.

By way of illustration of the dynamics of this trend, we focus on the case of mathematics and science curricular reform policy in the United States after the first TIMSS results were released the mid-1990s, since it continues to have major implications for education policy in this nation even today. We describe how in the middle of the last decade American policy makers embraced an image of the international competitiveness of the nation's mathematics and science test scores that led to a rationale for curricular reform. We then present some of our own analyses of this image with the TIMSS data, and show how *underwhelming* the empirical case really was for these curricular reforms in the United States. Our analyses suggest that if there had been more thorough appreciation of how complicated the empirical relationship is between quality of curricula in nations and level of achievement of students, a more balanced set of reforms might have been developed from TIMSS. We then speculate on the institutional nature of educational reform cycles in nations and worldwide.

From Comparison to Competition to Reform

National school systems seem always to be in the shop for repairs, or for what educators boldly like to call "reforms." In an interesting volume on *The Impact of TIMSS on the Teaching and Learning of Mathematics and Science*, twenty-nine national experts report on the effect the release of TIMSS test scores results had on educational policy in particular nations (Robitaille, Beaton, and Plomp, 2000). One is struck by constant reference to the need for nations to improve mathematics. Each nation has its own story of how TIMSS brought a particular problem to light that needs to be fixed and is now being addressed in this way or that. Remarkably, this is as true for the top-scoring nations as it is for low-performing ones. For example, high-scoring South Korea sees a national gender difference in mathematics that it says needs fixing, and even top-scoring Singapore manages to admit that there is "room for improvement" in mathematics and science education.

Modern systems of public mass schooling appear to travel a continuous cycle of identifying problems, constructing solutions, and implementing new reforms, only then to start the process all over again. But this description is too orderly for what really takes place; instead, most of the time reform cycles are running at different speeds around various parts of the system all at the same time. There is simultaneously much problem identifying, solution seeking, and reform implementing happening throughout educational systems. International comparative data have often been the spark to set off a cycle of this kind. National educational crises start as easily as the common cold spreads—the right sneeze in public, so to speak, and the cycle begins.

Even though continuous reform is common in all national education systems, discussion about educational problems, solutions, and implementation takes on a particularly national tone and image. Educational problems are often discussed as though they are truly unique to a particular nation, needing unique solutions made chiefly from homegrown ideas, spread through a unique national process of implementation of solutions, all operating within a national polity made up of indigenous political enemies and champions of any particular educational reform.

But even a cursory look across nations defies the image of struggling with one's own unique problems and solutions. Although cycles of problem identification and reform are national in the simplest sense, their overall volume across nations is so large that it is likely a world trend. Furthermore, it looks irrational as a solely national enterprise; for example, top-performing nations in past international mathematics and science studies launch into reforms as frequently as do poor-performing nations, sometimes deciding on reforms that take high- and low-performing nations back toward each other without even recognizing it![1] As the TIMSS volume on national reaction illustrates, a national ministry is never heard publicly proclaiming that everything is just rosy in the nation's education system and there is no need to fix anything. To do so is political suicide, and politicians know it, since they believe in the centrality of the educational process as much as the rest of society.

In our times, educational reform is perpetual and self-reaffirming. There is remarkably little cynicism about the educational reform cycle in society; it is widely and strongly believed in. Given this, we wonder if there is not a larger institutional logic behind reform that would explain the continuous high volume in nation after nation.

The Policy Trap

Several years ago with colleagues we wrote a paper entitled "The Policy Trap," about how misinterpretation stemming from rushed and underdeveloped analyses of international test results trapped nations into misidentifying problems and aiming reform issues in less-than-productive directions (LeTendre and others, 2001). The American reaction to TIMSS on a policy level illustrates this interesting phenomenon.

To simplify and make a long story short, an initial set of reasonably good academic Olympiad standings for the United States in the TIMSS fourth grade sample were dashed by internationally mediocre eighth grade results reported some time after the fourth grade results. The main message for American education policy makers that emerged from the highly publicized results was that the mathematics and science curricula had to be raised to international standards if America's educational achievement level were to also rise internationally. Comparison of what American students learned from

1. Compare, for example, how Japan, after scoring high in international studies in the 1980s, took to heart interpretations of its results that suggested too much emphasis was placed on basic computational skills and then sought reforms that put more high-order thinking in the mathematics curricula, while the United States, after scoring in the middle of the pack, sought reform for more basic skills as an interpretation of how to "catch up" with Japan.

elementary grades to middle and high school scores was disheartening and widely covered in the national media. For example, Table 10.1 shows an estimate of what students from a number of nations learn from fourth to eighth grade. The United States is at the bottom of the international rankings of how much mathematics is learned by eighth grade, although the American eighth grade mean is among average-performing nations. Results of this kind, coupled with the heated-up interest in the idea that mathematics and science education even at the most elementary level leads to national economic well-being, quickly kicked off a major cycle of problem identifying,

TABLE 10.1

Estimated Increases Between
Fourth and Eighth Grades on Science and Math

Nation	Science	Nation	Math
Iran	234	Thailand	168
Thailand	220	Singapore	159
Kuwait	213	Iceland	149
Singapore	210	Japan	148
Israel	179	New Zealand	146
Hungary	175	Hong Kong	141
Portugal	165	Norway	138
Czech Republic	164	Korea	137
Slovenia	164	Czech Republic	135
Greece	161	Iran	134
Cyprus	154	Canada	133
Netherlands	150	England	130
Norway	150	Israel	128
Ireland	149	Greece	128
England	149	Hungary	127
Iceland	148	Slovenia	127
New Zealand	147	Kuwait	125
Hong Kong	142	Australia	121
Japan	140	Austria	119
Austria	138	Ireland	116
Scotland	133	Portugal	115
Latvia	130	Scotland	115
Canada	130	Cyprus	108
Australia	127	Latvia	105
US	113	Netherlands	103
Korea	105	U.S.A.	93

SOURCE: Martin and others 1997.

solution inventing, and reform implementing in the United States. What happened next is what created the education policy trap we have observed in other nations as well: celebration of a solution waiting for a problem.

For some time now in the United States, mathematics and science educators have thought that what is taught across public schools in the nation is not too demanding a curriculum, and that more rigorous and better-implemented curricular materials would improve national achievement. Dating back to the 1960s' "new math" era and even before during the Sputnik crisis, there has been a long-standing wish on the part of mathematics and science curricular specialists in the United States to get a real chance at improving, strengthening, and standardizing curricula throughout the nation. This venerable interest in reform of American mathematics and science curricula was in the mid-1990s the solution waiting for a problem to attach itself to, and the media buzz about the "slump" in the TIMSS results from fourth to eighth grades became this problem—and a politically perfect one at that.

Educational reform cycles seem to occur most rapidly in the United States when there is a pending sense of educational doom (Cross, 2003). From Sputnik through the report *Nation at Risk* to the first release of the TIMSS results decades later, nothing seems to spell doom in American education quite like internationally inadequate mathematics and science education. In fact, this is probably the case in most nations.

Policy analysts and makers quickly seized on the idea that U.S. math and science curricula were "broken" and that this was the chief cause of the nation's slump in achievement compared internationally. Major national and local mathematics and science forces, such as the National Science Foundation, the U.S. Department of Education, nongovernmental organizations of curricular expert professional associations, state Departments of Education, and some local school districts, were all ready to spring into action upon hearing about this problem. Of course, they had the solution already in mind: curricular reform.

The mobilization of the American education establishment over mathematics and science curricula reform was primed by two well-established ideas about the educational performance of the nation and its economic well-being that had been widely disseminated in the media and even in scholarly works since publication of *A Nation at Risk*, in 1983. One idea was that the level of achievement of a nation in technical fields such as mathematics and science is directly linked to the nation's economic productivity. For example, two decades of concern over failing economic competition led to the national "economic threat" from superior East Asian (Japan, South Korea) national educational achievements. The other idea was that American public mass schooling was failing the nation as a producer of technically capable future workers. Both of these ideas were powerful in terms of policy, even though research on them suggests that national economic productivity is far more complicated than a one-to-one link with the performance of the school system.

By the time the TIMSS results were released in the mid-1990s, these ideas were already driving the highly ambitious federal government's "GOALS 2000" reforms. The GOALS legislation contained little in the way of concrete plans for improving education, but it laid out a clear set of lofty (if unrealistic) ambitions. The United States was to become "first in the world" in math and science by the year 2000; this was actually a goal borrowed from the George H. Bush administration. GOALS 2000 implicitly made the nation's performance on international tests a referendum on the quality of the entire educational system and promulgated the belief that a higher ranking was indicative of greater national economic competitiveness.

Note both the rhetoric of anticipation of an educational problem waiting to be solved as well as a dramatic call to reform schooling—in a press release from a powerful NGO interested in American science production. It is illustrative of the kind of statements made throughout this period:

The American Association for the Advancement of Science (AAAS) is saddened but not surprised by the disappointing scores of U.S. high school seniors in the Third International Mathematics and Science Study (TIMSS), released today by the Department of Education.

"As a country dependent on science and technology, we must see this poor performance as a call to action," said Richard Nicholson, AAAS's executive officer. "AAAS urges every community across the nation to launch into a forthright discussion about the implications of these scores and how we can improve the current system of education in science and mathematics. It will take a concerted effort by all of us—schools, parents, industry, government, and science communities—to ensure that future results are much more encouraging."

February 24, 1997—Washington, D.C, AAAS Press Release

The politics behind this case of educational reform in the United States turned on two main assumptions. First, the American mathematics and science curricula were indeed broken and in need of reform as compared to other nations. Second, if we managed to fix our broken curricula we would improve the nation's educational competitiveness internationally.

Broken Curricula?

Influential reports, using past and current international data to evaluate the state of the American mathematics and science curricula, portray in dramatic terms an image of broken national mathematics and science curricula, including "a broken spiral," "an underachieving curriculum," "splintered," and "a mile wide and an inch deep" (McKnight, Crosswhite, and Dossey, 1987; Schmidt, McKnight, and Raizen, 1997). In the immediate post-TIMSS environment in the United States, the latter image—namely, that a pressing national educational problem is its "mile wide and an inch deep" mathematics and science curricula, was the main message. This image really took hold as being an identifiable problem easily described in media and accepted among influential stakeholders interested in American science and technology production. The American mathematics and science curricula at the eighth and twelfth grade levels in the 1990s were thought to cover too many topics in too superficial a manner to ensure effective learning among the nation's students. The solution, of course, was already known—reform the curricula—but how to get this across to the broad spectrum of policy makers in the highly localized American educational system?

Mathematics and science curricular experts, among them William Schmidt, the chief author of many influential and official American TIMSS reports, led a media campaign, often with the support of the National Science Foundation, to spread the broken mathematics and science curricula message throughout the nation. Here, for example, is how Schmidt and a colleague describe the broken curricula image in 1997: "These results [from TIMSS] point out that U.S. education in the middle grades is particularly troubled; the promise of our fourth-grade children (particularly in science) is dashed against the undemanding curriculum of the nation's middle schools" (Valverde and Schmidt, p. 60).

But were the U.S. mathematics and science curricula truly broken, as in being a mile wide and an inch deep? If they were broken and then fixed, would American achievement be likely to improve compared to other nations? To foreshadow a bit, neither of these key assumptions driving American policy about the mathematics and science curricula reform since the release of the initial TIMSS results is supported by the very data that are often attributed in identifying the problem in the first place.

Assessing National Curricula: Breadth, Depth, and Repetition

An abundance of international data on curriculum and what happens to it in the classroom from the 1980s onward has taken the curricular theorist out of the classroom and into the world of nations and politics. For example, many important past ideas about curriculum tended to be about classroom processes, such as the idea of a "hidden curriculum," or the things that get taught unintentionally during the classroom process (see Bowles and Gintis, 1976; Eckert, 1989; Goldman and McDermott, 1987). Even Bruner's influential ideas (1962) about effective spiraling curriculum were conceived in terms of a teacher who anchors her material around key concepts and then spirals upward as she goes through the year. Cross-national surveys, particularly the IEA-type data sets (like TIMSS), which have always been designed with considerable input from curricular experts, expanded the image of how the whole curricular process works in a nation beyond just the content or very micro ideas about teaching. It is taken for granted that curricula are organized at several levels in a nation, each level with its own name.

On the first level are national curricular guidelines and national textbooks representing the *intended* or *ideal* national curriculum. On the next level is the national *implemented* curriculum, which is what is actually taught in the nation's classrooms. Last, the national *achieved* curriculum is what is actually learned by a nation's students from the intended curriculum. An expanded notion of a nation's curriculum and the flow of international data increased policy makers' interest in international comparisons of achievement, as well as curricular explanations for any cross-national differences.

Most countries in the world create national curriculum guidelines and use standardized textbooks regarding what should be taught in their schools. In this respect, the United States is notable in lacking any national curricula or guidelines. Intended curricula in the United States are only partially the domain of individual states, with a large amount of the control of content residing at the district or even the school level. This administrative arrangement certainly contributes to the belief among American curricular experts that a lack of formal standardization in intended curricula, as well as localized and hence perhaps weak quality control over the implemented curricula in the nation's classrooms, is the cause of the nation's mediocre eighth grade and twelfth grade mathematics and science compared to many other nations.

But these strongly held beliefs among American educators have never really been put to an empirical test at the cross-national level. Our TIMSS analysis project colleague and educational psychologist Erling Boe, in a policy brief in 2001, describes the astonishing lack of evidence about the relationship between national characteristics and national achievement, including the intended and implemented curricula, in the official American TIMSS reports that caused such concern about the image of broken mathematics and science curricula in the first place:

It is not surprising, therefore, that a critic of TIMSS (Bracy, 2000, p. 5) could claim legitimately, four years after the first release of data, that publications issued by the U.S. Department of Education had not offered any explanations about which differences in national education systems have produced the differences in observed achievement. In fact, none of the official reports of TIMSS findings issued to date have contained a quantified bivariate relationship between any specific predictor variable and any national-level achievement score, nor has there been publication of any multivariate models of national differences in math or science achievement. This observation applies to all of the many reports issued [by] the TIMSS. [Boe and others, 2001, pp. 1–2]

Boe's observations are all the more ironic because the TIMSS study was specifically designed to examine claims like those of the broken American curricula argument. Consequently, using the TIMSS data for what they were partially intended for, we investigate the characteristics of the implemented American eighth grade mathematics curriculum to see if it is indeed "broken" in comparison to curricula in other nations. Then we refer to the Boe report's results about the relationship between national curricular characteristics and national achievement. Our example here is limited to just mathematics, but we find roughly the same empirical situation exists for the science curriculum as well.

In keeping with the metaphoric image of "mile wide and inch deep" put forth by American mathematics curricular experts, we examine the "breadth," "depth," and repetition (broken spiraling) of the curriculum implemented in American classrooms as compared to other nations.

Simply measured, breadth is the number of topics covered in a school year and depth is the time spent on each topic. The mile-wide-and-inch-deep image suggested American teachers try to cover too many topics, and it is often thought that if a teacher covers too much content this robs emphasis and detracts from achievement. Similarly, if too many topics are repeated there is no upward spiral of learning of mathematics concepts at a more advanced level.

Nations where teachers cover a lot of topics could be said to have a broad curriculum. So is it true that the United States has an extremely broad mathematics curriculum?

As shown in Table 10.2, the average American eighth grade teacher teaches between seventeen and eighteen mathematics topics during the eighth grade. Although the U.S. average is among those nations with broader curricula, one could hardly call it extremely broad. Most nations have relatively broad curricula; for example, high-scoring South Korea has an average of more than nineteen topics. There are only eight relatively "narrow streams" in the world of national mathematics curricula captured by these TIMSS nations. Overall, most nations are quite similar in the number of topics taught in eighth grade mathematics.

The second column shows an indicator of how similar or dissimilar teachers within a given country are in terms of how many mathematics topics they teach in a school year. There is some variation within many nations. For example, Greece has the least variation among teachers (.27), meaning that most teachers cover about the average of nearly twenty topics. In the United States, at .68, some teachers cover fewer topics and some

TABLE 10.2

Math Breadth for the Implemented Curriculum:
Average Number of Math Topics Taught This Year

Country	Math Breadth Mean	Coefficient of Variation for Math Breadth
Hungary	21.6	0.36
Greece	19.8	0.27
New Zealand	19.5	0.52
Korea	19.4	0.36
Australia	18	0.57
Slovenia	17.59	0.47
U.S.A.	**17.51**	**0.68**
Portugal	17.5	0.38
Canada	16.8	0.64
Spain	16.7	0.56
Lithuania	16.2	0.67
Romania	16.1	0.73
Belgium (Flemish)	15.9	0.47
Iran, Islamic Rep.	15.9	0.7
Colombia	15.6	0.61
Slovak Rep.	15.6	0.6
Hong Kong	15.5	0.54
Netherlands	15.3	0.61
Singapore	15.2	0.3
Belgium (French)	14	0.6
Switzerland	13.9	0.79
Austria	13.8	0.58
Germany	13.7	0.8
Iceland	13.6	0.7
Czech Rep.	13.2	0.72
Israel	11.1	0.58
Latvia	11	0.73
Sweden	10.4	0.85
Russian Federation	9.5	0.07
Thailand	7.18	1

NOTE: Nations in same shaded area have averages that are statistically similar.
SOURCE: TIMSS 1995.

TABLE 10.3

Math Repetition for the Implemented Curriculum:
Average Topics Taught in the Past Year and This Year

Country	Math Repetition Mean	Coefficient of Variation for Math Repetition
Singapore	14.4	0.35
Romania	10.8	0.89
Hungary	10.3	0.88
Lithuania	9.3	0.8
Slovak Rep.	8.8	0.85
Slovenia	8.4	0.84
Iran, Islamic Rep.	8.3	0.97
Spain	6.7	0.98
Austria	6.5	0.96
Portugal	6.4	0.95
Germany	6.1	1.18
Greece	6	1.11
Israel	6	0.92
Korea	5.7	1.2
Russian Federation	5.7	0.08
Czech Republic	5.5	1.14
Latvia	5.3	0.98
U.S.A.	**5.1**	**1.46**
Hong Kong	4.9	1.33
Netherlands	4.9	1.33
Australia	4.6	1.43
Colombia	4.6	1.34
Belgium (Flemish)	4.4	1.25
Canada	4.2	1.67
Switzerland	4.1	1.31
Belgium (French)	3	1.38
New Zealand	3	2.01
Iceland	2.3	2.01
Sweden	1.8	2.34
Thailand	...	...

SOURCE: TIMSS 1995.

teachers cover more topics than the national average of 17.5 in the school year. But this level of variation in the United States is neither very large in absolute terms nor the largest among these nations.

If we carry on with the analogy of the river that proved so useful in making the case for curricular reform among American policy makers, the U.S. curricular stream is no wider than most countries, but it has many channels and backwaters. U.S. students, depending on their teacher, may experience a broad or narrow range of topics. Conversely, students in nations such as Greece and Singapore receive a more uniformly broad mathematics curricula over the eighth grade year.

Much of the variation in the exposure to mathematics topics in classrooms arises from processes within nations more than processes between nations. To be precise, about 70 percent of the variation we see among these nations in terms of the breadth of the math curriculum from classroom to classroom comes from within the countries themselves, leaving only 30 percent being between the nations. Most cover a lot of topics, and in many nations the amount of topics varies some from teacher to teacher.

If the average implemented curriculum in most nations is broad, what about depth? As just one indicator of depth, we find that the average amount of instructional time given to topics did not vary greatly across these nations, and again the American implemented mathematics curriculum as a whole is not extremely shallow in its coverage. At the same time, the average American eighth grade mathematics teacher is not more prone to topic repetition than other nations' teachers are, at least not to the extent that it might create the broken spiral described in the broken curriculum literature. Actually, as Table 10.3 shows, the average U.S. teacher is less repetitious than the average teacher across the whole TIMSS sample.

So it would appear that if the implemented American eighth grade mathematics curriculum is broken, it is no more broken than in most other nations. Although there is cross-national variation on these characteristics of the curriculum, the United States is not extreme in any sense. This leads to the next question: What if nations are able to have narrower, deeper, and less repetitious mathematics intended and implemented curricula, would this mean higher national achievement?

National Curricula and National Achievement

Boe and colleagues (2001) examined this question in great detail. They looked at achievement both across the full mathematics test given by TIMSS as well as with several types of subscore that focus on several parts of mathematics achievement. They studied characteristics of the national intended curriculum using special curricular data over several grades (Schmidt, McKnight, and

Raizen, 1997; Schmidt and others, 1997), as well as other curricular data. As a supplement to the Boe report, we analyzed measures of the implemented curricula broadness, depth, and repetition described earlier (national averages and within-nation variation).

In all of these analyses, on a range of characteristics of national intended and implemented curricula in both mathematics and science virtually *no* national qualities of curricula are related to any of a range of indicators of national achievement in eighth grade. High-performing nations are not more likely to have curricula with a particular set of characteristics in terms of both intended content and implementation in the classroom. Whether it is for the full mathematics and science tests or focused subscores, or for indicators of the intended or implemented curricula, there is no pattern of association between the qualities of national curricula and national achievement. The only exception is a moderate relationship between the coverage of algebra in nations and the cross-national level of algebra achievement.

So does this mean that curriculum is not important in the schooling process? Clearly not, but given the widely held belief that the curriculum plays a primary role in driving the national achievement level, these findings may astound some. How can they be explained?

One answer might be that curriculum really isn't important in producing the national level of achievement; another might be that the TIMSS curricular data were so flawed as to be unable to show this relationship. But we find little evidence to support either interpretation. Schmidt and others (2001) find significant correlations between curricula subtopics taught and achieved *within nations* (not among countries)—suggesting, as one would expect, that if students were not taught something they tended not to get problems of that type right on the TIMSS achievement test. Also, the TIMSS data were collected under rigorous scientific standards, so we doubt they could be so flawed as to be "hiding" major relationships between national curricula and achievement. Rather, a more global view of national curricula and national achievement helps to explain these results.

Assuming that if students are not taught something they tend to know less about it than ones who are taught, what would account for this lack of across-national association between curricula and achievement? Let's consider the intended curriculum first.

A plausible answer seems to be that every country in the TIMSS intends for its students to learn roughly the same knowledge base in mathematics and science, significantly reducing cross-national variation in the intended curriculum. A convergence of curricula means that the curricular content of eighth grade mathematics and science from one nation to the next is not large. In fact, research on historical curricular trends shows precisely this; national intended curricula continue to converge on similar content over time and across nations (see, for example, Benavot and others, 1991; McEneaney and Meyer, 2000). There has come to be much greater homogeneity in terms of recognized core knowledge—content for curricula—at least through the end of primary schooling across nations. Although nations vary with regard to the emphasis they place on numerous subtopics in the intended curriculum, virtually all nations teach mathematics and science with an increasingly standard notion of the essence and components of these subjects. In the elementary years, most students worldwide are exposed to core concepts, so it is understandable that there is no association between intended curriculum and achievement across nations. Even the one set of cross-national associations there is (those between algebra curriculum and achievement) is for a relatively distinct subtopic of mathematics that nations either do or do not teach in eighth grade. This case demonstrates what would be the case with the TIMSS data if there were significant differences in what nations intended to teach.

This isomorphic-curricular argument also explains why cross-national differences in implementation of curricula are not related to cross-national differences in achievement. We suspect there is not really much difference across nations in average implementation, particularly as compared to variation within nations. As we pointed out, considerably more variation in implemented curricula occurs among classes within nations than among nations. No nation—and certainly not the United States from the perspective of the TIMSS data—appears to have a wildly broken curriculum in terms of its average implementation. Finally, purely curricular-based reasons for national differences in achievement have been questioned for some time on the grounds that a host of curricular processes show only minor differences across nations and tend not to be significantly related to achievement (see Stevenson and Baker, 1996; see Valverde and others, 2002, for an opposite argument).

Institutionalized Policy Reform

What is interesting here beyond the specifics of this case of international educational competition and curricular reform is not just that our analysis finds little evidence for characterizing American curricula as broken, or that we find almost no evidence of an association between characteristics of national curricula and national level of achievement. Instead, the whole case illustrates how relatively easy it is for modern education systems to jump on a reform cycle. During the years that this American case unfolded, few seriously questioned the veracity of the two main assumptions about the broken American curricula and their role in national achievement. The cycle was easily launched and then wrapped in the scantiest of real evidence; there was a long-standing solution waiting for a problem, and this led to reform.

Although it may be too early to assess the long-run impact of curricular reforms in mathematics and science in the United States, we suspect that the general ideas stemming from the TIMSS case will have a significant effect on American educational policy at the national, state, and local levels for some time to come. Educational reform never happens in a vacuum; there is always some connection to past reforms, and each has some imprint on future ones. We wonder what those who will look back on the Bush administration's No Child Left Behind legislation will say about its connection to the ideas stirred up by the mathematics and science curricular reform issues of the 1990s.

Was it wrong after the release of the TIMSS initial results to be concerned about the nation's curriculum, or to have wanted to improve it to match the best in the world, or to want to try moving teachers to implement curricula in a more effective way? Of course not. Along with other professional educators, we would encourage any nation to implement the best curriculum that can be designed, and to continuously monitor it and make improvements where possible.

What we have described here is not some sort of scandal; quite the opposite. It was the result of multiple good intentions of many powerful stakeholders in educational policy in the United States. Everyone involved had the best of intentions of improving the nation's schools. We doubt that even timely, in-depth analyses of curricula and national achievement showing some of the flaws and overstatements in the original assumptions, as we show here, would have deterred this exuberant outbreak of mathematics and science curricular reform in the United States. There was just too much anticipation of the solution of reform in these areas for too long a time. What is most likely the cost of this laserlike focus on curricular reform was a chance to discuss a number of other educational problems in the United States that are identifiable with the TIMSS data—the resource inequality and disadvantaged students discussed in Chapter 5 being notable.

The American case is just one of many that illustrate a similar process about educational reform. We began this chapter with the image of a reform-crazed educational world, which often uses studies like TIMSS to adopt solutions and new approaches to prevailing concerns about a nation's schools in general. So how can we make sense of this from a more global perspective? We have already suggested that it is not just a process by which education is considered useful and everyone wants the best they can find. If this were so, it would be hard to explain why even top-performing nations are about equally prone to cycles of reform as are nations with poorer performance.

There are two productive ways to think about an educational world dripping with the political motivation for finding problems, creating solutions, and enacting reforms. One is about how education is a sector made up of many formal organizations constantly mixing with the realpolitik of social policy within a nation. The second is on a deeper institutional level, about what education has come to represent in society.

EDUCATIONAL REFORM AS AN ORGANIZATIONAL PRODUCT

As an institution, mass schooling in every nation is made up of a dense population of formal organizations of stakeholders in contrast to, say, the institution of the family, which comprises informal organizations. Schools, local education units, ministries of education, NGOs of professional educators, teachers' unions, and so forth are cast into a thick web of formal organizations, all of which have an interest and some influence in producing educational policy. As such, the institutional ideas behind education shape organizational behavior as much as they do the behavior of individuals participating in these organizations (Meyer and Jepperson, 2000). But how organizations behave is somewhat different from how individuals do, and this difference plays a role in producing the high volume of educational reform.

A relatively new and important school of thought about the interaction between formal organizations and the characteristics of the institutional sector they are in suggests some useful ways to think about constant worldwide educational reform. Observers of formal organizations from a neoinstitutional perspective (Richard Scott, John Meyer, Brian Rowan, and others) show us how constrained and even ritualistic organizations can be by the institutionalized world of common meaning and appropriate actions that they function in (Powell and DiMaggio, 1991).

As an organization, a school behaves more as the people within it think a school should behave than it does according to some unique rationalized plan of action. This is also true for governmental agencies, unions, and NGOs of all types within the educational sector. Certainly, formal organizations are bureaucracies and there are considerable rationalized processes within them, but formal organizations also conform to institutional ideas as to what they should be rational about and even how to be rational.

Taking this idea a step further, a fellow theoretical traveler of this viewpoint and organizational theorist, James March, finds that organizational processes such as problem identification, solution finding, and implementing are themselves ritualized to a degree. He convincingly argues that in real organizations, particularly large ones, each of these activities runs in a separate stream within the organization and generally does not occur in the order one would assume. Hence organizational solutions wait for the right problems, methods of implementation wait for the right solution to spread, and so forth (March and Olsen, 1979). One needs only to ask an astute older colleague in a large organization about the history of computerization and its effect on the organization's integrating this technology to hear stories of solutions waiting for and trying to find problems, or technology waiting for applications, or implementation strategies looking for solutions to distribute, and so forth.

An insightful way to think about the American TIMSS case, as well as similar reform activity in other nations, is not to attribute the reform cycle to the actions of just one or even a few organizations (a ministry, or a union, or even the statistical branch of a ministry that helps produce studies like TIMSS). Instead, attribute the actions to a web of numerous organizations, all of which in one way or another take part in the production of problems, solutions, and implementation strategies.

As we have described, a legacy of reaction to past international studies and the image of a problematic American mathematics curriculum led expert groups of mathematics educators, federal mathematics and science policy makers, and so forth to be receptive to a curricular interpretation of the United States's placing in the academic Olympiad of TIMSS even though this interpretation is not well supported by other parts of the TIMSS data set. In the mid-1990s, use of the TIMSS international scores was really just the spark, much as Sputnik and *Nation at Risk* functioned for earlier reform cycles. The web of organizations was loaded like a compressed spring aimed at a reform cycle; American performance on international tests (which in study after study is usually in the midrange, and rarely extremely bad) released this reform energy.

The point is that institutions like education, comprising to a high degree webs of formal organizations all producing streams of problems, solutions, and implementation, are capable of generating intense motivation for collective rationalized action aimed at a specific target. For example, American organizations such as the AAAS or the NSF, made up of high-profile experts and given the public charter to monitor and recommend ways to improve American technology and science, can generate collective motivation to look for solutions, find problems, and rally around implementation of reforms. Never do we see such an organization in the United States make a public statement that all is fine with its charge.

Certainly nations differ in the exact nature in which educational policy is made and reform is started. Nations with stronger centralized political parties organize approaches to reform differently from the American system of education with its highly disconnected, localized governance system. Such political-structure variation across nations probably has some relationship to the frequency of reform cycles across them. For example, the United States, with its very high ratio of educational organizations (other than schools) to students, yields a nation often primed for reform (Tyack and Cuban, 1995). Some other nations may have slightly less frequent rounds of reform, but overall the process we describe leads to considerable reform activities worldwide. Last of all, there is evidence to suggest that, as with the case here, use of external information from other nations is more frequent when policy debates are about highly contested issues (Steiner-Khamsi, 2002; Schriewer, 1990).

REFORM AS AN INSTITUTIONAL VALUE

The image of reform as an institutionalized value helps us think about educational policy reform as a worldwide experience that stems directly from the institutional character of mass schooling. So far in this book, we have discussed the power of education in modern society as an institution, how central it has become to so many important things about the future of our children and our nations. We have shown how as an institution it surpassed even the vital role of the family in many aspects of childrearing and the passing down of advantage to future generations. For better or worse, mass schooling is among a relatively small number of central institutions in modern society, and our tales so far have documented some of the things that are happening worldwide in this powerful institution. Yet when we try to explain the world trend of educational reform, we encounter a paradox.

As sociologists have long pointed out, when institutions reach their height of power and influence on human behavior they organize meanings and norms that are highly resistant to change. However, constant educational reform seems to move in the opposite direction. The powerful institution of mass schooling appears entirely open to change.

One way out of this paradox is to suggest that reform really doesn't change much; what occurs is merely surface change, while the main values of the institution remain stable underneath. Certainly there is some truth in this image, and we don't want to equate all reform with major institutional change. Yet as various histories of educational reform in the United States have shown, reform often does lead to profound institutional change (Tyack and Cuban, 1995). Reform is not necessarily always trivial or faddish.

Perhaps a better way out of the paradox is to consider how the tendency for continuous reform cycles is built into the institutional fabric of education. Institutional theorist Meyer has thought the most about this aspect of mass schooling. In a provocative chapter (in a book celebrating the academic career of David Tyack) titled "Reflections on Education as Transcendence," he discusses how the institutional origins of mass schooling are strikingly religious in form (Meyer, 2000). This no doubt sounds like a strange thing to say about public schooling, which usually meticulously separates out religious beliefs from public instruction. But Meyer is not referring to the teaching of religion; rather, he refers to the idea that in its institutional form mass education takes on religiouslike power in modern society. He points out that schooling's mission to transmit major knowledge about how the world works and its ability to transform students into "educated adults" in a universalistic fashion (see Chapter 2 on gender, for example) gives the institution transcendental qualities. It is not that public mass schooling is about religion; instead, it has powerful institutional components that make it like a religion in modern society.

Reform gets built into core values about education in modern society. The word *reform* itself, of course, derives from the idea of reforming the universal Catholic Church. Not radical restructuring but constant reform gives the institution a certain dynamic power. It is not static; it is open to some change, to the flexible exercising of basic institutional ideas in developing a better school system. This quality of schooling is what drives so much reform.

Its power as an institution is in large part derived from the belief held by many in modern society that schooling is a key component in producing the good society. Technically, morally, and civically, education is called upon to provide the masses with the right stuff to form a productive, just, and orderly world. When social problems arise, the call for an educational solution is not far behind. A powerful modern ideology is that society itself is a project, and one of the fundamental parts of the project is to use education to achieve society. Seen this way, it is no wonder that reform to improve the basic ideas, goals, and operation of mass schooling is nearly continuous and publically welcomed—exactly as it appears to be across so many nations.

THESE TALES COVER a set of phenomena about the schooling and learning of mathematics and science in many nations. They are not, nor are they meant to be, a comprehensive set of trends about all aspects of schooling. As we described in the beginning chapter, there are three subplots running through all of them to varying degrees that nevertheless make them part of the picture of what is happening in mass public education.

The subplots revolve around three main ideas: (1) over its relatively short history mass schooling has become an exceedingly successful institution worldwide; (2) it has generated a world culture of education shaping similar values, norms, and even operating procedures in schools across all kinds of quite contrasting nations; and (3) most educational change right now is a result of deepening of existing institutional qualities more than the effect of outside forces. We have tried to point out how these ideas filter down and shape the daily actions and beliefs of students, parents, teachers, administrators, and national leaders of education, who all take part in this massive human activity we call schooling. Additionally, some of the tales have led us to play with notions about why sometimes a nation will fully incorporate a part of the world educational culture, while at other times it will react idiosyncratically to a world norm, or even resist it. All of these thoughts not only helped us understand the many findings from our empirical studies and write these interpretive essays; we used them extensively in planning the analyses of the TIMSS data from the very beginning of our project.

We don't want to give the impression that these ideas were all worked out and that the analyses just fell into place behind them. Rather, these thoughts were part of a general institutional perspective that helped us develop hunches and hypotheses that were tested with the data. As we have described in a number of the chapters, the findings often surprised us in ways that led us to expand and alter our original thoughts about how things work institutionally.

Over the past three decades, most of the scholarship on understanding how schooling develops as an institution has been about the historical spread of mass schooling as a distinctly new way to organize education. Therefore it documents the spread of schools for all children; growth in enrollment rates; development of similar curricula across time and place; and the values, norms, laws, and shared meanings driving this world educational project in diverse nations over the course of the last century. This research leaves an astonishing historical and cross-national record of the use of an increasingly similar organizational form of schooling throughout the world. As with the business firm, the military, and the social welfare system, nations adopted mass schooling in a remarkably similar organizational form. Even so, it is too simplistic to say that schooling operates in the same way in all nations; this is just not true. The image we prefer is one of a world culture presenting the rules of the game, but within these basic rules how the game is played in each nation can become quite elaborated. Both the potency of its rules and the complicated ways they get worked out in different places attests to how dynamic schooling can be as an institution.

Our tales take off from this point and bring an institutional perspective to the complex and messy world of how schools operate, students learn, teachers teach, administrators administer, and stakeholders take interest in education across many nations. From an institutional perspective, "complex and messy" means less than fully agreed upon. The basic organization of mass schooling and the assumptions behind it are similar worldwide, but how this gets worked out in practice in nations is far from uniform. For example, a culture of cognitive achievement, where mathematics and science are among a few valued subjects, a culture of schooling aimed at universalism and social justice along with cognitive performance, and even the operational relationship between schools and the national government are all complex processes well beyond the basic organizational structure of mass schooling. Therefore throughout our tales we dealt with both similarities and differences across nations and tried to make sense of the pattern of both. So it is not surprising that our tales are a bit messy too. They do not neatly sum up the idea of one monolithic form of schooling, teaching, and learning in operation everywhere; instead they add up to a fair amount of evidence of a strong current of world culture pulling many aspects of schooling, teaching, and learning in the same direction everywhere.

The data from the TIMSS study are extremely useful in this regard; among them one finds a wealth of both cross-national similarities and interesting national differences. The data enabled us to enter into an ongoing and fertile dialogue among educational researchers, sociologists, and anthropologists about cross-national similarities and differences, and what each means for a comparative perspective on schooling. On one side are many informative studies describing how and why the organization of schooling becomes more homogeneous over time everywhere—what we might call the isomorphic argument (Baker, 1999; Benavot and others, 1991; Fuller and Rubinson, 1992; Boli, Ramirez, and Meyer, 1985; Ramirez and Boli, 1987; and Thomas, Ramirez, Boli, and Meyer, 1987). On the other side of the debate are equally useful studies documenting distinct or blended differences in the operation of schools and even norms about schooling and instruction from nation to nation, or what we might call the creolization argument (recalling the discussion in Chapter 9; elsewhere see, for example, Anderson-Levitt, 2001; LeTendre and others, 2001; Mills and Blossfeld, 2003; Stevenson and Stigler, 1992). Looking at our tales of schooling, we see no immediate end to the debate, and we welcome fruitful continuation of it. It would be fair to say that in telling these tales we have leaned harder on an isomorphic argument than on creolization. But obviously both have merit, and they end up not being so much stark opposites as they are complementary viewpoints.

This final chapter does two more things. First, we comment on what our tales mean for understanding what causes some nations to produce higher mathematics and science scores than others. We also speculate on what our tales hold for the future of mass schooling and the teaching and learning of mathematics and science.

Why Nations Perform as They Do

We are often asked what all of our analyses say about why nations perform as they do, and what nations can do to improve their academic competitiveness in the future. Frequently the question gets asked specifically as "What is *it* that matters cross-nationally?" The *it* in the question is telling as it calls attention to how people think about cross-national achievement differences in mathematics and science—namely that cross-national differences result from some single, powerful factor. In all of the analyses of international data on school achievement we have done, and in all that we have read about others' analyses, it is safe to say that no one has found *the* one factor that makes some nations perform higher than others. We strongly suspect that no such master factor exists. Rather, the picture is one of a combination of factors, none of which is overly powerful, that add up to some degree of national advantage in students' learning mathematics and science.

We say "some degree" of national advantage because it is important to keep in mind that, like many social phenomena produced chiefly by individuals, students' mastery of mathematics and science differs the most from student to student, followed by a lower level of difference from school to school, and on to the least difference from nation to nation. What one eighth grader knows about mathematics compared to another can vary quite a bit, but what the average student in one nation knows compared to the average student in another nation differs far less. Given what we have described in our tales, this makes intuitive sense as well; here is a dramatic consequence of a powerful world culture of schooling. None of the nations participating in TIMSS operates some radically different schooling process. Whatever educational innovation there is at the national level, it is carried out safely within the same basic operation of schooling found in other nations. This means that not only should one not expect to find a single master national factor; one should also realize that cross-national differences in achievement likely stem from moderate national influences on the distribution of achievement, not from some nationally unique and highly powerful determinant of individual achievement.

Given the context we have just described, our answer to the question of why nations perform as they do comes in two parts. First, a number of national factors that people in the past have thought caused achievement differences do not. The trail of the search for what matters nationally is littered with ideas that did not pan out. School uniforms, classroom diversity in student background, religious-cultural background, and so forth are not associated with cross-national achievement. Our tales here add to the list. For example, as we described in Chapters 4 and 9, how centralized or decentralized the governance of schooling is in a nation has no association with the national achievement level. The same is probably true for use of national high-stakes tests, heavy reliance on shadow education in a country, and national norms about assigning homework. As we described in Chapter 10, we doubt that some national factor in the intended or implemented mathematics and science curricula in nations causes cross-national differences in achievement. Again, we should emphasize that this is not to say that many of these factors are not important in the schooling process of individuals; they clearly can be. But as factors that make nations produce differing levels of achievement, these things do not associate with the national level of achievement. Much of the reason for this is that nations do not differ greatly from one another in the basics of the schooling process of mathematics and science. Or if they do differ, say in the use of shadow education, no one has found a particularly potent national factor that causes national differences in achievement.

Second, there are, however, two national factors that have a consistent (albeit not too powerful) association with achievement. First, wealthier nations outscore poorer ones in mathematics and science, but not always because the effect is modest. Second, substantial inequality in the distribution of educational resources across schools can limit a nation's overall production of achievement. Both lead to some interesting speculation about what nations do educationally to influence patterns of achievement among their students.

Students in wealthier nations *on average* have richer learning environments both at school and at home. Higher national wealth tends to mean better-funded schools, higher-paid teachers, and higher average educational attainment of parents. We don't want to overstate the importance of resource differences across nations because, as we described in Chapter 3, the impact is probably declining over time with the general drive for school quality in many nations. Nevertheless, through various mechanisms national resources influence national achievement.

As we described in Chapter 5, negative things can happen in a national school system that in one way or another produces persistent inequality in terms of access to school quality. Low achievement among socially disadvantaged students and a greater rate of student violence in school are two trends related to inequality described here, but there are certainly many others. For a nation to stay internationally competitive, it must not only worry about the average student and school (or the best students and schools) but also focus ever more on the weakest sections of its system.

So what does this mean for giving advice to nations in terms of improving mathematics and science achievement? The first message is that there is no easy fix. There is no single crucial practice employed among the highest-performing nations that can simply be imported to improve a nation's achievement output. The whole schooling process needs to be made the best that a nation can afford. The second message, interestingly enough, is in terms of the in-school activities a nation needs if it is to keep up with the pack, so to speak. Undoubtedly each nation has its own idiosyncratic features in the school system that stand in the way of moving along with the rest of the world educationally. Whether it is extreme local funding in the case of the United States, adherence to traditional educational streaming in Germany, heavy examination pressures in South Korea, or skimming the most talented students into private schooling in Chile, all nations have educational processes that result in being out of sync institutionally with the rest of the world in some aspect of schooling. As we saw in Chapter 10 on the United States and curricular solutions, educational reform runs wild in nations today. Much of it is aimed at changing things that are at some odds with central institutional values about mass schooling circulating around the world at any point in time. To the degree that a nation can bring real change in its more negative idiosyncratic features, this will help it compete internationally.

But at the same time, educational competition is more a game of staying in the pack than striving to be a leader. Striving to outcompete other nations in one particular aspect of schooling may actually be a source of problems for a country in the future. Our thoughts in Chapter 8 about homework and its heavy use in the United States raise concerns about what advantage we as a nation receive for waves of recommendations to assign more homework. Excessive emphasis by nations on academic competition, particularly in just a few academic areas, or emphasis on building a national student elite, or excessive recommendation of widespread use of just one teaching practice can undermine many of the positive effects of mass education. Considerable public funds spent on narrow reforms that might boost national achievement scores in one subject by only a few points at one time can come at the cost of not improving other school factors that may in the long run hurt a nation's competitiveness. Nations would be better served by reforms that improve access to quality education for all students, including access to rigorous teaching, best curricula, and similar resources.

Future of Mass Schooling

As the trends have led us to do throughout the book, we take a particularly bullish perspective on the future of mass education in general. Bullish in the sense that the institution, in a relatively short time, has become so dominant in most places in the world that we see little to suggest that it will not continue to be so into the near future. It is a future where a deepening of existing institutional values about education will generate some dynamic institutional change from within the education sector itself, but most likely not as much from without. What, then, do our tales about cross-national trends in schooling of mathematics and science suggest for the future of the institution some forty or fifty years hence?

To start with, it is highly likely that national governments will continue to pour vast amounts of public funds into education; barring some worldwide economic or military crisis, the relative proportion of public funds used for education will increase. The belief in extensive technical and social benefits of education for all people is too embedded within nations to forecast any real decline, and since the pattern worldwide continues to be steady linear growth, we predict sustained growth in funding. In modern society, governments seem never to turn away from better (and more) schooling as a solution to all sorts of social problems and as a proposed way to realize collective dreams of national progress. The defining of social problems as something that education can solve in turn stimulates even more reliance on education to achieve the good society.

Expanding resources will lead to greater efforts to make educational opportunity as universal and even across populations as possible, as described in Chapter 3 in discussing the changing dynamics between families and schools. The effects of a widespread revolution in school quality will most likely continue as national governments commit more resources to education. There are always political interests pulling in the opposite direction, but the trend so far has been for mass schooling to expand universality both technically and socially. The fascinating story of declining achievement differences between boys and girls in mathematics attests to the power of expanding educational universalism and the effect it can have on student motivation to master important academic subjects.

Similarly, resources for quality instruction among nations' poorest schools will continue to inch up, resulting in even smaller differences among schools. As a result, it is obviously a safe bet to predict that a Coleman pattern of larger family effects than school effects on achievement will spread throughout the world over time (it may already have done so), and differences among families will continue to contribute to achievement differences among students. But as we presented in Chapter 3, an alternative speculation is that differences among families could also decrease. Schooling will continue to take the lead in the symbiotic relationship between the family and the school as institutions, but it is a highly dynamic relationship and will certainly continue to be a point of innovation.

Although it is not specifically part of any of the trends, a significant portion of increased public resources will be used for expansion of mass schooling in several other predicable ways, given how the institution has expanded over the past hundred years. First, schooling will expand downward, incorporating even younger children than it does now. Currently, public preschooling (pre-K) is a reality in only a few nations, but we see no clear organizational or institutional barriers stopping a worldwide spread. The logic of sending young children to school, including teaching them academic curricula about reading and mathematics and even science, is already a formable institutional idea within mass schooling. In the past, every time educators assumed that some young age limit had been reached, the institution pushed it down even further. One can also see substantial evidence of continued educational expansion up the age ladder as well.

Governments will not be the only ones spending more money on education in the future. In modern society, education is a good that people can't seem to get enough of. Families of the future will likely spend more resources and time on education for their children, particularly resources aimed at enhancing the child's cognitive achievement as much as possible. Continued inequality in education will be generated by differences in families' resources, access to political power, and knowledge. As discussed in Chapters 3 and 5, it is not clear if the offsetting trend to produce greater uniformity in quality across schools can ever fully counter high motivation for families to enhance achievement generated by the singular advantage of academic credentials that schooling as an institution has created and maintained.

One can easily predict that the culture of cognitive achievement in schools and the motivation it generates for families to assist in it will foster the continued growth of related professionals who sell services to families to assess problems and recommend paths to greater learning potential, including even the growing use of pharmacological aids for children to "behave better" in school and hence learn more of what is intended. In the next twenty years, these trends, which are prominent among upper-middle-class families in some nations, could easily spread across nations and families. Similarly, the expansion of education and the pressure of families to seek advantage for their children can continue to create elite pathways to better education that governments will have to deal with.

Shadow education will play a key future role in the changes in schooling. As discussed in Chapter 4, as shadow education expands in many nations it could have a number of influences on what happens in schools. Similarly within families: many, maybe even most, students everywhere in the future will routinely use some form of shadow education. Although South Korea may not be the exact future of all nations, it is likely that systems of shadow education will continue to expand in all nations. Many future students will likely be using a range of services augmenting formal schooling. Also, in some systems shadow education may expand to the point that students do not do much traditional homework from school.

Nations will need to walk a careful line between increasing educational access and providing equal education in the face of intense pressure from families to control their children's educational trajectory. As nations strive to be more competitive, they run the risk—as in Japan and Korea—of alienating large numbers of children, creating the phenomenon of "school refusal." Once schools become too dominated by academics, and so too competitive, many children may simply opt out of schooling, creating significant problems. Also, if nations continue to differentiate (as do the German and Japanese systems) within the elementary and secondary systems, they will run the risk of further accentuating formation of exclusive pathways to elite tertiary education. The resulting differences in academic achievement will generate more school violence or school apathy, again creating a drain on the system. Finally, all nations will face challenges to equality on the basis of differences in regional economic development within nations. This may occur on a large scale, as when a city or a region undergoes economic decline and the schools suffer. But it may happen on a small scale across a nation, as when a local elite dominates certain schools, maximizing public and private funds to increase school quality.

Student violence and aggression in school will continue to be persistent problems for nations in the future. If we extend out our findings literally, a world with greater resources put into education and the tendency to slowly do away with gross resource inequality across schools should lower the rate of everyday violence in many nations. Those nations that can marshal the political will to achieve these goals will reap the benefits of a lower rate of school violence and probably come to exert pressure for change on other nations wishing to emulate their success. However, some nations will not be able to challenge effectively entrenched systems of differentiation, or they will lack the political will to truly distribute resources evenly. These systems will continue to be bogged down in reforms aimed at eliminating school violence. Some countries, or regions in countries, could even run the risk of having the basic process of schooling undermined by chronic violence. To address these problems nations will require more than just changes in educational policy. Nations will have to coordinate economic stimulus efforts, social service packages, and educational support to address serious inequalities within the national system.

If current trends persistent, what happens in a classroom in Seoul, Paris, Santiago, Cleveland, or Tunis will be remarkably similar, most likely even more so than now. In the near future, curricular content for standard subjects such as mathematics and science, for example, will hardly vary at all cross-nationally. The globalization of curricula and its implementation in classrooms will exert a soft but steady pull on nations toward a world norm, to the point where little variation in curricula exists across nations. What differences remain will be mostly across schools within nations for intentional reasons and some idiosyncratic variation introduced by teachers.

As we have seen, in nations with dissimilar histories and cultural backgrounds teachers working in schools come to think about their job in similar ways. Certainly, specific conditions of the job will be determined locally, but the understanding of the role of teacher and what that means for how a teacher approaches his or her job shows remarkable similarity across nations, and this will only continue into the future. The definition of teaching may shift, with new ideas or even greater institutionalization of current ones, but the point is that we are rapidly heading toward a worldwide faculty moving more or less in the same direction.

Schooling in the future will increase in administrative complexity. As schooling takes on ever more importance in the lives of families and the plans of politicians, demands for better and more accountable schooling will grow overall. Administrators will not only have to manage more programs; they will have to maintain a higher degree of accountability. We have already seen evidence of a high degree of nominal decentralization at the school level in many nations. A reasonable prediction to make is that as an institution schooling will continue to become even more central and standard in beliefs and practices throughout the world, and as a result a certain amount of administrative decentralization will go along with it. In other words, the paradox we point out in Chapter 9 of centralized decentralization will likely become even more embedded within most national systems, and hence make them much more complicated to administer.

Last, the transcendental nature of schooling in modern society means that school reform will continue unabated into the future in most nations. As schooling takes on more meaning for people, both for individuals and for society in general, the religionlike nature of its powers links it to all types of highly valued qualities in modern society (Meyer, 1977, 2000; Pallas, 2000). Schooling becomes synonymous with the project of forming the good society that gives modern nations a sense of meaning. This is not say that we have some Pollyanna view of the power of schools to do all good all the time; clearly that does not happen, but the fact that so many in society have such ideas about modern mass schooling imbues it with special power. This creates the interesting paradox about schooling as an institution that we have played with throughout this book: namely, that into the future its social power will continue to sustain the kinds of trends we see here, as well as furnish the logic for educational change.

Bibliography

Akiba, M., LeTendre, G., Baker, D., and Goesling, B. "Student Victimization: National and School System Effects on School Violence in 37 Nations." *American Educational Research Journal*, 2002, *39* (4), 829–54.

Anderson, L., Ryan, D., and Shapiro, B. *The IEA Classroom Environment Study*. New York: Pergamon, 1989.

Anderson-Levitt, K. *Teaching Culture*. Cresskill, N.J.: Hampton Press, 2001.

Ariès, P., and Béjin, A. *Western Sexuality: Practice and Precept in Past and Present Times*. New York: Blackwell, 1985.

Astiz, F., Wiseman, A., and Baker, D. "Slouching Toward Decentralization: Consequences of Globalization for Curricular Control in National Education Systems." *Comparative Education Review*, 2002, 46, 66–88.

Aurini, J., and Davies, S. "The Transformation of Private Tutoring: Education in a Franchise Form." *Canadian Journal of Sociology*, 2004, *29*(3).

Baker, D. "Schooling All the Masses: Reconsidering the Origins of American Schooling in the Postbellum Era." *Sociology of Education*, 1999, *72*(4), 197–215.

____. "Should We Be More Like Them? American High School Achievement in Cross-National Comparison." *Brookings Papers on Education Policy*. Washington, D.C.: Brookings Institution, 2002.

Baker, D. P., Akiba, M., LeTendre, M. G., and Wiseman, A. "Worldwide Shadow Education: Outside-School Learning, Institutional Quality of Schooling, and Cross-National Mathematics Achievement." *Educational Evaluation and Policy Analysis*, 2001, *23* (1), 1–17.

Baker, D., Goesling, B., and LeTendre, G. "Socio-Economic Status, School Quality, and National Economic Development: A Cross-National Analysis of the 'Heyneman-Loxley Effect' on Mathematics and Science Achievement." *Comparative Education Review*, 2002, *46* (3), 291–312.

Baker, D., and Holsinger, D. "Human Capital Formation and School Expansion in Asia." *International Journal of Comparative Sociology*, 1996, *37* (1–2), 159–73.

Baker, D., and Jones, D. "Creating Gender Equality: Cross-National Gender Stratification and Mathematical Performance." *Sociology of Education*, 1992, *66*, 91–103.

Baker, D., and LeTendre, G. "Comparative Sociology of Classroom Processes, School Organizations and Achievement." In M. Hallinan (ed.), *Handbook of Sociology of Education*. New York: Plenum, 1999.

Baker, D., LeTendre, G., and Goesling, B. "Educational Resource Inequalities Among American Schools and Cross-National Differences." Working paper, Education Policy Studies Department, Pennsylvania State University, 2002.

Baker, D., Riegle-Crumb, C., Wiseman, A., LeTendre, G., and Ramirez, F. "Shifting Gender Effects: Opportunity Structures, Mass Education, and Cross-National Achievement in Mathematics." Under review.

Baumgartner, F. *Conflict and Rhetoric in French Policymaking.* Pittsburgh: University of Pittsburgh Press, 1989.

Benavot, A., Cha, Y., Kamens, D., Meyer, J., and Wong, S. "Knowledge for the Masses: World Models and National Curricula, 1920–1986." *American Sociological Review*, 1991, 56, 85–100.

Benbow, C., and Stanley, J. "Sex Differences in Mathematical Ability: Fact or Artifact?" *Science*, 1980, 210, 1262–1264.

Benjamin, G. *A Year in a Japanese School Through the Eyes of an American Anthropologist and Her Children.* New York: New York University Press, 1997.

Bennett, W. "Implications for American Education." *NASSP Bulletin*, 1987, 71, 102–108.

Berger, P., Berger, B., and Kellner, J. *The Homeless Mind.* New York: Random House, 1974.

Berkovitch, N. *From Motherhood to Citizenship: Women's Rights and International Organizations.* Baltimore, Md.: Johns Hopkins University Press, 1999.

Bishop, J. "Do Curriculum-Based External Exit Exam Systems Enhance Student Achievement?" *CPRE Research Report Series RR-40.* Philadelphia: Consortium for Policy Research in Education, Graduate School of Education, University of Pennsylvania, 1998.

Blair, C., Gamson, D., Thorne, S., and Baker, D. "Rising Mean IQ: Cognitive Demand of Mathematics Education for Young Children, Population Exposure to Formal Schooling, and the Neurobiology of the Prefrontal Cortex." *Intelligence*, 2005, 33 (1), 93–106.

Boe, E., Barkanic, G., Shin, S., May, H., Leow, C., Singleton, C., Zeng, G., and Borouch, R. *Correlates of National Differences in Mathematics and Science Achievement: Evidence from TIMSS.* (Data Analysis Report 2001-DAR1.) Philadelphia: Center for Research and Evaluation in Social Policy, University of Pennsylvania, 2001.

Boli, J., Ramirez, F., and Meyer, J. "Explaining the Origins and Expansion of Mass Education." *Comparative Education Review*, 1985, 29, 145–170.

Boli, J., and Thomas, G. *Constructing World Culture: International Nongovernmental Organizations Since 1875.* Stanford, Calif.: Stanford University Press, 1999.

Botrel, J. "Decentralización y Desconcentración en el Sistema Educativo Francés." *Novedades Educativas*, 1996, 68, 52–65.

Bourdieu, P. *Cultural Reproduction and Social Reproduction: Knowledge, Education, and Cultural Change.* London: R. Brown Tavistock, 1973.

Bowles, S., and Gintis, H. *Schooling in Capitalist America.* New York: Basic Books, 1976.

Boyd-Barrett, O. *Structural Change and Curriculum Reform in Democratic Spain. Educational Reform in Democratic Spain.* New York: Routledge, 1995.

Bracy, G. "The TIMSS 'Final Year' Study and Report: A Critique." *Educational Researcher*, 2000, *29*, 4–10.

Bradburn, N., Haertel, E., Schwille, J., and Torney-Purta, J. "A Rejoinder to 'I Never Promised You First Place.'" *Phi Delta Kappa*, June 1991, pp. 774–77.

Bray, M. *The Shadow Education System: Private Tutoring and Its Implications for Planners.* Paris: International Institute for Educational Planning, UNESCO, 1999.

Bray, M., and Kwok, P. "Demand for Private Supplementary Tutoring: Conceptual Considerations and Socio-Economic Patterns in Hong Kong." *Economics of Education Review*, 2003, *22*, 611–20.

Bruner, J. *On Knowing: Essays for the Left Hand.* New York: Atheneum, 1962.

Buchmann, C., and Hannum, E. "Education and Stratification in Developing Countries: Review of Theories and Research." *Annual Review of Sociology*, 2001, *27*, 77–102.

Burlamaqui, L., Castro, A., and Chang, H.-J. (eds.). *Institutions and the Role of the State: New Horizons in Institutional and Evolutionary Economics.* Northampton, England: Edward Elgar, 2000.

Campbell, J., Hombo, C., and Mazzeo, J. *NAEP 1990 Trends in Academic Progress: Three Decades of Student Performance.* Washington, D.C.: National Center for Education Statistics, U.S. Department of Education, 2000.

Carnoy, M., and Rhoten, D. (eds.). "Special Issue on Globalization and Education." *Comparative Educational Review*, 2002, *46*, 154–55.

Ceci, S. "How Much Does Schooling Influence General Intelligence and Its Cognitive Components? A Reassessment of the Evidence." *Developmental Psychology*, 1991, *27* (5), 703–22.

Chabbott, C. *Constructing Education for Development: International Organizations and Education for All.* New York: Routledge Falmer, 2003.

Charles, M., and Bradley, K. "Equal But Separate? A Cross-National Study of Sex Segregation in Higher Education." *American Sociological Review*, 2002, *67*, 573–99.

Cohen, A. *Delinquent Boys.* New York: Free Press, 1955.

Coleman, J. Ernest, Q., Campbell, C., Hobson, J., McPartland, J., Mood, A., Weinfall, F., and York, R. *Equality of Educational Opportunity.* Washington, D.C.: Government Printing Office, 1966.

Collins, R. *The Credential Society: An Historical Sociology of Education and Stratification.* New York: Academic Press, 1979.

Conley, D. 2004. *The Pecking Order: Which Siblings Succeed and Why.* New York: Random House/Pantheon, 2004.

Cooper, H. *Homework.* White Plains, N.Y.: Longman, 1989.

Corno, L. "Homework Is a Complicated Thing." *Educational Researcher*, 1996, *25*, 27–39.

Cross, C. *Political Education: National Policy Comes of Age.* New York: Teachers College Press, 2003.

Dale, R., and Robertson, S. "The Varying Effects of Regional Organizations as Subjects of Globalization of Education." *Comparative Education Review*, 2002, *46* (1), 10–36.

Eccles, J., and Jacobs, J. "Social Forces Shape Math Attitudes and Performance." *Signs: Journal of Women in Culture and Society*, 1986, *11*, 367–80.

Eckert, P. *Jocks and Burnouts*. New York: Teachers College Press, 1989.

Elmore, R., and Fuhrman, S. "Governing Curriculum: Changing Patterns in Policy, Politics, and Practice." In R. Elmore and S. Fuhrman (eds.), *The Governance of Curriculum*. Alexandria, Va.: Association of Supervision and Curriculum Development, 1994.

Farkas, G. *Human Capital or Cultural Capital?: Ethnicity and Poverty Groups in an Urban School District*. Hawthorne, N.Y.: Aldine de Gruyter, 1996.

Fiala, R., and Gordon-Lanford, A. "Educational Ideology and the World Education Revolution, 1950–1970." *Comparative Education Review*, 1987, *31*, 315–33.

Finnemore, M. "Norms, Culture, and World Politics: Insights from Sociology's Institutionalism." *International Organization*, 1996, *50* (2), 325–47.

Fiske, E. *Decentralization of Education Politics and Consensus: Directions in Development Series*. Washington, D.C.: World Bank, 1996.

Fukuzawa, R., and LeTendre, G. *Intense Years: How Japanese Adolescents Balance School, Family, and Friends*. New York: Routledge, 2001.

Fuller, B. "What School Factors Raise Achievement in the Third World." *Review of Educational Research*, 1987, *57* (3), 255–92.

Fuller, B., and Rubinson, R. (eds.). *The Political Construction of Education*. New York: Praeger, 1992.

Gambetta, D. *Were They Pushed or Did They Jump? Individual Decision Mechanisms in Education*. Cambridge, England: Cambridge University Press, 1987.

Gill, B., and Schlossman, S. "A Sin Against Childhood: Progressive Education and the Crusade to Abolish Homework, 1897–1941." *American Journal of Education*, 1996, *105*, 27–66.

____. "A Nation at Rest: The American Way of Homework." *Educational Evaluation and Policy Analysis*, 2003a, *25* (3), 319–37.

____. "Parents and the Politics of Homework: Some Historical Perspectives." *Teachers College Record*, 2003b, *105* (5), 846–71.

Giroux, H. A. "Theories of Reproduction and Resistance in the New Sociology of Education: A Critical Analysis." *Harvard Educational Review*, 1983, *53* (3), 257–93.

Goldman, S., and McDermott, R. "The Culture of Competition in American Schools." In G. Spindler (ed.), *Education and Cultural Progress*. Prospect Heights, Ill.: Waveland Press, 1987.

Gornick, J., Meyers, M., and Ross, K. "Public Policies and the Employment of Mothers: A Cross-National Study." *Social Science Quarterly*, 1998, *79* (1), 35–54.

Hanson, E. "Decentralization in Colombian Education." *Comparative Education Review*, 1995, *39*, 100–119.

Hansot, E., and Tyack, D. "Gender in American Public Schools: Thinking Institutionally." *Signs: Journal of Women and Culture and Society*, 1988, *13*, 4.

Hanusek, E. "A Jaundiced View of 'Adequacy' in School Finance Reform." *Educational Policy*, 1994, *8* (4), 460–69.

Hedges, L., Laine, R., and Greenwald, R. "Does Money Matter? A Meta-Analysis of Studies of the Effects of Differential School Inputs on Student Outcomes." *Educational Researcher*, 1994, *23*, 5–14.

Heyneman, S. "Influence on Academic Achievement: A Comparison of Results from Uganda and More Industrialized Societies." *Sociology of Education*, 1976, *49* (3), 200–211.

____. "Resource Availability, Equality and Educational Opportunity Among Nations." In L. Anderson and D. Windham (eds.), *Education and Development Issues in the Analysis and Planning of Post-Colonial Societies*. Lexington, Mass.: Lexington Books, 1982.

Heyneman, S., and Loxley, W. "Influences on Academic Achievement Across High and Low Income Countries: A Re-analysis of IEA Data." *Sociology of Education*, 1982, *55*, 13–21.

____. "The Effect of Primary-School Quality on Academic Achievement Across Twenty-Nine High- and Low-Income Countries." *American Journal of Sociology*, 1983, *88*, 1162–94.

Hinds, M. *Violent Kids: Can We Change the Trend?* Dubuque, Iowa: Kendall/Hunt, 2000.

Hirschi, T. *Causes of Delinquency*. Berkeley: University of California Press, 1969.

Hopper, E. "Educational Systems and Selected Consequences of Patterns of Mobility and Nonmobility in Industrial Societies." In E. Hopper (ed.), *The Theory of Educational Systems*. London: Hutchinson, 1971.

Huber, E., and Stephens, J. "Partisan Governance, Women's Employment, and the Social Democratic Service State." *American Sociological Review*, 2000, *65*, 323–42.

Husén, T. *International Study of Achievement in Mathematics: A Comparison of Twelve Countries*. Stockholm: Almqvist and Wiksell, 1967.

Ingersoll, R., and Smith, T. "The Wrong Solution to the Teacher Shortage." *Educational Leadership*, 2003, *60* (8), 30–33.

Janssens, M. "Maternal Influence on Daughters' Gender Role Attitudes." *Sex Roles*, 1998, *21*, 13–26.

Karen, D. "Achievement and Ascription in Admission to an Elite College." *Sociological Forum*, 1991, *6*, 349–80.

Katsillis, J., and Rubinson, R. "Cultural Capital, Student Achievement, and Educational Reproduction: The Case of Greece." *American Sociological Review*, 1990, *55*, 270–79.

Kelly, D. "How the School and Teachers Create Deviants." *Contemporary Education*, 1977, *8*, 202–5.

Kelly, D., and Grove, W. "Teachers' Nominations and the Production of Academic Misfits." *Education*, 1981, *101*, 246–63.

Kerckhoff, A. "The Realism of Educational Ambitions in England and the United States." *American Sociological Review*, 1977, *42*, 563–71.

____. *Getting Started: Transition to Adulthood in Great Britain*. Boulder, Colo.: Westview Press, 1990.

Kinney, C. "Building an Excellent Teacher Corps: How Japan Does It." *American Educator*, Winter 1997–98, 16–22.

Kozol, J. *Savage Inequalities*. New York: HarperCollins, 1993.

Kravolec, E., and Buell, J. *The End of Homework: How Homework Disrupts Families, Overburdens Children, and Limits Learning*. Boston: Beacon Press, 2003.

Lareau, A. *Home Advantage: Social Class and Parental Intervention in Elementary Education*. Lanham, Md.: Rowman and Littlefield, 2000.

Larson, R., and Verma, S. "How Children and Adolescents Spend Time Across the World: Work, Play, and Developmental Opportunities." *Psychological-Bulletin*, 1999, *125*, 701–36.

Lawrence, R. *School Crime and Juvenile Justice.* New York: Oxford University Press, 1998.

Leahy, E., and Guo, G. "Gender Differences in Mathematical Trajectories." *Social Forces,* 2001, *80,* 713–32.

Lee, K. "The Best of Intentions: Meritocratic Selection to Higher Education and the Development of Shadow Education in Korea." Doctoral dissertation, Pennsylvania State University, 2003.

Leithaeuser, T., Exner, M., Haack-Wegner, R., Schorn, A., and von der Vring, E. *Gewalt und Sicherheit in Oeffentlichen Raum* (Violence and Safety in Public Spaces). Giessen, Germany: Psychosocial-Verlag, 2002.

Lemann, N. *The Promised Land: The Great Black Migration and How It Changed America.* New York: Random House, 1991.

LeTendre, G. "Distribution Tables and Private Tests: The Failure of Middle School Reform in Japan." *International Journal of Educational Reform,* 1994, *3,* 126–36.

____. "Constructed Aspirations: Decision-Making Processes in Japanese Educational Selection." *Sociology of Education,* 1996a, *69,* 193–216.

____. "Social Background and Educational Attainment in Japan: A Review of Research in the Post-War Period." *Research in the Sociology of Education and Socialization,* 1996b, *11,* 203–32.

____. "Emotional Choices: How Schools Affect the Educational Decisions of Young Adolescents and Their Families." Paper presented at the National Academy of Education Fall Meeting, Pittsburgh, Oct. 1999.

____. *Learning to Be Adolescent: Growing up in U.S. and Japanese Middle Schools.* New Haven, Conn.: Yale University Press, 2000.

LeTendre, G., Akiba, M., Baker, D., Goesling, B., Fabrega-Lacoa, R., and Zhao, H. "Why Schoolwork Goes Home: Cross-National Factors and International Trends in Homework Usage in 37 Nations." Paper presented at the Comparative and International Education Society, Orlando, Fla., Mar. 2002.

LeTendre, G., Akiba, M., Goesling, B., Wiseman, A., and Baker, D. "The Policy Trap: National Educational Policy and the Third International Math and Science Study." *International Journal of Educational Policy, Research and Practice,* 2000, *2* (1), 45–64.

LeTendre, G., Baker, D., Akiba, M., Goesling, B., and Wiseman, A. "Teacher's Work: Institutional Isomorphism and Cultural Variation in the U.S., Germany, and Japan." *Educational Researcher,* 2001, *30* (6), 3–16.

LeTendre, G., Hofer, B., and Shimizu, H. "What Is Tracking? Cultural Expectations in the U.S., Germany and Japan." *American Educational Research Journal,* 2003, *40* (1), 43–89.

LeTendre, G, Rohlen, T., and Zeng, K. "Merit or Family Background? Problems in Research Policy Initiatives in Japan." *Educational Evaluation and Policy Analysis,* 1998, *20* (4), 285–97.

Lin, C. "The Republic of China (Taiwan)." In R. Thomas and T. Postlethwaite (eds.), *Schooling in East Asia: Forces of Change.* New York: Pergamon, 1983.

Loveless, T. "The Tracking and Ability Grouping Debate." *Fordham Report,* 1999, *2* (8), 1–27.

Lucas, S. *Tracking Inequality: Stratification and Mobility in American High Schools.* New York: Teachers College Press, 1999.

MacLeod, J. *Ain't No Makin' It: Aspirations and Attainment in a Low-Income Neighborhood.* Boulder, Colo.: Westview Press, 1987.

Maguire, K., and Pastore, A. "Sourcebook of Criminal Justice Statistics." Albany: School of Criminal Justice, State University of New York at Albany, 1995. Accessed July 14, 2004 (www.albany.edu/sourcebook).

March, J., and Olsen, J. *Ambiguity and Choice in Organizations.* Bergen, Norway: Universitetsforlaget, 1979.

Marini, M., and Brinton, M. "Sex-Typing in Occupational Socialization." In B. Reskin (ed.), *Sex Segregation in the Workplace: Trends, Explanations, Remedies.* Washington, D.C.: National Academy Press, 1984.

Marshall, G., Swift, A., and Roberts, S. *Against the Odds? Social Class and Social Justice in Industrial Societies.* Oxford, UK: Clarendon Press, 1997.

Martin, M., Gregory, K., and Stemler, S. *TIMSS 1999 Technical Report.* Boston: International Study Center, Boston University, 1990.

Martinez, M. *Education as the Cultivation of Intelligence.* Hillsdale, N.J.: Erlbaum, 2000.

McClelland, K. "Cumulative Disadvantage Among the Highly Ambitious." *Sociology of Education,* 1990, *63,* 102–21.

McDonough, P. *Choosing Colleges: How Social Class and Schools Structure Opportunity.* Albany: State University of New York Press, 1997.

McEneaney, E., and Meyer, J. "The Content of the Curriculum: An Institutional Perspective." In Hallinan, M. (ed.), *Handbook of Sociology of Education.* New York: Kluwer Academic/Plenum Publishers, 2000.

McKnight, C., Crosswhite, F., and Dossey, J. *The Underachieving Curriculum: Assessing U.S. School Mathematics from an International Perspective.* Champaign, Ill.: Stipes, 1987.

Meyer, J. "The Effects of Education as an Institution." *American Journal of Sociology,* 1977, *83* (1), 55–77.

___. "Reflections on Education as Transcendence." In L. Cuban and D. Shipps (eds.), *Reconstructing the Common Good in Education.* Stanford, Calif.: Stanford University Press, 2000.

Meyer, J., Boli, J., Thomas, G., and Ramirez, F. "World Society and the Nation-State." *American Journal of Sociology,* 1997, *103,* 144–81.

Meyer, J., and Jepperson, R. "The 'Actor' of Modern Society: The Cultural Construction of Social Agency." *Sociological Theory,* 2000, *18* (1), 100–120.

Meyer, J., Ramirez, F., and Soysal, Y. "World Expansion of Mass Education, 1870–1980." *Sociology of Education,* 1992, *65,* 128–49.

Meyer, J., and Scott, R. (eds.) *Institutional Environments and Organizations: Structural Complexity and Individualism.* Thousand Oaks, Calif.: Sage, 1994.

Mickelson, R. "The Attitude-Achievement Paradox Among Black Adolescents." *Sociology of Education,* 1990, *63,* 44–61.

Mills, M., and Blossfeld, H. "Globalization, Uncertainty and Changes in Early Life Courses." *Zeitschrift fur Erziehungswissenschaft,* 2003, *6* (2), 188–218.

Mitchell, R. *Pupil, Parent and School: A Hong Kong Study.* Taipei, Taiwan: Orient Cultural Service, 1968.

Mosteller, F., and Moynihan, D. *On Equality of Educational Opportunity.* New York: Random House, 1972.

Newman, G. *Global Report on Crime and Justice.* New York: Oxford University Press, 1999.

Nijboer, J., and Dijksterhuis, F. "Education and Delinquency: The Relationship Between Performance at School and Delinquency." *International Summaries.* Washington, D.C.: National Institute of Justice, 1983.

Oakes, J. *Keeping Track: How Schools Structure Inequality.* New Haven, Conn.: Yale University Press, 1985.

Office of Educational Research and Improvement (OERI). *The Educational System in Japan: Case Study Findings.* Washington, D.C.: U.S. Department of Education, 1998.

___. *The Educational System in Germany: Case Study Findings.* Washington, D.C.: U.S. Department of Education, 1999a.

___. *The Educational System in the U.S.: Case Study Findings.* Washington, D.C.: U.S. Department of Education, 1999b.

Ogbu, J. *Minority Education and Caste.* New York: Academic Press, 1978.

Organization for Economic Cooperation and Development (OECD). *The Well-Being of Nations.* Paris: OECD, 2001.

___. *Education at a Glance.* Paris: OECD, 2003.

Orloff, A. "Gender in the Welfare State." *Annual Review of Sociology,* 1996, *22,* 51–78.

Pallas, A. "The Effects of Schooling on Individual Lives. In M. Hallinan (ed.), *Handbook of Sociology of Education.* New York: Kluwer Academic Press, 2000.

Polk, K., Frease, D., and Richmond, F. "Social Class, School Experience, and Delinquency." *Criminology,* 1974, *12* (1), 84–96.

Polk, K., and Pink, W. "School Pressure Toward Deviance: A Cross-Cultural Comparison." In K. Polk and W. E. Schafer (eds.), *Schools and Delinquency.* Upper Saddle River, N.J.: Prentice Hall, 1972.

Pong, S., and Post, D. "Trends in Gender and Family Background Effects on School Attainment: The Case of Hong Kong." *British Journal of Sociology,* 1991, *42* (2), 249–71.

Powell, W., and DiMaggio, P. *The New Institutionalism in Organizational Analysis.* Chicago: University of Chicago Press, 1991.

Ramirez, F. "Global Changes, World Myths, and the Demise of Cultural Gender: Implications for the USA." In T. Boswell and A. Bergesen (eds.), *America's Changing Role in the World System.* New York: Praeger, 1987.

___. "World Society and the Political Incorporation of Women. *Kölner Zeitschrift für Soziologie und Sozialpsychologie,* Oct. 2001, 356–74.

Ramirez, F., and Boli, J. "The Political Construction of Mass Schooling: European Origins and Worldwide Institutionalization." *Sociology of Education,* 1987, *60,* 2–17.

Riddell, A. "An Alternative Approach to the Study of School Effectiveness in Third World Countries." *Comparative Education Review,* 1989, *33* (4), 481–97.

___. "Assessing Designs for School Effectiveness Research and School Improvement in Developing Countries." *Comparative Education Review,* 1997, *41* (2), 178–204.

Riegle-Crumb, C. *International Gender Inequality in Math and Science Education: The Importance of Gender Stratification Across Generations.* Doctoral dissertation, University of Chicago, 2000.

Riordan, C. *Equality and Achievement: An Introduction to the Sociology of Education.* White Plains, N.Y.: Longman, 2003.

Robitaille, D., Beaton, A., and Plomp, J. *The Impact of TIMSS on the Teaching and Learning of Mathematics and Science*. Vancouver, B.C.: Pacific Educational Press, 2000.

Rohlen, T. *Japan's High Schools*. Berkeley: University of California Press, 1983.

Rubinson, R. "Class Formation, Political Organization, and Institutional Structures: The Case of Schooling in the United States." *American Journal of Sociology*, 1986, *92*, 519–48.

Rubinson, R., and Browne, I. "Education and the Economy." In N. Smelter and R. Swedberg (eds.), *The Handbook of Economic Sociology*. Princeton, N.J.: Princeton University Press, 1994.

Schafer, W., Olexa, C., and Polk, K. "Programmed for Social Class: Tracking in High School." In K. Polk and W. Schafer (eds.), *Schools and Delinquency*. Upper Saddle River, N.J.: Prentice Hall, 1972.

Schaub, M. *Parenting Cognitive Development: The Institutional Effects of Mass Education on the Social Construction of Childhood and Parenting*. Doctoral dissertation, Department of Sociology, Pennsylvania State University, 2004.

Schiller, K., Khmelkov, V., and Wang, X. "Economic Development and the Effects of Family Characteristics on Mathematics Achievement." *Journal of Marriage and Family*, 2002, *64*, 730–42.

Schmidt, V. A. *Democratizing France: The Political and Administrative History of Decentralization*. Cambridge, England: Cambridge University Press, 1990.

Schmidt, W., McKnight, C., Houang, R., Wang, H., Wiley, D., Cogan, L., and Wolfe, R. *Why Schools Matter: Cross-National Comparison of Curriculum and Learning*. San Francisco: Jossey-Bass, 2001.

Schmidt, W., McKnight, C., and Raizen, S. *A Splintered Vision: An Investigation of U.S. Science and Mathematics Education*. Lansing, Mich.: National Research Center for the Third International Mathematics and Science Study, Michigan State University, 1997.

Schmidt, W., McKnight, C., Valverde, G., Houang, R., and Wiley, D. *Many Visions, Many Aims: A Cross-National Investigation of Curricular Intentions in School Mathematics*. Norwell, Mass.: Kluwer Academic, 1997.

Schoon, I. "Is There a Class Ceiling? Persisting Inequalities in Educational and Occupational Attainment." Paper presented at symposium, EARLI Conference, Padua, Italy, Sept. 2003.

Schriewer, J. "The Method of Comparison and the Need for Externalization: Methodological Criteria and Sociological Concepts. In J. Schriewer and B. Holmes (eds.), *Theories and Methods in Comparative Education*. Bern, Switzerland: Lang, 1992.

Schümer, G. "Versuche zur Aufklärung von Leistungsunterschieden zwischen Schülern aus verschiedenen Ländern." In S. Gruehn, G. Kluchert, and T. Koinzer (eds.), *Was Schule macht: Schule, Unterricht und Werteerziehung: theoretisch, historisch, empirisch*. Weinheim: Beltz, 2004.

Scott, W., and Meyer, J. "Institutions and Organizations: Toward a Theoretical Synthesis." In W. Scott, J. Meyer, and others, *Institutional Environments and Organizations*. Thousand Oaks, Calif.: Sage, 1994.

Seymour, E., and Hewitt, N. *"Talking About Leaving: Why Undergraduates Leave the Sciences*. Boulder, Colo.: Westview Press, 1997.

Shavit, Y., and Blossfeld, H. *Persistent Inequality: Changing Educational Attainment in Thirteen Countries.* Boulder, Colo.: Westview Press, 1993.

Skowronek, S. *Building a New American State: The Expansion of National Administrative Capacities, 1877–1920.* Cambridge, England: Cambridge University Press, 1982.

Spillane, J., and Thompson. "Reconstructing Conceptions of Local Capacity: The Local Education Agency's Capacity for Ambitious Reform." *Educational Evaluation and Policy Analysis,* 1997, *19,* 185–203.

Spindler, G. *Education and Cultural Process: Toward an Anthropology of Education.* Austin, Tex.: Holt, Rinehart and Winston, 1974.

Spindler, G., and Spindler, L. *The American Cultural Dialogue and Its Transmission.* New York: Falmer Press, 1990.

Spindler, L. *Culture, Change, and Modernization: Mini-Models and Case Studies.* Prospect Heights, Ill.: Waveland Press, 1977.

Stage, F., and Maple, S. "Incompatible Goals: Narratives of Graduate Women in the Mathematics Pipeline." *American Educational Research Journal,* 1996, *33,* 23.

Steiner-Khamsi, G. "Re-Territorializing Educational Import." In A. Novoa and M. Lawn (eds.), *Fabricating Europe: The Formation of an Education Space.* London: Kluwer Academic, 2002.

Stevenson, D., and Baker, D. "Shadow Education and Allocation in Formal Schooling: Transition to University in Japan." *American Journal of Sociology,* 1992, *97* (6), 1639–57.

____. "Does State Control of the Curriculum Matter?" *Educational Evaluation and Policy Analysis,* 1996, *18,* 339–43.

Stevenson, D., Schiller, K., and Schneider, B. "Sequences of Opportunities for Learning." *Sociology of Education,* 1994, *67* (3), 198.

Stevenson, H., Lummis, M., Lee, S., and Stigler, J. *Making the Grade in Mathematics: Elementary School Mathematics in the United States, Taiwan, and Japan.* Reston, Va.: National Council of Teachers of Mathematics, 1990.

Stevenson, H., Parker, T., Wilkinson, A., Bonnevaux, B., and Gonzalez, M. "Schooling, Environment, and Cognitive Development: A Cross-Cultural Study." *Monographs of the Society for Research in Child Development,* 1978, *43*(3), 175.

Stevenson, H., and Stigler, J. *The Learning Gap.* New York: Summit Books, 1992.

Stigler, J., and Hiebert, J. "Teaching Is a Cultural Activity." *American Educator,* Winter 1998, 4–11.

____. *The Teaching Gap: Best Ideas from the World's Teachers for Improving Education in the Classroom.* New York: Free Press, 1999.

Stinchcombe, A. *Rebellion in a High School.* Chicago: Quadrangle Books, 1964.

Storey, J., and Edwards, P. *Managers in the Making: Careers, Development and Control in Corporate Britain and Japan.* London: Sage, 1997.

Sweeting, A. "Hong Kong." In R. Thomas and T. Postlethwaite (eds.), *Schooling in East Asia: Forces of Change.* New York: Pergamon, 1983.

Thomas, G., Ramirez, F., Boli, J., and Meyer, J. *Institutional Structure.* Thousand Oaks, Calif.: Sage, 1987.

Tilly, C. *Coercion, Capital, and European States.* Cambridge, Mass.: Blackwell, 1990.

Tobin, J., Wu, D., and Davidson, D. *Preschool in Three Cultures: Japan, China, and the United States.* New Haven: Yale University Press, 1989.

Tsang, M. "Public and Private Costs of Education in Developing Countries." In M. Carnoy (ed.), *International Encyclopedia of Economics of Education*. Oxford, UK: Pergamon Press, 1995.

Tsukada, M. *Yobiko Life: A Study of the Legitimation Process of Social Stratification in Japan*. Berkeley: University of California Press, 1991.

Turner, R. "Sponsored and Contest Mobility and the School System." *American Sociological Review*, 1960, 25, 855–67.

Tyack, D. *The One Best System: A History of American Urban Education*. Cambridge, Mass.: Harvard University Press, 1974.

Tyack, D., and Cuban, L. *Tinkering Toward Utopia: A Century of Public School Reform*. Cambridge, Mass.: Harvard University Press, 1995.

Tyack, D., and Hansot, E. *Learning Together: A History of Coeducation in American Schools*. New Haven, Conn.: Yale University Press, 1990.

U.S. Department of Education. *Measuring Classroom Instructional Processes: Using Survey and Case Study Field-Test Results to Improve Item Construction*. Washington, D.C.: National Center for Education Statistics, 1999.

____. National Commission on Excellence in Education. *A Nation at Risk*. Washington, D.C.: U.S. Government Printing Office, 1983.

U.S. Department of Education and U.S. Department of Justice. *1999 Annual Report on School Safety: A Joint Report Prepared by the U.S. Department of Education and the U.S. Department of Justice*. Washington, D.C.: Government Printing Office, 2000.

Valverde, G., Bianchi, L., Wolfe, R., Schmidt, W., and Houang, R. *According to the Book: Using TIMSS to Investigate the Translation of Policy into Practice Through the World of Textbooks*. New York: Kluwer Academic Publishers, 2002.

Valverde, G., and Schmidt, W. "Refocusing U.S. Math and Science Education." *Issues in Science and Technology*, 1997, 14, 60–66.

Werum, R., and Baker, D. "Inequality and Schooling as an Institution: Future Directions in the Comparative Study of Educational Stratification." (Commentary.) *Annual Review of Sociology of Education*, 2004, 14, 275–84.

Westbury, I., and Hsu, C. "Does State Control of the Curriculum Matter? A Response to Stevenson and Baker." *Educational Evaluation and Policy Analysis*, 1996, *18*, 343–47.

Willis, P. *Learning to Labor: How Working Class Kids Get Working Class Jobs*. New York: Columbia University Press, 1977.

Wray, H. "Change and Continuity in Modern Japanese Educational History: Allied Occupational Reforms Forty Years Later." *Comparative Education Review*, 1991, 33, 447–75.

Wrigley, J. *Education and Gender Equality*. London: Falmer Press, 1992.